'... touching, angry, uproarious tale sustains
... because it never lets go of the notion
that as one day follows another something more
than a pop group's career might be at stake'

Greil Marcus

'Finally ... a Clash book worth its salt ... a
magnificent, roller coasting rock'n'roll read, and
completely essential to Clash City Rockers old
and new' Ian Fortnam, *NME*

'Fucking great!' Joe Strummer's builders

'Is it authentic? Yes ... Here it all is, London
calling from the top of the dial – the low-life
liggers, the bags of cash, the cops, the coke, the
quarrels, up and down the Westway in and out of
the lights, the great bass speakers, the driving
rain and reggae, expectation, expectoration and
the cosmic live gigs ... This is a witty tribute to
the only lastingly listenable punk band'

Liz Young, *Independent*

'*A Riot of Our Own* is written from inside the eye
of the storm. Johnny Green captures the essence
of The Clash. He's pretty funny, too ... *A Riot of
Our Own* enables you to smell the leather, the
hairspray, the sweat and the spliff. It could
quite happily sit alongside Kerouac, Kesey and
Ginsberg in terms of its celebration of living life
on a knife edge' Ben Myers, *Melody Maker*

A RIOT OF OUR OWN

Johnny Green has a degree in Arabic and Islamic
Studies from Lancaster University. After leaving
the music business he eventually became Kent
county education adviser on sex and drugs.

Garry Barker is a Clash fan. He has a degree in
English from London University and is now a
freelance writer and journalist. They both live in
Kent.

Ray Lowry was an artist and cartoonist for the
NME, the *Observer*, *Punch*, *Loaded* and *Mojo*. He
died in 2008.

A Riot OF OUR OWN

NIGHT AND DAY WITH THE CLASH – AND AFTER

Johnny Green
and Garry Barker

Illustrations by
Ray Lowry

WEIRD shit
Coming down...

W&N
WEIDENFELD & NICOLSON

First published in Great Britain in 1997 by Indigo
Reissued in 2000 and 2003 by Orion
This paperback edition first published in 2019 by Weidenfeld & Nicolson
an imprint of The Orion Publishing Group Ltd
Carmelite House, 50 Victoria Embankment
London EC4Y 0DZ

An Hachette UK Company

1 3 5 7 9 10 8 6 4 2

Text copyright © John Broad and Garry Barker 1997, 2019
Illustrations copyright © Ray Lowry

A RARE Moment of self doubt...

A CIP catalogue record for this book is available from the British Library.

ISBN (paperback) 978 1 4746 1118 3
ISBN (ebook) 978 1 4746 1119 0

Designed and typeset by Production Line, Minster Lovell, Oxford
Printed in Great Britain by Clays Ltd, Elcograf S.p.A.

MIX
Paper from
responsible sources
FSC® C104740
www.fsc.org

www.orionbooks.co.uk

To **Polly**, **Lewis** and **Basil**,
who had a riot of their own
around our feet.

Foreword by **Joe Strummer**

*A*nd to me falls the pleasure of introducing our humble narrator to his readers.

Picture a rain-lashed night on the banks of the Thames. Jutting out from Battersea Park some hundred feet into the river is a pier where the Queen alights should there be some function in the park. At the end of this jetty the Clash have set their stage gear up – three mikes, three monitors, three amps and a drum kit.

The video for *London Calling* has been recorded by director Don Letts. The band have completed their run-throughs and left for various destinations. Enter, from stage left so to speak, a tall, studious-looking man, wearing glasses suitable for a librarian in Macclesfield.

The man is clearly not happy. But he does not scream or shout. Instead he has a look of grim determination about him. He strides to centre stage and grabs hold of the nearest speaker cabinet. With all his strength he lifts it above his head and casts it deep into the dark, flowing river. The lights twinkle from the Embankment and the Houses of Parliament. He does not look. He is too busy throwing mikes, amps and drums into the River Thames.

This, ladies and gentlemen, is my friend, and your narrator: Johnny Green.

MR. BASS MAN

Mick

JOE SINGER.. THE filth and the FURY!!!.

THE ENgine ROOM......

THE BAKER.
MAN of dRUMS...

THE GREENING OF the BROAD...

PUNK RooocK!

THE EYE OF TIME

1

We were broke. The Clash then had no manager and were lurching from one financial crisis to the next. The band was recording *London Calling* at Wessex Studios, although the crisis of confidence between record label CBS and the Clash was so deep that no one was sure if the record would ever be released.

Joe Strummer, Mick Jones and Paul Simonon had no money. Topper Headon certainly had none. Neither had I or the Baker, who between us shared in all the band's decisions, did all of the Clash's administrative tasks and lugged around and set up the amps and PA. CBS was trying to soften the Clash – toning down the band's image and its political stance – by withholding money. The last-minute offer to appear at a music festival in Finland was a chance to earn some cash which was too good to miss.

But it had to be cash. We owed money to banks, and all accounts had been frozen pending a deal with former manager Bernie Rhodes. The Clash's appearance at the Russrock Festival, Finland, had been set up by Ian Flooks. He had recently set up his own agency, Wasted Talent, and was touting for trade, with a watchful eye on the managerless Clash. I had to impress on him that we were not interested in cheques or banker's drafts, just British pound notes – up front, in the hand.

I conducted lengthy negotiations from the wall-mounted telephone in the corridor of Wessex Studios. Eventually the fee was agreed. That left just one more problem – equipment. All the Clash's gear had been set up in the studio for the recording session. There wasn't time to dismantle it and send it to Finland. And anyway it had taken three days to get the right sound, and we just couldn't afford the cost in studio time to go through the whole process again.

From phone calls to Scandinavia, I achieved a personal coup through Thomas Johansen, Abba's road manager, who agreed that we could use Abba's PA and sound equipment. Abba were the only group which had ever made me star-struck. I anticipated the tingle of excitement when I would plug my jack-plug into Agnetha's amp ... As it turned out, I received more than a tingle.

We flew to Finland with the minimum crew. Rob Collins, a sound engineer whom we had used before was called in at short notice, and Jeremy Green, the tape operator at Wessex Studios, was recruited on the spot to look after the guitars and amps. With the lift-off of the plane we all felt the lifting of pressure on the band. A kids-out-of-school atmosphere took over, which lasted for the whole trip. We were away from the pressures of recording and our money problems, with the prospect of earning cash-in-hand. We were on holiday!

The festival site just added to the holiday feeling. The changing rooms were some caravans behind the stage, next to a beautiful lake, with fir trees and sunshine. It was a long way from the streets of Notting Hill and the garages of Camden Town – the subject matter of most Clash songs. And the band were playing outdoors, in the daytime – almost unknown for them. The Clash had second billing at the festival, after Graham Parker and the Rumour. They hadn't played support for any band since the Sex Pistols on the Anarchy in the UK tour of December 1976. We knew Graham Parker and his gang, and they couldn't understand it: 'How come you're playing support? How much are you getting paid?'

We played dumb and giggled up our sleeves.

Shortly before the Clash were due to play, the band asked: 'Where's the money?'

'It's OK. It's safe back at the hotel,' said the organizers, surprised at the demand.

'No, we want it now, in our hands, before we go on.'

I was dispatched to the hotel with one of the Finnish promoters to fetch the money. He found it hard to believe that I was standing in the hotel room counting out £7500 in sterling, all wrapped in £100 bundles. This wasn't the normal way of doing business. The festival was funded by the Finnish government, under a youth arts development programme, so it was unlikely that they would have paid us short. But we had learnt from long experience not to trust anyone. Satisfied that it was all there, I bundled the notes into my atomic pink flight case and rushed back to the stadium.

'We've got the cash, lads. On you go!'

The band prepared to run on-stage when I noticed a buzz from the PA. I rushed on to connect a loose jack-plug, grabbed a mike-stand with my other hand and performed a backward flip across the stage as an electric current took a short cut

across my chest. The crowd went mad with excitement. They thought my acrobatics were part of the act. I went mad. Grabbing the microphone, I yelled abuse about incompetent Finnish technicians and generally called for the whole of Scandinavia to plummet into an obscene hell, led by the cheering folk in the audience. They loved this even more, and as I went backstage to resume my grip on the case full of cash, the Clash went on-stage to a huge roar. The band put on a good show, fuelled by the Finnish vodka they'd demanded backstage before the set.

After the set the holiday mood continued. We watched Graham Parker's band from the stage wings, shouting encouragement and taking the piss. I had a cheap camera, and went on-stage and asked Parker to smile for a photo mid-song. He would sing a line and then say, 'Fuck off, fuck off', to me out of the corner of his mouth.

After the concert all the bands and their entourages went to a huge banquet in the dance hall of the hotel. Everyone was working hard at getting wrecked – Finnish beer is state-licensed, and labelled with one, two or three stars according to strength. We went for three-star. As was my way, I got more wrecked than most, and fell into a stupor, still with a dead-man's vice-like grip on the case of cash.

Eventually Joe and Paul decided to carry me to the bedroom. They told me the next day that they couldn't lift me and had had to drag me across the floor to the lift. My back had the carpet burns to prove it. As Joe passed Graham Parker, pulling me and the pink cash bag, Parker had shouted to him: 'Who is that cunt?'

'He's our road manager,' said Joe. 'He's looking after us.'

Waiting at Turku airport for our return flight, we were still in high spirits. We felt like we had got away with a bank heist. As photographer Pennie Smith said later: 'Being on the road with the Clash is like a commando raid performed by The Bash Street Kids.' During the flight I sat with the briefcase on my lap and handed out wads of cash, making a real game of it.

'One for you, one for you, one for me ...'

Everyone stuffed wedges of notes into their pockets, to the shocked astonishment of the other passengers and flight staff. We had cash at last and wanted to flaunt it. We had bypassed our creditors and the banks, and had been fellow conspirators throughout the gig. Little did Graham Parker and the Rumour know that although we had played support, we had been paid more than them.

We changed planes at Stockholm, and each of us bought a copy of *Playboy* for Tony Sanchez's exposé of Keith Richards and the Rolling Stones. Mick Jones was a 'Keef' lookalike, and he knew it, but his attempts to live a Keef-like lifestyle were better hidden from the public gaze. He leant across and swiped me across the back of the head with his rolled-up *Playboy*. 'Don't you ever do the same thing to us, Johnny,' he said.

And now I have. When I told Mick about this project he had no objections.

'Don't worry, I won't go on about the cocaine and the birds,' I said.

'That's a pity,' said Mick. 'I could do with the credibility.'

'Fuck authority,' said Joe. 'I loved that, "Who's in charge?" "He is ..." and there was you completely out of it,' and he leapt on to the burning log straddling the bonfire, sparks and flames leaping up around his fire-dance, his frame, still sporting a fine quiff, silhouetted in the aureole surrounding the eclipsing full moon. He looked just slightly older, slightly wiser, than the figure he cut on stage twenty years previously.

And I clicked and slipped backwards. The Clash were filming a video for *London Calling* ...

The Baker and I had turned up at Battersea Park at midday. A bright spark at the council had thought of installing sleeping policemen in the park road, presumably to slow down runaway wheelchairs. It was murder manoeuvring the Clash's atomic pink flight cases of amps and speakers over them to the floating jetty, grandly called Battersea Pier, which bobbed up and down with the tide. Don Letts, who was doing the filming, turned up on a motor launch, dreadlocks flying, with the film crew. We set up the backline as if we were playing at the Lyceum – amps, leads, mikes, stands, PA to roll back the sound. And we waited and waited for the band to arrive. We buttoned our coats against the growing cold of the afternoon and even Letts' good humour began to wane. Cold hours passed and the sun set. It began to rain and the Clash turned up. All the band's equipment was standing in the drizzle getting soaked. Don had sent out for some lights and I sent out for some Rémy Martin. I wanted to pack up and go home. The boat pulled out, riding the swell of the river, and Letts was shouting instructions to the band through a megaphone, like he was at the Boat Race.

'All right, hold it. When we do that section again all gather around the mike then spread ...'

It was so weird it cheered me up, and the band ran through it again and again, patiently and professionally, looking urban and urbane, and wet. It was as if they had known it was going to rain, and known it was going to be filmed at dusk. Joe wielded his faithful old guitar, with its 'Ignore Alien Orders' sticker. Paul sported a wide-brimmed gangster hat; Mick was in a dark suit, with a red tie and handkerchief sending off flashes of colour. Every time Topper hit the drums spray bounced up into his face, sparkling in the artificial light. Between takes I mopped at their rain-soaked guitars and faces with towels in a little wooden hut nearby, as they slugged Rémy and hugged each other against the cold.

Finally, it was done and the band pissed off in a cab. Baker and I, cold, wet and starving, were left to pack everything away, without even the roar of the crowd to see us home.

Baker whinged. 'Look at this stuff – it's soaked. How are we going to dry it off? It's ruined."

 I grabbed a mike-stand and dumped it into the water. Anger welled into strength, and I picked up a wedge monitor, hired from Maurice Plaquet, and with a roar hurled it into the Thames. To our surprise it floated, and, rocking with laughter, we watched it bobbing under the fairy lights of Chelsea Bridge.

2

I fell in with the Clash almost by accident – through a series of those strange coincidences of being in the right place at the right time with the right people.

I quickly became friendly with the band. I was twenty-seven and had been around a bit. I could tune into their different wavelengths. I chatted to Joe Strummer about politics, to Topper Headon about drugs, to Mick Jones about music history and to Paul Simonon about art – and I could hustle with the characters in Camden High Street at 1 a.m. if necessary.

Strummer was seen by many as the inspirational force behind the Clash, but he wasn't that much more forceful than the others within the dynamics of the band. He was seen as a man who would punch someone out if he didn't like them. I suppose he might have done, but he would think about it first. When we arrived at a venue the others would go for a drink or watch TV. He would go for a walk alone. At twenty-five, he was the oldest of the band.

Paul was twenty-one, a shy guy, very cool. He was the real hard man of the band. He was so hard he didn't have to demonstrate it very often. He was stylish, a beautiful mover on-stage. But at first he couldn't play his instrument – he was given the bass because it was easier to learn, with only four strings. He thought that the more he moved about the stage and the cooler he looked, the less people would notice that he couldn't play. Not that he cared, really. He was interested in appearances and visuals, and that was an important part of the Clash. Give him a new guitar and within minutes he had painted it and carved his name on it. That was important to him. He was largely responsible for the look of the band, and his love of reggae and ska was another strong influence on the Clash.

Jones was a real poodle. He was the most instantly likeable, but also the most irritable if things didn't go the way he wanted. He was a musician, and had always wanted to be in a band.

At twenty-two Mick had been a member of Malcolm McLaren's and Bernie Rhodes' original pool of musicians, from which the Sex Pistols and the Clash emerged, and Mick had recruited the other Clash members. In many ways, the Clash were 'his' band. He certainly thought so.

Topper was the new boy at the time. He was also twenty-two, and a professional drummer. He had been in bands before. The other guys wore Clash-style clothes – at the time: black, with lots of zips, and stencilled-on slogans – as a fashion statement. Topper wore them because the other guys did. If he had been in Showaddywaddy he would have dressed like Showaddywaddy. He wasn't interested in politics or philosophy, just having a laugh and a good time. He always wanted someone at his shoulder. If he wanted a drink in a hotel bar he would have to persuade someone, usually me, to go with him just to keep him company. But he was a terrific musician, and held the band together on-stage.

In the autumn of 1977 I was planning on going to the Middle East to explore the culture and make some money. Instead I found myself in Belfast, doing a bit of work for Clash manager Bernie Rhodes – unpaid, of course – before I quite knew what was going on. And I found myself loving it.

I was first and foremost a Clash fan. I had been running a club in Lancaster, playing punk music. Me and Stevie were DJs, wired up on speed, working without speaking, communicating through amphetamined telepathy. Janet, a friend with blousy, long blond hair and the seedy punk look later

21

associated with Nancy Spungen, objected to a sex-jealousy number we were playing. She threw a glass, which just missed my head and exploded on the wall behind, showering the turntables with splinters. I immediately played 'Cheat' from the first Clash album, about violence and drugs. Vinyl became reality. Music merged with the moment.

I had booked the Sex Pistols and the Clash to play at Lancaster University on the Anarchy in the UK tour, which the students' union cancelled on the totally unfounded grounds that punk music was 'sexist'. I had tried to see the Clash play live twice before, but each time I had been in the wrong place with the wrong people. I went with a bottle of whisky and Lisa, a twelve-stone lesbian with bright pink hair to catch the Anarchy tour in Manchester. I got drunk, saw the local band, the Buzzcocks, then went outside for some fresh air. This was soon after the infamous Bill Grundy interview with the Sex Pistols, which had been followed up by the tabloid press with shock stories about punks. Consequently there was any number of cops patrolling outside the venue, the Electric Circus – a very rough old church hall, covered in graffiti. I had an argument with Lisa, she whacked me on the chin and the cops kicked me into a van, trod on my glasses and hurled me into a cell. The next morning I appeared in court without specs. I couldn't see a yard in front of me. I was fined £11 for being drunk and disorderly and went straight to Manchester Royal Infirmary with bruising to the head and two cracked ribs. I later hitched to see the Clash on the White Riot tour but was stranded on the M6 and missed the show.

Perhaps in a way it was Bernie Rhodes and I who were responsible for getting the first Belfast gig cancelled. I was just hanging around after helping to unload the equipment at the hall. There was a crowd of street kids outside the hall, and Bernie loaded me up with three boxes of Clash badges to hand out. Badges were always given away free at gigs. The kids saw me and mobbed me. The boxes went up in the air, and there was a mad scramble for badges. Three Army Land Rovers came around the corner, each with a machine-gun mounted at the back manned by a squaddie. The kids all hit the deck. I just stood there. A squaddie came and prodded me with a rifle.

'Oy, what's going on? You're English? You'd better get inside. Now.'

When the patrol moved on the kids went wild in a spontaneous riot, smashing windows at the venue. The insurance company was contacted, they came and had a look, and the gig was cancelled.

That night in Belfast I slept in the truck in a bunk bed behind the driver's seat. I was woken by armed police who thought I was mad.

An RUC man said, 'A lorry like this is a prime target to be nicked. You'd go with it, and that'd be the last we'd have seen of you.'

I hadn't thought of the risk. I thought I was in Great Britain. This was the United Kingdom.

The Clash were the first band from the mainland to visit Belfast for years – apart from the Rory Gallagher band that is, and Rory was Irish. It was, Joe told me later, a deliberate decision by the band to start the October 1977 Out of Control tour in Belfast. They had their photographs taken next to British squaddies in combat gear on the streets. The visit made a lasting impression on me, and the band, who would return to play Belfast several times. The image of armed British troops on the streets became as vivid for the band as the charging policemen in Portobello Road, which Paul, Joe and Bernie had witnessed at the Notting Hill Carnival the previous year, and which formed the backdrop for their stage set on the tour as well as for the cover of *The Clash*, their first album.

I had gone to Belfast for the ride. I had bumped into an old mate who had graduated from doing removals around Notting Hill in a Transit to running three lorries, making monthly trips taking, of all things, three miles of chocolate Swiss roll to Saudi Arabia. He said he also moved bands around. 'People like Gentle Giant. And I've got a new band, the Clash, lined up for next week.'

This was my chance to see the Clash at last. I asked if I could tag along, and three days later we were heading for Stranraer and the ferry to Belfast. After the debacle in the north, I went with the band's gear to the south and finally got to see the Clash play at the university in Dublin. One of the lighting guys asked what I was doing, and I said I was just hanging around.

'Can you work a spot?'

'Sure.'

Well, I watched what the other guys were doing, and followed Strummer around the stage with the spotlight that night. The show was just terrific. I had seen plenty of rock bands before, but nothing like this.

After the gig the lighting crew asked if I wanted a job. The next show of a six-week tour was in a few days in Dunfermline. Yes! I went back to Lancaster for a couple of nights then caught a train to Scotland. I arrived at the concert hall as the band's gear was being unloaded. One of the lighting crew said, 'Oh no, he's turned up.' They hadn't expected me to show, and had given the job to someone else.

I thought I would stay and see the show and then push off home. The support band for the tour were American punks Richard Hell and the Voidoids, who were hanging around, looking nervous and pissed off. One of the band said to me, 'We need another roadie. Can you do a backline?'

'Sure.'

Well, I watched the other guys, and they helped me. They said, 'You're hired. Come on the tour. We'll pay your hotel bills.'

Which they didn't. But I dossed down where I could, and I didn't mind too much. I was up and running. I was hooked.

I did this for a few days, then the Clash's regular roadie, Roadent, left them. He was an intelligent guy but very off-the-wall. He had earned money selling Bibles, then lived for a while under the M6 sliproad at Coventry. He used to spike his hair with boot dubbin. He had been at odds with the Clash for some time, and at Edinburgh he simply got on a train and went to work with the Pistols in London. I took his place. And after about a week of that the Clash's driver-minder felt homesick. He was a seriously hard man – but he missed his wife in Walsall and went home to her. So I took his job.

I had been known as Johnny Greenglasses, because I wore green specs, but it was about this time that I acquired my name for the next few years. By the time we roadies had loaded out after a gig it was in the small hours when we lurched into a hotel. I usually showered in one of the other guys' rooms and slept in the truck. At the Merrion Hotel, Leeds, one of the sound engineers, Dave South, looked at the register of reserved but unfilled rooms and spotted 'John Green, Dagenham Plastics'. I gave the clerk his name and secured a bed for the night, and from then on became Johnny Green.

Up to this point I had hardly spoken to the Clash members. Then they said, 'Can you drive a minibus?'

'Sure.'

Within three weeks I had gone from fan to one of the band's intimate entourage. The first time I got behind the wheel of the minibus, with the Clash in the back, I felt a bit awestruck. Then Ari Up, from the Slits, jumped on to my lap wearing just tights and knickers over the top, and a tampon as an earring.

'Go! Plymouth, next stop!' she screamed.

I drove.

Next time someone screamed 'Go' I was just as quick off the mark, but in the wrong direction. Promoter Dave Cork had

Drive, he said!....

briefed me: 'It has to be a runner. We haven't got the dough for the hotel.' He was sweet-talking the manager, then jumped in the van and screamed, 'Now!' Everyone was braced for the acceleration – but not backwards on to the main road. Heads jerked. We waved as we sped off, the manager staring, jaw open. We left Sheffield by the back roads, looking for the cop car in the mirror.

Apart from such escapades, touring, as opposed to gigging, was pretty dull for the band. But not so for me, having to concentrate on driving. They argued about the seating arrangements like children: 'He sat in the front last time; I always sit in the back.' We stopped at service stations to break the monotony. Punk still wasn't widely known about, despite the Grundy interview and the tabloids. People stood and pointed at us, or said in hushed tones, 'There's some of those punk rockers we've read about.' I had never felt I was a part of a movement – or a part of anything – before. The nearest I had come to that feeling was standing at the Stretford End, baying for a penalty. I had a degree from Lancaster University but I had never seen that as conforming with society's expectations. I had simply collected my degree certificate and stuffed it in my back jeans pocket, like a rolled-up *Daily Mirror*. Its only use was to make dead-ends into motorways. I had never felt part of society – and here I was at some shabby service station with new-found kindred spirits. And I was excited. We were vivacious about being outside of society, and proud of it, enjoying the horrified glances from other drivers.

But generally in the van there was a lethargic atmosphere, with people sprawled across the seats, reading or rolling joints. Someone would shout: 'Drive like an undertaker,' so their hands wouldn't be jolted while skinning up.

I once deliberately slammed on the brakes as a wind-up, and Rizlas, tobacco and dope showered on to the floor. I didn't care. Cannabis was not my drug of choice. Joe spoke in whispers because his singing style hurt his throat, and he complained about the thick dope smoke in the van – although he also smoked the joints. I wound the windows right down, also to wind the band up. Topper had an air-pistol and would fire at targets from the window as we drove – road signs, cows. And there were always books and newspapers about. And always music and a scramble to gain control of the tape machine. We would discuss songs or slag them off in a matey sort of way if it was a 'rival' band. And sometimes the van contained a fan or two along for the ride.

The band were always keen to meet whatever fans there were, and there weren't huge numbers at that time. One of my first instructions was to make sure kids could come into the dressing room once the band had grabbed a cold drink and dried off the sweat and spittle after a performance. The band didn't want to sign autographs and then push off, they wanted to meet their fans. This was all new to me. Part of the mystique of rock musicians at the time was that they wore glamorous clothes, led glamorous lives and stayed aloof from the common people who bought their records and went to their concerts. The Clash were the opposite. They wore the same clothes on-stage that they had been wearing all day, and they wanted to be accessible. Kids could talk to them – they could talk about drum skins with Topper, or the unwelcome rise of the National Front with Joe.

Joe wanted to know about the towns he was visiting. What it was like to grow up in Sheffield, or Newcastle. He used to chat to me in the van about Lancaster, and compare it with his time with a rockabilly band in Newport, Wales, where he was known as 'Woody' (we used to wind him up about that). Fans would ask where we were playing tomorrow, and Joe kept a notebook of their names, telling doormen to put them on the guest list at gigs. He would ask where they were kipping, and we always ended up with a few kids coming back to our hotel to sleep. The floor of my room would always have people asleep on it. But so would Joe's, unless he had a woman with him, which was fair dos. Being accessible to fans was all part of the punk movement, or at least the Clash's version of it. They encouraged other burgeoning bands. 'We did it, why don't you? Get up and play.' If some lads wandered in during a soundcheck and said they played in a band, there'd be a fair chance they would be invited to do an opening half-hour set that night.

This was the band's first big tour of the country, and we were staying in quite plush hotels. It was wonderful for the guys to wander in after a gig with a little crowd of fans. Mick was still living with his nan at Wilmcote House, a tower block off the Harrow Road. Joe and Paul were in squats, and Topper was in a rented flat off the Seven Sisters Road. And here they were in a luxury hotel! It was like they had won the pools. The band and fans would festoon the bar. Fans went to the bedrooms and the band were saying, 'Woa! Look what we got. Come and share it. Have a bath. Have a shower. Call room service.' They didn't really think that they would have to pay – which led to problems later. The hotels were about cushioned luxury. The band didn't smash the places up, Keith Moon or Led Zeppelin-style, but they weren't respectful, either, particularly to the sort of people who thought staying in a hotel gave them some sort of status. We had fun, we had a laugh. At the Atlantic Tower in Liverpool Joe and I went along the corridor howling like dogs, and then we started acting like dogs, going on all fours and nibbling at leftovers from room-service trays left outside doors. There was disgust and disbelief on the faces of some of the other guests.

Another of my early jobs was to smooth the way for the band to leave in the mornings. They had been caught and prosecuted for stealing towels from the Holiday Inn, Newcastle, on their previous tour – something that probably every travelling sales rep has done, but which turned into a big thing because 'punk rockers' were involved. So there were bag searches when we left a hotel, often with the police involved.

My other chief job was to make sure everything was ready for when the Clash hit the stage – including the band, who I gee-ed up minutes before each show, like a football manager giving a team talk. I loved the sheer magnitude of the panic attack that took hold as the time for the set approached. Junkies talk about the rush of smack being like six white stallions galloping up the spine to the brain. This was better. This was pressure, building and building from the inside, but just knowing that it was worth doing made me learn to ride it out, until surfing on the lip of the tidal wave of anxiety became a buzz in itself. And the feeling was usually amplified with amphetamine or Methedrine.

Spitting – 'gobbing' – became a problem on this tour. The custom has become one of the clichés of punk-rock behaviour, and it was rife at punk gigs in 1977, although none of the bands, with the possible exception of the Sex Pistols, encouraged it. Who wants to be spat at? Gobbing reputedly started because Pistols' singer Johnny Rotten used to spit on to the stage floor, footballer-style, and occasionally into the audience, some of whom spat back. It was disgusting to be on the receiving end of volley upon volley of phlegm. Professional roadies and sound engineers with long hair, beer bellies and big bunches of keys jangling from their flared jeans would refuse to do their job, and so I had to, returning to the wings with everything – clothes, hair, specs – covered in mucus. The band would have to dash to the side for me to wipe the guitar frets because they'd become too slippery to play. The band continued to wear their day clothes to play in, but they had to take fresh clothes to change into immediately after they came off stage. They washed their clothes in the hotel sinks, trying to scrub out the mucus. After the tour Joe Strummer went down with hepatitis and was treated at Fulham Hospital. People tend to associate hepatitis with needle-use – which was never in evidence. Joe is convinced he got the disease from spittle from the audience. I certainly remember him coming off stage somewhere in the Midlands and saying, 'Christ, Johnny, that was horrible. I copped a real greenie right down the back of my throat when I was singing.'

When we went to the Manchester Apollo, the audience were going wild before the gig and ripping out the seats. Seats stopped people from dancing, and the Clash didn't want to perform to people sitting on their arses and admiring their musicianship. They wanted to interact with the audience. So they didn't like seated venues, and watched the antics from backstage with disaffected amusement. We were even running a little sweepstake on how much damage would be caused.

'I reckon they'll trash them all up to row G.'

'No, look at that bloke go. They'll easily reach J.'

As the mayhem continued, Richard Hell wandered up to me

and mumbled, 'Where are we tonight?' Americans particularly like to come on stage yelling, 'Hallo, Sheffield!' (or wherever).

'Leeds,' I said.

He went on-stage with his band.

'Hallo, Leeds!'

The stalwart Lancastrians, already hyped up, seethed. He saw someone heave a bit of broken seat at him and leapt into the crowd wielding his sky-blue bass. He was showered with punches and gob and retreated across the stage pushing over the amps and the drums as he ran. Some of the crowd set off after him, and he dodged missiles until he reached the dressing-room toilets – his usual safety zone – and made his escape through the window, eventually cowering in the car park.

Richard Hell didn't know what had hit him, but this was British punk rock. He had always claimed to be the founder of punk. Bernie Rhodes and the Clash had brought him and the band over from New York for the Out of Control tour, and he had been prominent in the New York underground 'punk' scene long before the British punk explosion. So perhaps his claim could be supported. But if punk ever had anything to do with relating to working-class kids rather than striking a pose, then count Richard Hell out as its founder. But he did have a lot of style, and his pinned eyes revealed access to seriously good drugs.

Then the Clash came on-stage, thriving on the adrenalin-charged atmosphere, feeding off the near-riotous audience. Chaos and disorder seemed to bring out the best in the Clash.

The tour came to an end. I never did get paid by Richard Hell for the work I had done. But I asked him for a book of his poems, written under his real name of Richard Meyers. He gave it to me, and I was pleased. I haven't got it now.

More importantly, I had become friends with the Clash. I'm not a shy fellow. They paid me off, said, 'Thanks very much for your help. See ya.' And I went to see my parents for Christmas.

But I was hooked. Energy was at the hub of everything with the Clash. From the start of a gig they ran on-stage – it was like the gun going off at the start of a sprint – grabbed their instruments, then 'one two three four' and in. There was lots of jumping about, running, bumping into each other. It was charged-up music – not necessarily fast, in fact some of the reggae-influenced tunes were fairly slow – but full of bursts of angry energy. The music was confrontational and so were the band. They didn't look at each other while they were playing, didn't smile at each other thinking, Hmm, nice guitar lick. They were looking at people in the audience, thrashing the guitar strings, pounding the drums and straining their throats with a message. Strummer's 'electric leg' would be pumping up and down. And those in the audience didn't interact with each other, beyond bouncing off one another while dancing. It was too loud to talk, there was too much to see and take in.

I had been a part of all that, helping to make it all happen, and I wanted more. But I had been paid off. Dave South, a professional soundman who had worked for every band around, had said to me, 'You want to watch out. Being on the road is like going to sea for a sailor. It gets into your blood and you feel you can't do without it.' I didn't know what he meant.

3

*C*hristmas 1977, and my thoughts strayed to Belle Vue funfair, Manchester, which I had visited each winter as a child on a coach trip run by Cadishead British Legion to see the circus.

Belle Vue, where I had seen Bob Marley play the year before. Belle Vue, a funfair with fifties-style dance halls, where a few weeks previously we had done a gig to be filmed for *So It Goes*, the TV music show produced by Tony Wilson ...

The hall where the Clash played was all scuffed velvet and theatre boxes, in which the film crew set up lights and cameras. Steep spiral stairs led from the dressing rooms to the stage, which was crammed with the Clash's equipment. The soundchecks took ages, and there was more delay as the film crews set up.

The foyer was like that of a cinema, full of glass windows and doors. It was just not the right venue for a punk gig, and the promoters didn't know what was going to hit them. The crowd, waiting in the deserted funfair, heard snatches of the soundcheck. They weren't nice polite youngsters; they were punk rockers, or certainly would be after the gig. It was something of a baptism, or confirmation. London – everywhere – was burning with boredom.

Windows smashed, doors burst open, and teenagers scurried in, heading for all corners of the hall like rats in a fire. The security guards reacted like characters in an Ealing comedy, simply pushing back their peaked caps and scratching their heads in bewilderment. After half-hearted attempts to catch

EL LIOUXpy....
SiOUXSiE aNd the
BULLShits...A
WiZARd, a tRUE PAIN iN
thE ARSE...

some of the rushing punks they gave up. The excitement
turned to fear. Security men made themselves scarce, while
the roadies and film crew saw it all as a bloody nuisance –
damned kids getting in the way of their highly technical
work. But the exuberance of the crowd filled the Clash with
delight as they peered at the mayhem from backstage. I was
out front, striding up to the foyer and back every so often to
report to the band what was going on. Tony Wilson seemed to
appreciate the theatre of the moment too.

Siouxsie Sioux, McClaren's protégé, and her band the Banshees, formed from the fashionable Bromley Contingent, were playing support. They were Malcolm's fashion statements, riding on the ripped coat-tails of the Pistols. Siouxsie, bored and listless, was crammed on to a tiny area of the stage which was otherwise filled with the Clash's gear. She had to stand almost on top of the drums, and was sulking like a spoilt child at a party. She wore thigh-high boots and fishnets, and a cold white face. She cut no ice with the highly charged crowd and was unable to cope with the audience's energy and dynamism. She ran through her set and quit the stage, kicking petulantly but violently at the wedge monitor as she left.

The Clash were just itching to get out there, desperate to join in. Running on-stage they were frustrated by the spiral staircase, and tripped over their guitars, their feet, and each other in the rush. They played a dynamic set, fed from the audience's energy. The band were just not used to the heat from the extra film lights. They never appeared on *Top of the Pops* because they refused to mime. Strummer collapsed. The 'Garageland' drum beat started. Joe bashed the rhythm on the wooden drum rise and leapt up like a voodoo jack-in-the-box. He was manic . . . he launched into the vocal. Everyone yelled along with the chorus. The Clash took the crowd's energy and gave it back. The interaction and fusion was a total contrast to Siouxsie's action and audience reaction.

Afterwards I was asked to run Siouxsie and her band to the station to get their train. She didn't want to stay for a drink. We climbed into the Clash's filthy minibus on a foul Manchester evening. The rain dripped off her black dyed hair on to her schoolgirl mackintosh, which was wrapped around her, her body language signalled rejection. She was silent – totally pissed off as we drove through the dark rainy city.

I tried to talk to her – I was charged up by the show and everything that had happened: the riot, the music, the response. I didn't get a word of reply. I dropped her at

35

Piccadilly station and didn't even get a 'thank you'. What an old bag. I rushed back to the hotel to join the band celebrating in the bar with a whole load of fans drinking jelly-beans, high on adrenalin from the gig. A jelly-bean – every white spirit in the bar plus Pernod and black and lemonade – was a serious drink for angry times. This was the high life.

Dawn was in the late morning in Camden Town. It found me, soon after Christmas, on a borrowed, damp, stained mattress on the bare floorboards of the first-floor office of Rehearsal Rehearsals. Light entered lazily and dustily through the grimed and cracked windows, seven feet up the wall. I had to stand on a chair to look out on to a cobbled, former British Rail goods yard, now dotted around the sides with garages and lock-ups. I didn't bother very often.

I reached for my specs and began the ritual of brewing tea on a Camping Gaz stove, then dragged my mattress and sleeping bag into the huge bare backroom, which was like an empty classroom. I wandered to the toilet to piss, brushing against one of the gangster movie posters and *Evening Standard* bills screaming of deviant crimes which plastered the walls, loosening the Sellotape on one corner so that it slowly tried to roll itself up before falling with a swish to the floor. I quickly washed in the sink, fed with water running straight in from the roof through a broken fan-light into the tank, nourishing the strange plants growing in it. Rehearsal Rehearsals was an old Customs warehouse, with thick, black, damp walls. Bernie Rhodes leased it – no one knew how. It was impossible to tell what kind of day it was outside so I switched on the three-bar electric fire anyway and gulped my tea in my daily race to get out.

The doorbell rang. I knew it was the Baker, come to chivvy me along. It was typical of Bernie that I was the only person with a key to the place. No one else was trusted. I wasn't trusted, but I lived there.

36

The Baker. Paul gave him the name – some said unkindly, because he looked like a lump of dough. But he did look exactly like he should work in a bakery. Everyone knew he was called Barry, but only his mum called him that. He was my fellow non-musician in the Clash entourage. We were mates but like chalk and cheese. I loved rock 'n 'roll, the Elvis Sun sessions. He preferred the O'Jays and the Philly sound to punk rock. He was short and chunky and transpontine – he lived over the bridge in Barnes with his mum and cacti. He had left school early and started an apprenticeship as a printer but jacked it in when his school mates formed a band. He became their driver and roadie – simply because he had the wheels. When Subway Sect signed up with Bernie he came as part of the package and it didn't take the Clash long to figure out that he was a man who got things done. He was a very practical bloke, as practical as I wasn't, and as straight as I was a drugs fiend. He hardly ever drank because he was driving all the time. I drove as well as drank. The joke was that I ran a school of drink-driving.

Topper was the first to arrive, as always, with his dog, Battersea, a dark, wiry, jumpy and nervy, smooth-haired mongrel from Battersea Dogs' Home. Topper was very fit and always raring to play, but would often want to shoot over to the pub for a quick drink first to calm his nerves.

Paul entered. The epitome of cool, spot on from his barnet to his boots, you knew he had taken a good look at himself before walking out the front door.

'All right, Johnny? Christ, your jeans are a bit tight. As tight as Bernie.'

He was always making Bernie jokes, and I could never understand how much a serious, tough-minded man like Bernie could be upset by such silliness. But at that point Paul's jokes had taken on a harder edge. He was struggling to learn the bass-lines, note by note, to Joe and Mick's new songs, and we were all constantly broke, despite the Clash's deal with CBS and the success of the first album.

I left Paul and Topper mucking about on the little pop-pop moped Paul had left at Rehearsals when we moved out. They were riding up and down the tunnels behind the railway track, goofing around on the bike like the kids that they were.

I set off in the Baker's little yellow Renault 5 to pick up Mick. He insisted on being collected from Wilmcote House, the tower block where he lived with his gran. The Baker hated doing it, so it usually fell to me. It was a job that needed patience. It meant hanging around for the lift with dodgy people who wouldn't look you in the eye; the place smelling of piss ... clichéd, but true. His gran had a high-pitched voice and called him Michael. He hated it. He treated her like a hired help he couldn't sack. He was surly and shouted orders. Music blasted out in this tiny little flat and she always shouted: 'Turn it down, Michael, it's much too loud.' She didn't care that he had been on the front page of *NME*. She'd say: 'I'm making tea, Michael, would he like some?' She never spoke directly to me. He always took ages getting ready. His dressing ritual had got gradually longer, and would continue to do so. He checked his wardrobe, carefully washed and dressed. Later, much later, the Baker asked me whether we should have nipped all this in the bud. Maybe, but we didn't.

I looked out the window over the Westway, thinking that the punk classics from the first album were written on this balcony. Mick chose an outfit in his bedroom. He emerged, looking like a rock star. Down the pissy lift and into the yellow Renault.

Meanwhile, Strummer had arrived by bus. Often he walked from his room in Albany Street, stopping on the way in record and book shops. By the time he arrived Mick was hungry.

'Let's go down the café.'

'Oh, for fuck's sake, let's get on,' said Joe's hoarse voice.

38

'No, I want to eat. I can't play if I'm hungry.'

'None of us can play if we spend all our time in the café.'

We collected a paper from over the road, strode past the lock, down Chalk Farm Road, over the canal, past the Caernarvon Arms and into George's Café, a home from home, run by an Italian family who ran a slate for us when we were skint – which was often. Their daughter, Gaby, had eyes that just melted you, huge dewy eyes. We were all in love with her. A deer-like girl. I don't think anyone ever made the remotest move towards her. It was our home base, and we used it for music-press interviews.

Back at Rehearsals it was cold and damp, as always, and the strip lighting made it seem colder. There were electric fires but we might as well have just lit matches for all the effect they had. One of the first things I did on taking control was to get a big Calor Gaz heater.

There was no daylight in the rehearsal room, just a row of barber's chairs that were too damp to sit on. These stood against the back wall, on which Paul had painted a bleak mural of the Westway and a car dump. There was a jukebox, with an eclectic range of music, from the earliest Elvis to obscure ska and reggae. But to everyone's utmost frustration, it didn't work any more.

The room was tiny but all the gear was laid out as if on-stage. I didn't realize until other roadies came round to see me that other bands rehearsed quietly and comfortably. To me, and the Clash, it seemed natural to rehearse at full pelt as if doing a gig.

By now it was mid-afternoon. They were on edge, as always before a rehearsal, pacing like boxers pacing the ring before a bout, moaning at me about the cold room. They began slowly, not knowing what to do with the pent-up energy, but with instruments in their hands I didn't exist for them until they wanted something: a plectrum, drumsticks, a cup of tea. With minimal vocals, they rattled through a few old favourites to

39

build up a head of steam: 'Pressure Drop', 'Protex Blue'. Mick's voice came over the PA: 'Johnny, come and skin up.' Although I didn't smoke dope I rolled a better joint than any of them. I returned to the office upstairs. 'Johnny! Guitar string!' Joe went through a lot of guitar strings, even rehearsing. They treated their guitars like weapons, not instruments. I slapped a couple of strings on the amp. 'You break them, you change them.' 'White Man in Hammersmith Palais' leaked out through the wooden loading bays. After school the Camden Town Ferrets – a bunch of giggling schoolgirls – assembled outside. They never wanted to come in, they just stood listening and clucking. The band said hello to them when they went out for air, and they were happy with that. Sometimes they'd go to the café and sit at the next table, giggling.

The Clash played the song straight through, then shouted at each other, then played it again. Topper was still not sure of his position with the band. He knew what he was doing with the drums and did it well, but he did what he was told and did not make any creative suggestions. Mick was the muso. The main concern was keeping the tempo, hitting a crescendo together, attacking the notes. Joe shouted at Mick: 'Too many fiddly bits. It don't need a long solo.'

Mick to Paul, 'Keep up.'

'Fuck off, cunt.'

That was Paul's catchphrase. Not very witty, but often effective. He said it quietly, sometimes in jest, sometimes with menace. But the music was good. They knew it was good. They worked at it. When they rehearsed, they rehearsed. They didn't fuck about, and although they smoked prodigious amounts of dope, somehow it made them more hyped-up instead of relaxed. I never heard them jam. They played songs.

The Baker drove Mick home, the rest wandered off. I swept up the fag ends, emptied ashtrays, and prepared the room for the Subway Sect, who were coming in to rehearse that evening. The Subways were another band Bernie was involved in, along with the Coventry Automatics and Dexy's Midnight Runners. I was supposed to sit there with them, but when they arrived I told them I wanted to go over the pub, so I'd lock them in.

'Eh? Fuck off. It'll be like prison. And it's freezing.'

'I'm not sitting here all night listening to you lot.'

They phoned me at the pub later from the Rehearsals payphone.

'We've finished. Let us out.'

'You'll have to wait. I've just got another beer.'

Later, with Rehearsals locked, my nostrils full of speed, I headed for Dingwalls, and after that closed wandered the streets near Regent's Park, eerie animal noises from the zoo filling my ears. I went back to Rehearsals to defy the amphetamine and the cold to sleep.

Sometimes my nights were enlivened by telephone calls from Gordy, a lad we had met in Belfast. He seemed to represent all those alienated, isolated and afraid people out there.

'What's the band up to?' he'd say. 'How's Joe? Is there a new song coming out?'

He was there in the Falls Road among soldiers and guns, knee-cappings and fear, ringing Clash HQ for inspiration, for escape. He thought he was in personal touch with London rock'n'roll and the bright lights. What did he get? Me, sitting on my own in a hovel, speeding. He thought he was calling paradise, and maybe for him it was.

I also fielded frequent calls, day and night, for Paul, from Patti Smith, whom he had met the previous spring. She rang from the various European cities she visited on tour. It was obvious she wasn't ringing to discuss the weather in Turin. If Paul was there when she phoned he'd wave his hands and say: 'Tell her I'm out.' But he didn't want me to get rid of her, and I developed a gradual telephone relationship with her. When she came back to London, I went to see her at the Portobello

41

Hotel, as well as at the Rainbow gigs. But generally I preferred talking to Gordy.

I was taken aback when I once took a phone call for 'John'. It put me on my guard. 'Who is it?'

'It's his mother.'

'Oh, you mean Joe. He's not here.'

'Is he well? Is he looking after himself? Could you ask him to get in touch.' And she confided in me how much she worried about him, and I filled her in with the news – I didn't mention the hepatitis – and nagged Joe gently to contact her himself.

Rehearsal Rehearsals had been my home since I turned up in London and asked for a job. Previously it had been the Clash's nest, their home. Paul and Joe had lived there, and it was the garageland of the song. It was threatening, dark and unpleasant. But to me it felt like home.

One day my morning ritual was interrupted by the phone. I got calls from Bernie any time of the day or night.

'Liss-ern, liss-ern. Do you realize the situation?' (We used to mimick his lisp and his catchphrase.) 'People just put up with it. Piles of rubbish everywhere. What do you feel about this? What are you going to do about it?'

In '78 there were strikes aplenty. I was only just awake and not in the mood for Bernie's typical probing. 'I don't know, Bernard. Fuck knows.'

'Fuck knows ain't good enough. Things won't change unless you react. Grab hold of the situation … Come and collect this package. It's got to be at CBS. Now.'

Everything had to be immediate with Bernie, but I was quite pleased. It was a chance to go up west, maybe look in on Roadent. Robin Crocker, who had stayed the night at Rehearsals, decided to come with me, and a glint of kindness made me invite Topper along. He had asked me round to his gaff the night before to play pool. Set up in the room was a kid's pool table. There was not enough room for the

42

cues. But he was pleased I had visited him. Pathetic, really.

Speeding, and bearing in mind Camden's one-way system, it was quicker to walk to Bernie's. He had a top-floor flat in Camden Road, near Holloway Prison, where he lived with his partner Sheila and his son, although I hardly ever saw him – I don't know if anyone did. Sheila, thin and stooping, was always pleasant and apologetic. She answered the door, and kept me waiting ten minutes on the doorstep before handing over the package. I'd only been in the flat a couple of times before. Once, I was invited to sit down, but the only place to sit was on stacks of *Marxist International*. The flat had been piled high with boxes of T-shirts and hundreds of copies of

the original *Capital Radio* EP, which was supposed to be a rarity. Bernie was short and balding, with bad posture. He tended to peer up at me through his aviator glasses. He always wore a leather motorbike jacket, tight Levi's and creepers – a bit of a Teddy Boy image that never quite looked right. But it was brave of him to try. Caution wasn't a part of his make-up, except in parting with money. He had hidden depths – like his car. He had asked me to run his British racing green Renault home for him one night, and I nearly got whiplash when I tickled the accelerator. He had a Ferrari engine beneath the family-car bonnet.

We were always treated with disdain by the uniformed doormen at CBS in Soho Square. We were never made to feel welcome at that place, except by the press officer Ellie Smith, a thin North American who always wore full lipstick and make-up. She was probably nice to all the bands with CBS, but she gave the impression that she was being specially nice to you. We were hoping for a cold beer from the fridge in the office, but she offered tea. As if to make up, she nodded towards a corner. 'There's some promos there.'

She left the room and we dived in. Topper was adept at loading himself with as many albums as he could. I chose only Abba releases and Country albums.

Topper and Crocker, staggering under the weight of albums marked 'For promotional use: Not for resale', headed straight for Cheapo's record shop just round the corner, where they sold them.

We found Roadent, as expected, decked out in bondage gear in the Pistols' studio in Denmark Street, two minutes from Soho Square. In the middle of the street of music shops, down an alley and in a side door, the studio was really a tiny terraced house, and Roadent occupied the back room. His huge, black-booted feet were on the desk. The room was minute compared with the Rehearsals warehouse, and his boots were the dominant feature. I liked him and often visited

44

to swap tales about the best place to buy guitar strings. I had stepped into his shoes, and there was a friendly rivalry between us. Of late he hadn't had much to do. The Pistols had been thriving on their notoriety, but hadn't been producing much, while the Clash had been rehearsing hard. The Pistols had played a few gigs under the name of the Spots at tiny clubs the previous year. I'd been to Wigan Casino with my arm in a sling and a sophisticated recorder concealed under the masses of bandages to bootleg the gig, but they hadn't turned up. They were now in America, and the news that filtered through was of outrageous behaviour and fights within the band.

'Looks like leaving the Clash was a mistake, mate,' I said.

'We'll see,' he smiled, not giving anything away.

The Clash camp followed the Pistols' career with interest and a mixture of jealousy and scorn. The Pistols had found fame and notoriety and were in America, while we were in cold Camden, working hard at material for the second album. Sid Vicious had hung around with Paul and Mick and the punk pool of talent which Bernie had pulled together in early 1976. Bernie had also worked with ex-Pistol Glen Matlock, Steve Jones and Paul Cook, giving direction to the embryo band. He had got Rotten into the Pistols.

Roadent came with us to the Centrale, a café for cheap eats next door to a strip joint, and a West End haven for the Clash when walking around in punk gear could be dangerous. We all waited, smirking, for Roadent to order first.

'Jam pudding and custard. Then egg, sausage, beans and chips. Then tea.'

He always ordered, and ate, in reverse order. He preferred his meals that way.

We went to the Cambridge, just past St Martin's college on the Charing Cross Road. We used the separate bar upstairs, where Malcolm held court. Punks came and went, stopping to pass a few words with us. It was a place where ideas were

MELCOLM AND The SEX
PUPPets.. OR
So he would
have us believe..

swapped, but with a competitive edge. Malcolm and Bernie
were there. To see them together was always interesting. They
were pals from their mod days, and always alluding to 1968
and the Paris Commune. Bernie, normally so opinionated,
seemed to be in Malcolm's shadow. With hindsight perhaps he
was simply being cagey and keeping his cards close to his
chest. Malcolm's conversation hinged around musicians and
women. When he talked, others kept quiet. They kept their
distance from us, but watched across the bar.

'Takes you back,' said Crocker.

The bar had been a regular haunt for the Pistols, Clash and the small core of punk rockers throughout 1976 and 1977. Now 'punk' had caught on, most of the original crew drank elsewhere.

Bernie and Micky Foote, his sidekick, often used to sit across the bar. Occasionally Footey would come across with a message from Bernie. Something like: 'Johnny, don't stay in here all night. The Subways are at Rehearsals soon, you've got to let them in.'

Micky Foote had come into the Clash circle with Joe, his mate from his days in South Wales, and later the soundman with Joe's old band, the 101ers. Bernie now spent little time with the Clash, and when he did see them there were usually rows about money, with Jones leading the way. These would turn into screaming matches, with Micky backing up Bernie, although he lived with Joe at Albany Street.

Micky's crime, though, was to varispeed up *Clash City Rockers* while Mick and Joe were in Jamaica writing new material. Jones was furious, and that was the end of Micky Foote.

About a week after this outing to the West End, the Pistols split up. The Clash were ready to step into their shoes.

O n Fridays – pay day – Bernard usually called in at
Rehearsals with my wages – fifteen quid. I always had to
ask for the money, but this week he hadn't showed up, and I
had tried to contact him all day. I was desperate for money to
score and buy beer – it was the weekend.

I finally got through in the late evening, and said, 'Where's
my pay?'

'You should have come up here and got it. You've got to
learn to go and get what you want. I wanted you to learn
that.'

'What? You've kept me waiting all day to teach me some
rotten lesson?'

We all learnt with the Clash to know what you want and
grab it. It was no use being polite.

We were all getting pissed off with Bernie, who rarely
showed his face. The Clash were featured nearly every week in
the music press, they were recognized in the street, but were
getting fifteen quid a week from Bernie. It was more than the
dole, but it wasn't enough for the rock'n'roll lifestyle that
Mick had always wanted and now felt he had earned. We had
to prise the cash for a new set of guitar strings from Bernie,
but we also had to admire his touch:

Like with the Marxist gig in Paris. We had flown to Charles
de Gaulle airport, and throughout the flight Joe had interro-
gated Bernie, unsuccessfully, about the gig.

'What's it all about?'

'Listen, it's right up your street. You'll love it.'

'Yeah, but what is it? What's it in aid of?'

48

'I know about Paris. I know about revolution. The way you stand is an act of revolution, you know.'

'Who are we playing to?'

'You'll meet a lot of fascinating people.'

The venue was like a huge circus top. We had travelled light, me and Micky Foote, former soundman and producer of *The Clash*, with the guitars, and the Baker with the traps case for Topper's kit. Me and the Baker checked the equipment on stage – it was ropy – but we couldn't do a soundcheck. There were four guys with beards on stage singing French folk songs, and the Clash were on next.

Bernard gave me a can of Halford's red spray paint and peered up through his aviator specs to provide instructions.

The singers were about to launch into another melody. I walked on stage.

'Come on. *Allez*. Fuck off. The Clash are coming on now. Fuck off.'

I approached the backdrop – huge pictures of Lenin and Marx, and with the can at arm's length, sprayed over it: THE CLA— The hall exploded with indignation and there was a surge towards the stage. The Clash ran on and drowned the angry roar. Smoke canisters flew through the air and I ran about kicking them off stage. Police appeared at the back of the hall. The crowd surged towards them. The police charged, and the crowd headed back towards the stage. The band were playing manically, grinning and crying from the gas. I glanced at Bernie. He was standing calmly, with a satisfied grin.

Afterwards he said, 'Come with me,' and we picked our way through broken glass to see the organizers.

A bearded radical said, 'That was mayhem.'

Bernie half-smiled. 'What do you expect when you hire the Clash? A folk band?'

'There's a lot of damage. How can we pay you? We'll have to come to an arrangement.'

I grabbed him in a neck lock, and we were paid a big bundle of cash in a canvas bag.

He said, 'Look at this,' and produced a medieval-style mace – a wooden pole with chain and ball attached. 'We took it from one of your fans.' Which was probably bollocks.

Bernie said, 'It's lovely. Can we have it?' I put it under my coat. We smuggled it through Customs in Topper's traps case, and he hung it on the wall of his flat. He liked things like that.

But not having felt much of Bernie's touch for a while the Clash were feeling the pressure. *Clash City Rockers* had just been released, and the varispeeded-up treatment had brought back Mick and Joe's resentment that their recording had been tampered with by Micky Foote. It also brought back their anger with CBS for releasing 'Remote Control' as a single without their consent. They hadn't wanted a single that was also available on an album, and although they felt they had set the record straight and regained artistic control by insisting on 'Complete Control' as the third single, they now distrusted the record company. And CBS were now hassling them to record a second album.

With the Pistols gone, the Clash were left as the standard bearers of punk. But it was a frustrating time. Joe was in hospital for a month with hepatitis – which at least gave Paul time to learn by rote the bass line to 'Safe European Home'. He stayed late at Rehearsals, practising with headphones on, tongue pressed to top lip in concentration, while I pulled faces and waved two fingers at him to wind him up. The music press, and fans, were also waiting for the next album. There was another slanging match with Bernie, who had made a rare visit to Rehearsals.

'Listen, don't you realize the Subways are coming to rehearse in an hour? Johnny, get this place sorted out.'

Mick said, 'Fuck the Subways. What about us?'

'What do you mean? They rehearse here as well, you know.'

'Yeah, well perhaps you should be spending more time sorting us out with a recording studio. And they ain't using our gear.'

'It ain't your gear.'

Which shut Mick up, because it wasn't.

Joe came out of hospital and straight back to rehearsing. He was weak. He had gone yellow in hospital and was still jaundiced. One evening when the Baker had taken Mick home from Rehearsals, I suggested nipping over the boozer.

'I'll give it a miss. How much orange juice can you drink in a day?' Joe said.

He had quit drinking until he was fully recovered. It was an alien concept to me.

'What do you do when you go out, then?' I asked. 'I can't imagine a night on the town without booze.'

He looked at me straight. 'It's boring. And it gives you itchy feet. We'll go out tomorrow and I'll show you.'

Me and Joe went clubbing and I matched him, sticky orange juice for orange juice. Bands I usually enjoyed sounded crap. Conversations with acquaintances didn't flow. I looked straight through the scene I usually enjoyed. We went from Dingwalls to the Music Machine to the Speakeasy, looking for the familiar buzz that wouldn't come without drugs and alcohol.

'See?' said Joe. 'What next? What next?'

Dr Alimantado's 'Born for a Purpose' was on the sound system. Joe was on the wagon to become strong, to get the strength to be the singer with the Clash – to get the strength to be Joe Strummer.

Joe wasn't the only one getting impatient. The music press was biting back, with sniping pieces about Joe's White Mansion – 31 Albany Street, where he had moved the last autumn. I had dropped Joe off there between tour dates. I couldn't believe this big white fifteen-bedroom house fronting

Regent's Park. At the back, it was just a tall terraced building.
I was never allowed to use the front door.

Bernard did. It was leased by Sebastian Conran, son of
Superwoman author Shirley Conran and Habitat owner Terence.
He had swirled into the lobby of Albany Street one day like a
ludicrous and arrogant Georgian prince, to see 'the boys',
Jasper and Sebastian. The curl of his lip seemed to indicate
that he didn't rate us very much. It was mutual. But it was his
house. Bernie had wanted it to be the nerve centre of Clash
operations. Alex Michon, who designed punk clothes, worked
there, sometimes with Paul, developing the Clash 'look' and
designing T-shirts for the Clash and its entourage (not for
selling to fans – no attempt at Clash merchandising was made
at this stage). Another Albany Street resident, a big, chunky
photographer called Rocco, designed Clash stage backdrops.
One, put up at the Rainbow, showed an old woman sitting by
a gas fire in her council flat. Mick took one look at it and
said, 'I'm not getting on-stage until that's gone.' And it was
taken down and not used again. Mick thought it was taking
the piss out of him living at his nan's flat.

Bernie had started setting up an office in Albany Street,
but it never got further than placing a big desk in a big
white room with bare floorboards. Inside the house, it was
just like any number of squats, with weird people wandering
about. Joe had a small room right at the top, with just a
mattress in the corner and his records and books. The Lous,
a French lesbian junkie band, lived somewhere upstairs.
Sebastian didn't really do anything except design posters and
hang out with Joe. Jasper had a workshop and self-contained
flat in the basement, designing and making clothes. One
night when Crocker and me had run out of money the
amphetamines told us he would be a soft touch. We banged
on his door, and he simpered, 'Go away', while we bellowed:
'Let us in. Give us money.' Crocker broke the door in with a
lump of wood and we found Jasper in bed. He pointed to

his wallet. 'Take it and leave me alone.' Which we did.

The *NME* ran a piece about Joe living in luxury in the house of Sebastian, the wealthy Habitat heir. Joe moved out, into a squat near Edgware Road. Alex moved her sewing machines into the back room of Rehearsals, where I stowed my mattress, and we didn't see Sebastian after that.

In contrast to Joe's conscience-driven move to a squat, Mick moved to plush Pembridge Villas, off Portobello Road, with Tony James of Generation X. He took longer and longer to get ready when I picked him up for rehearsals, much to the irritation of the rest of the Clash, waiting to get on with it. Paul used to have a go: 'Where've you been? You and your mate Tony been playing with each other?'

In many ways it was me and Crocker who held the band together at that time. Crocker was Mick's old schoolmate. Crocker told me they had first met in a maths class, when they fought about who was the greatest – Bo Diddley or Chuck Berry. Crocker was always around, and was my mate in Camden. He did the things the other guys would have loved to have done had they dared. He had a daredevil air about him – gaunt, with prominent neck tendons like tree roots. Paul egged him on, the others liked hearing about his excesses. The Clash liked having him around. For one thing, he had been inside, and didn't mind talking about it. It gave them cred. We always called him Robin to his face: he said his surname reminded him of certain institutions.

Once, he had called at Rehearsals, wanting to go on a bender.

'I'm skint, mate,' I said.

'Don't worry, I'll buy. I had a stroke of luck today.'

We were off, drinking in the Camden pubs, then Dingwalls. He came back to sleep at Rehearsals. I found the key and lurched up to the office-cum-bedroom ... 'Where's all my fucking records?'

They had been Crocker's stroke of luck. He had shinned up

the drainpipe – a journey few others would have risked – through the landing window and had pinched them all, flogging them at Cheapo's. I confronted him. He admitted the crime.

'Yeah, but I got you pissed, and I got this speed.'

He made free with a mirror and razor blade. How could you get angry with someone like that?

On 30 March 1978, two of Topper's old mates from Dover, Steve and Pete Barnacle, arrived. Topper's first gig had been with their dad Bill's trad jazz band. They had brought a high-powered air rifle, with sights, to flog to Topper. He loved it. He had a fascination with guns. He had once called Paul and me into his hotel room in Birmingham to show us how he had written his name on the ceiling with air-pistol pellets. This had got us thrown out of the hotel.

Topper was haggling over the price when Crocker strutted in from the pub, rolling his shoulders like a man who owned the world.

'What do you think, Robin?'

'Yeah, it's nice.'

Crocker didn't play with guns – in the way that a chippie doesn't play with a chisel. He had done three years at Albany Prison, Isle of Wight, after holding up a bookie's in Streatham with a sawn-off shotgun.

Paul came in. 'Cor! Let's have a look,' and he wrested the rifle from Topper.

I left them to it. The Baker turned up with Mick and we started changing the drum skin on the snare.

I was shooting the breeze with Mick and Joe in the office, while rolling another spliff for them, when Mick suddenly got impatient:

'Where's Paul and Topper?'

'They went off to muck about.'

Then there were sirens and a screech of tyres. I jumped on the desk to peer out of the grimy window. A big Rover pulled across the entrance to the yard.

'Fucking hell, it's like *The Sweeney*.'

'What's going on? What's old Laurie been up to?' Mick and Joe were asking excitedly.

Laurie was the guy who ran the yard – a big, smartly dressed, heavy-looking London boy.

They grinned at the unexpected scene outside, while I stood on tip-toe to watch more cops pour out of cars, then crouched to look up at a police helicopter flying very low overhead. The office door was suddenly booted open.

'Don't move.' A big man in a suit pointed a pistol at us, *Sweeney*-style.

Cops poured in, shooting orders and questions from all sides: 'Let me see your hands ... Sit down ... How many are there? ... Where are the guns? ... What are they armed with?'

'What the fuck —?' Still on the desk, I glimpsed Paul and the others being herded into a van and driven away very fast. Joe and Mick were stoned. There was no need for dope-induced paranoia – this was for real. Joe was saying, 'What's going on?' while trying to hide his hash. The cops only wanted weapons, though. Mick was nearly hysterical when I told him what was going on. He screamed at me: 'Ask them, Johnny? Ask what's it all about? Ask where they're taking them.'

I managed to talk calmly to an officer in a cap. He said the others were being taken to Kentish Town for questioning. 'This is extremely serious. This is terrorism.'

Mick snapped into action. 'Something has got to be done here. Get Bernie.'

I fiddled with the pay-phone on the wall, using our 'secret' key to unlock the cash box to re-use the only 10p and 2p coins it contained. I got through to Sheila: 'He's out. I'll tell him when I see him.' Mick said, 'It's not good enough. All right, get Coon.'

Caroline Coon, ex-Clash-friendly *Melody Maker* journalist, Paul's girlfriend, and co-founder of Release, the legal-aid

CAROLINE COON
HOUSEWIFE,
SUPERSTAR
EX · MAYFAIR girl..

group for drug busts, rolled up in a taxi, and I shot us up to Kentish Town. Mick's leadership qualities came to the fore. He was now businesslike. He had me stop at several phone boxes on the way to try Bernie again and tell the record company what was going on. Bernie couldn't be found. Coon was in her element and welcomed the chance to prove her worth to Mick and Joe, who she knew regarded her as an ageing rich bitch.

'They're not letting anyone see them, and they're going to be remanded at Brixton.'

Coon sorted out bail, and next morning Mick and I went to pick them up from jail. Up the little side road to the prison, I said to Mick, 'I suppose this is all a bit unfamiliar to you.'

'What do you mean? I was brought up round here.'

'No. I meant being up and about at this time of day.'

'Huh,' he said. 'Well, Bernie should have been here.'

I pulled up to the gates of the prison like it was a stage door. Screws came running out. I'd started a security alert. 'You can't stop the motor there. Shift it.'

I walked back to the prison gates to meet Topper, Paul and Crocker as they came out. We milled about outside in the bleak morning air. You'd have thought they'd just done a ten-year stretch. Topper was still white and shaking. I walked away to get the car, and could hear Crocker saying, 'I never thought I'd see inside that place again. You asked me what it was like inside. Now you know ...'

They had been shooting at pigeons from the roof – not just any old pigeons, as it turned out. An old chap had built pigeon lofts up on one of the nearby warehouse roofs. He used to sit up there in a deckchair, surrounded by birds and run-down industrial buildings, a bit like Marlon Brando in *On the Waterfront*. I used to shout up to him: 'How's it going?'

'Great,' he'd shout down. 'Yourself?'

His birds were expensive racing pigeons. Topper, Paul, Crocker and the Barnacle brothers were charged with possessing an illegal weapon and attempted manslaughter. They had been seen with a rifle on the roof by officers of the British Transport Police, who had offices nearby. They had tipped off the Anti-Terrorist Squad, MI5, Flying Squad and the local cops that a bunch of anarchist guerrillas were taking pot shots at trains on the mainline to Euston.

A couple of weeks later I went to pick up Paul from his flat. He was grinning, pleased with himself, and beckoned me in.

'You'll never guess what I've done.'

He showed me his air gun and pointed across the road to the house of a woman he hated because she was always complaining about him.

'I opened the window just a little, just enough to poke the barrel out – and I shot her right in the arse!'

I had to laugh. I said, 'Don't you bloody learn?'

5

hose few pigeons caused us a lot of problems.

A condition of bail was daily reporting at local police stations. Me or the Baker had to take Topper and Paul there at some stage each day.

Paul had filled Rehearsals office – still my bedroom – with paint pots. He was painting a mural – a huge caricature of Bernie, surrounded by pigeons flying about his head and shitting on him. Paul and Topper hadn't forgiven him for doing absolutely nothing to help in the pigeon-shooting débâcle.

But we soon had other things to think about. The message had gradually filtered through that Bernie had been negotiating with CBS about the second Clash album. He had told us about the plans with an enthusiasm that was not really shared by the band. It was apparent that CBS, perhaps seeing the way that raw punk had mellowed into well-produced 'new-wave' music, wanted an album with no expense spared on production that would appeal to the American market and assimilate the Clash into the mainstream.

'They want Sandy Pearlman to produce it,' he told us.

Mick the muso was keen to play about in a 'proper' recording studio, and also for the Clash to break America. The others went along with him.

Pearlman had produced American rock band Blue Oyster Cult, who were touring Britain. CBS arranged for the Clash camp to see the band at Hammersmith Odeon. Sitting to watch a band at a huge rock venue strongly associated with early seventies 'progressive' rock acts wasn't the Clash's style. Topper watched the drummer, all the time tapping his hands on the seat-arms and his knees; Paul stared around the audience looking, vainly, for someone with style; Mick got into the music-making, if not the music, listening to where the guitars and drums kicked into the songs, checking what amps and guitars the band used. Joe and I sloped off to the bar mid-song. We found it almost deserted, ashtrays overflowing, the uniformed barman making towers of plastic glasses, striped with the yellow and brown dregs of unfinished pre-gig drinks. There were one or two Blue Oyster Cult fans with long hair, satin bomber jackets and stack heels strutting about.

I said, 'We're just watching an empty spectacle. There's nothing really going on there.'

Joe agreed: 'Yeah. How is it that American rock'n'roll bands don't cut it, when Elvis, Bo Diddley and all come from there? Now they ain't got no fire in their belly.'

'I hope you don't end up sounding like that with Pearlman producing the album.'

'No. Jones will see to that. We won't let him. I don't know nothing about production, but I trust Jones to take care of Pearlman. We know what we want.'

'Why the fuck are you working with him, though? He wears a baseball cap and Earth shoes!'

'It don't matter, Johnny. So long as we make our point. It's what we are saying and how we do it that counts, and the better it sounds the more people will hear it, y'see? He can't touch our music, only the sound of it. That's why we are here. That's why we are flirting with this stuff.'

I found it all repugnant – the Blue Oyster Cult T-shirts and merchandise for sale, the noise of the songs filtering through layers of fire doors into the bar, the veneer of American rock glamour. I knew what Joe was getting at, though, and hoped he wouldn't be let down.

Soon after the concert we all went to a reception to meet Pearlman and our American CBS stablemates. We were very out of place – the members of the other band were standing about sipping champagne, with their coiffured hair, flared suits and wives and girlfriends wearing cocktail dresses. They were all tiny; even in their stack heels they made Topper look tall. The whole do was very showbiz, very self-congratulatory; vol-au-vents and profiteroles were everywhere. We stood in a corner, sneering. We didn't like what we were seeing, and Bernie's doctrine, passed on to the Clash, was that the opposite of like was hate. We were not going to smarm around a man who had changed his name to Buck Dharma! Food started flying about. A guy spotted a cream cake hurtling towards him and ducked. His wife copped it, smack on the chest. Her day was ruined. He was angry.

'Who the fuck threw that?'

He squared up to us – a bunch of louts in the corner. We were used to confrontation. He wasn't. Dear Ellie Smith, the press officer, defused the situation with her charm. We left and headed for the nearest back-street boozer. Joe and Mick were still confident that they could use Sandy Pearlman to their own ends. Paul had loved the laugh. 'What a pompous balloon we burst!'

As always when the Clash faced a new challenge, they went back to their roots as a live band, and I was asked to set up a few impromptu gigs, which Bernie thought would also give Pearlman a chance to see the band perform and get a taste of what he needed to capture on record.

One of these was in the sports hall at Lanchester Polytechnic, near Coventry. The dressing room was a sports changing room, with tiled walls and floor. Someone had had the bright idea of putting Crocker on the door. It was hectic backstage, as with any thrown-together gig, but eventually we had improvised enough to get all the amps, lights and mikes set up, and I started clearing the dressing room of hangers-on so the band could prepare for their performance. There was a knock at the door. 'What?' said Crocker.

'It's Sandy.'

'Who?'

'Sandy Pearlman.'

'What d'you want?'

'I just came to say hi to the guys.'

'Well, you can't. Fuck off, mate.'

After some to-ing and fro-ing Pearlman burst into the room. He just had time to say hi before Crocker whacked him. Crocker could fight, as he had proved in many bars, gigs and motorway service stations. Pearlman went down, blood streaming on to his shirt and the floor. We all tried to stifle sniggers, except Bernie, who ran across to Pearlman, bent down and pulled out his linen handkerchief to dab at his face. He called for water and started cleaning him up. We were amazed. The Clash stepped over Pearlman's supine, groggy figure and hit the stage. It was usually my job to fire the band up before a gig. This time Crocker had done the job for me. I don't think he ever said sorry to Pearlman. So far, we had met Pearlman on his own territory, and he had met us on ours. Both times it had been a disaster.

This short Midlands tour helped to road-test the *Give 'Em Enough Rope* material, but I was sad about a missed opportunity. The TV show *Tiswas* was always a good reason for getting up on Saturday mornings. It was a kids' show, but acquired a cult following of adults. The Clash – the band that wouldn't do *Top of the Pops* – had really hustled to get on the show while we were in the Midlands. Eventually they were invited to appear, and were really excited about it. We were going to meet Chris Tarrant, Lenny Henry, Spit the Dog and Sally James, the sexy leather-clad co-presenter. It was a live show, and come that Saturday morning, Mick wouldn't get up. At a hurried conference, we decided that Joe and Paul would go to the show, Topper and Mick would stay behind. And I would stay to look after them. We kicked around the hotel in Birmingham, and watched the show on TV. Joe and Paul were 'put in the cage' on *Tiswas*. It looked great fun. I sulked and drank. I felt like someone had nicked my Cup-Final ticket. But Mick was unrepentant. For him, when he surfaced from bed, nothing had happened. He couldn't understand why I was upset. As far as he could see, this television show was just a silly aside to the main business of making music, and in a way he was right. But I was in it for the crack ...

•

A gig at the Manchester Apollo had gone down particularly well with the Mancunian crowd. Joe had said, 'Let's do another show here.' And it was left to me to organize it, on what was supposed to be a day off for me and the band. I found a small club willing to let the band play the next night. I had to find a smaller PA system, smaller lights, and get the Clash's backdrop,

The ANARCHY tour
ElECTRic CiRCUS, MANCHester
FRom MEMORY... 1976

designed by Paul, into the venue. News of the gig spread by word of mouth. It was all a lot of hassle, but it happened. The band were really enjoying themselves on-stage, spurred on by the impromptu nature of the show, and the crowd of devoted Clash fans – weekend punks wouldn't have known about the gig – who appreciated their efforts. Joe glanced at me and beckoned me with a jerk of his head. I thought a lead had come unplugged and bent down to check. Joe put his shoulder against my leg, straightened, and flipped me into the audience. I rode the crest of a wave in the sea of people. I yelled 'Baker' and managed to throw my specs to him, over Strummer's head, before sinking into the mass of ecstatic bodies, and swimming through the heaving, sweating audience to climb back on-stage. It was the first time I had seen the Clash from out front. They were good.

*T*he Clash were good, but it took a big event to make them realize just how big they had become.

The band were a late addition to the bill at the Anti-Nazi League rally in Victoria Park, London, which included Steel Pulse, X-Ray Spex, punk poet Patrick Fitzgerald and the Tom Robinson Band. We had already heard about and discussed the open-air concert, organized in response to the growing strength of the National Front. John Dennis, the ANL organizer, had approached Joe about doing the gig. His angle was flattering. He said the whole event would have more clout if the Clash were involved. The band agreed to do it, but were worried about the pure practicalities of playing to a huge crowd in a flat field in the middle of the afternoon – something we hadn't done before. We were always very careful to be in control of the music and how it was presented.

Mick said, 'Do they know what they're doing? Are they capable of organizing something this big?'

But that wasn't the real problem. The event was about more than just music, and we all realized that and discussed it endlessly. Just whose pole were the Clash tying their flag to? Was there a left-wing group behind the Anti-Nazi League? Would the Clash be seen to be endorsing their politics?

Bernie fanned the flames of doubt. 'Are they sure they know what they're doing?' he asked me on the phone. 'Do they really want to be knocking about with these student types? Isn't it all a bit safe and cosy? Aren't they preaching to the converted? And what's it going to achieve?'

It was all part of his strategy of keeping people on their

toes, making them ask questions, not just toeing the line, even if the line did appear to be radical. I told Joe Bernie's views.

He said, 'Yeah, but tell Bernie people have gotta walk before they run. If people get out of their bedsits for the day it'll have achieved something. If they think about politics just enough for 'em to know they hate fascists, that's something.'

John Dennis was mild-mannered, neat and conventional. He looked more like a lecturer than a student. He phoned me and fired questions: 'What will you need? What are your requirements backstage? What sound equipment will you need?' I said we would be all right with whatever the other bands were using. 'Don't worry about us, we'll fit in.' I reported his concern back to Bernie, who uttered the dreaded words: 'What about the backdrop?'

The bloody backdrop, of a fighter plane, was the bane of mine and the Baker's lives on the road, and a source of hilarity to the Clash. Not only was it heavy to lug into position on awkwardly shaped stages – and every stage was awkwardly shaped – we then had to cover it with black polythene sheeting, and, seconds before the band came on stage, balance precariously behind it on whatever we could find, ready to unwrap it, like the Queen unveiling a plaque at a hospital, just as the applause started – usually while Mick and Joe screamed for last-minute adjustments to their guitars ...

I had to get back on to Dennis and ask about the height of the stage roof, its width, how much room at the back ... He didn't know, and it threw a spanner in the works, leading to much practical and technical discussion. Soon it became the only thing about the show that Bernie cared about. Appearances were all-important to him. He had recently screeched to a halt beside me as I hurried up Parkway. 'Nice quiff, Johnny,' he said. I had just shelled out a fiver in Evans' gentleman's hairdressers for a two-back one-forward roll-over and press-brilliantined beauty with a DA at the back, so I was

66

chuffed. But he screeched off again before I could get down to business.

He called me just days before the show.

'Listen, can you get hold of a cheap van for the Victoria Park gig?'

'Yeah, I suppose so. What for?'

'You've got to take a film crew with you.'

On the morning of the show I had to go out and pick up the van – the cheapest I could find in Greater London – from a company known to us as Avawreck. It broke down three times on the way from Rickmansworth (via Camden) to Hackney, with the backdrop tied on the roof because it was too big to go inside. As we approached the park, the Baker started moaning.

'Oh, look at the state of that,' he wailed, pointing at a bloke with a beard in a grey woolly. The Baker was a bit of a snappy dresser in his own idiosyncratic style. He had had little contact with student life and confronting it en masse was a shock to him.

The gear was set up smoothly. This wasn't the sort of day for detailed soundchecks. Me and the Baker just used our judgement. We went to pick up the band. They were all excited about the show. As we drove in through the crowds it started to sink in that this was big – not just big, but huge. It was different to anything we had ever done before. There were columns of cops, blokes with collecting buckets, blokes selling *Socialist Worker*, giant trade-union banners, leather jackets, tweed jackets, green hair, no hair.

There was a jaunty atmosphere in the changing rooms of the old lido. All the performers were in there together, and there was a feeling of unity – united both behind the anti-National Front cause the show was promoting, but united in being part of the anti-Establishment. This wasn't Live Aid. There was a lot of good-natured banter. Mick walked in wearing a peaked cap, looking like a bus conductor. Someone shouted: 'Did you come by bus? Tickets please!' There was general mock horror when people realised he was going to wear it on-stage (eventually he threw it frisbee-like into the crowd after a couple of numbers). With all the musicians about we barely noticed the addition of Dave Mingay and his film crew to our team. They were starting filming what was to become *Rude Boy*. Bernie had vaguely mentioned something about the filming, and they were the last thing on my mind that day. It was a shambles backstage, like a huge student gig, except for the professional entourage of the Tom Robinson Band. They were a pro outfit, and as far as they were concerned it was the Anti-Nazi League starring the Tom Robinson Band. Now we liked the guy – we took the piss out of his ground-breaking homosexual stance by shouting: 'Backs to the walls, boys,' when he came in the dressing room. He laughed with us – it was his road crew that were the cold, clinical professionals. His band did what his roadies said, and it was our first whiff of organized efficiency – punk professionalism.

Minutes before the Clash were due on-stage, I was running up and down the steps at the back of the plank-and-scaffolding platform – the price paid to allow people at the back of the crowd to see the bands is having a very high stage. I was worried that Strummer might forget where he was and dive into the audience. A security man came up to me and said there was a woman looking for me.

'Ain't I lucky?'

'She says she's got your children with her.'

And there, peeping through the barbed-wire-topped fence at the far side of the stage was my ex-wife, who lived near the park with my two daughters. I organized with the security men to get them through, and settled them safely in the wings, where I wouldn't normally let anybody stand. There's a five-second glimpse of them in *Rude Boy*, as the Clash come on-stage. I felt quite proud that my kids had come to see Daddy at work. A guy in a silk tour jacket – a Tom Robinson roadie – said, 'Who let those kids up here?'

I said, 'I did. So what? Fuck off.'

Those Tom Robinson boys wanted to call all the shots. They couldn't handle our more maverick approach.

Master of ceremonies, Barry Myers, who we knew as a DJ at Dingwalls, introduced the Clash. They ran on-stage, fast as always, no twiddling with amps, straight into the first song. As always, I watched their faces closely, looking for any signals that they needed something. I saw their looks of delight freeze into fixed grins at the sudden realization of the size of the crowd, filling the park as far as the eye could see, heaving and bobbing to the music. The Clash's set was remarkable, but as I watched I became more and more aware that the Tom Robinson team were looking at their watches, shaking their heads, as cold as ice. Then, suddenly, the music stopped. Joe, Mick, Paul, all looked round at me. I didn't know what

THE CLASH RUSH the Stage at the ANTI-NAZI LEAGUE RALLY - VICTORIA PARK.

had happened. I was afraid. I knew nothing about electrics. I would have to go on stage in front of a crowd of 80,000 and try to fix ... whatever it was that was wrong. I saw the Scottish TRB road manager standing threateningly over the plug board. I knew immediately what had happened. I ran on-stage to Strummer saying, 'They've pulled the plug,' then back to the road manager. I shaped to hit him, then dived under him and replaced the plug. I grabbed Steve English, Johnny Rotten's mate and minder, and asked him to guard the plugs. No one would dare move him. Jimmy Pursey came on-stage, dressed like a reject from Billy Smart's circus, to join the Clash in singing 'White Riot'. The crowd roared once more. Pursey's band, Sham 69, were notorious for their skinhead following. The audience saw his appearance on stage at this gig as nailing his colours to the mast. I heard Jack Hazan, filming for Mingay just behind my shoulder, mutter, 'Unbelievable. The hair's standing up on my neck.'

Dave Mingay had grown mischievous. As I cleared our gear from the stage, he said to Ray Gange, whose part in *Rude Boy* was to be filmed as a Clash fan: 'You don't want to hear the Tom Robinson band. I bet the crowd don't either. Why don't you ask them?'

So Ray ran on-stage and started geeing up the audience. 'We want more Clash ...' Tom Robinson's road manager said, 'Get this idiot off.' And he was bundled away.

There was a slight sour taste in our mouths, but it soon disappeared in the jubilation backstage. We had done our set as arranged, and it wasn't our fault it had overrun. But the enormity of the event was such that a little egotism couldn't spoil it. Driving home with the band, everyone was delighted, excited and chattering. It was one thing to sell out a gig in a 1500 capacity hall, another to play before a crowd of 80,000, all going crazy. It began to sink in that the Clash were big. And Bernie's only input into the show had been quibbling about the backdrop.

7

I was standing on the doorstep of Pembridge Villas, holding a pack of hair dye I had just bought from round the corner in Westbourne Grove, waiting for a reply to my constant ringing. A third-floor window opened and Tony James's long, dark, floppy fringe appeared just long enough for him to glance down and fling me the keys. I let myself in and took the stairs two at a time up to the top flat of the plush converted house which Mick and Tony shared. I began work, emptying the ashtrays of last night's roaches, picking up the empty glasses. I put the kettle on for a cup of tea, poured Mick a glass of Ribena with ice cubes (it had to be just so). While the tea was brewing I found his stash and rolled him a five-skin joint, poured the tea, put the lot on a tray and knocked on his bedroom door. Mick slid his skinny bare torso up the bed.

'Morning, Johnny.'

Morning? It was two in the afternoon. He took a swig of his Ribena, put the joint in his mouth and waited for me to flick my Zippo.

'It's a good day for it,' I said. 'I've got your hair dye.'

He inhaled dope smoke deeply. A girl's form could be made out inert beneath the covers. I knew her name, but it was interchangeable with others – Kate, Ivy, Olivia – they were all good lookers. He exhaled and the room filled with smoke. I wanted to get out. I went back to the living room and pulled out the coke I had scored for him. I never cut his cocaine, like most middle-men would. True loyalty? I drew up a line for Mick on the glass-topped table, using the blade he kept for

Mick in Keef persona around 1978

splicing his tapes. I knew he was still going to be some time, so I picked a video from the small selection. Mick was one of only a few people I knew with a video recorder – he hadn't asked for it, he'd demanded it from Bernie. Paul followed suit fairly soon after. Topper waited quite some time for his. Joe hadn't wanted one. I made a small line for myself. The day seemed brighter and sharper as I settled in to watch the film. After a while I banged on the door again.

'Come on, Mick, recording studios cost money – yours!'

His chemical breakfast was still waiting for him on the table. At the third shout – 'Come on! You wanted me to do your barnet. I've got the dyeing gloves on' – he emerged wearing just his trousers, tight around his skinny calves and thighs. He wandered around the wall-to-wall record collection – not at all the collection of the punk rocker who sang about banishing Elvis and the Stones on '1977'. It revealed his comprehensive knowledge of pop music, black and white, Elvis albums sharing shelf-space with reggae and thirties blues and jazz. He selected Big Youth's 'Dreadlocks Dread', put it on the turntable, and gradually came to life, moving restlessly around the room, listening to the music, snapping questions. 'Do you hear that guitar sound? Wonder how they got that?'

Then Springsteen. He wasn't enjoying listening. This was serious. 'Listen how the drums come in ...'

He put on the demos from the Clash's session the previous night, playing the tape over and over, looking thoughtful and pacing the room. I wondered if I was going to have to grab him and hold him in the chair.

Tony James, fresh-faced bassist with Generation X, said hi as he passed through the room on the way to his band's office (which was all leather chairs and photos on the wall). He tried to look like a tough punk, but resembled a dressed-up schoolboy. He was a keen fell-walker, which didn't match with the punk image so he tried to keep it quiet. He sneaked off to go rambling the way others sneak off for a dirty weekend. He was a nice enough chap, all gushy and enthusiastic.

'Why do you share a flat with a wanker like that?' I asked Mick as he left.

'He has his uses.'

Mick was fiercely competitive with James, mocking his band, who once came round to Rehearsals in a stretch limo, cashing in on their good looks and the punk scene.

Mick was worried about his own looks. His hair was thinning, which was why he asked me round to dye it. His jaw structure bore an astonishing resemblance to Keith Richards's. He had grown his hair long, like Keith's, and was now dyeing it black like Keith's. He was copying Keith's cocaine habit as well.

73

So I started dyeing his hair and he was making a fuss: 'Make sure you wipe it off my forehead and neck.' I dabbed at the dribbling dye with a towel. Then he stopped me.

'Draw me up another line before we go any further.'

I got busy with the blade, and Mick bent over the table with a rolled fiver up his nostril, snorting the powder as black splashes from his head dropped all around.

He dried his hair, still pacing around the room, listening to music, vibing himself up. The demo tapes went into his attaché case, his leather shoes clicked efficiently against the pavement, and he meant business. We got into the car, drove the short walk to Basing Street studios, and he was out of the door before it came to a stop, across the red, black and chrome reception and into the control room. Joe, Paul and Topper were already there. Paul couldn't pass up the chance to take the piss out of Mick and Tony James. He came up to me, his big mouth and good teeth grinning gleefully.

'Here, was he there? Was he naked? Was he sitting naked on the coffee table with Mick lying underneath?'

Mick didn't care. He was in the control room, taking control.

Those sessions at Basing Street were interminable. Pearlman was a professional, and a perfectionist. He was staying at a hotel in Drury Lane, and I had to pick him up every day. He was always ready, bang on time, always chirpy. In the studio, every take had to be spot on. It would take forty attempts to get a guitar break right. To me this was excruciating. I never knew making a record could be so dull. Pearlman didn't find it exciting either. To him, dinner times were exciting, and they enlivened my day. He was a gourmet, and his Bible was a good-food guide to London. Pearlman looked on good food as a perk of his job, just as a businessman might treat himself to filet mignon after a hard day's geeing up his sales staff – except Pearlman's business was making records. He worked set hours. He never said, 'Wow, we're really grooving today, let's

♪ HAIR dyeing time!!..

keep at it.' He often ordered Indian takeaways from three different restaurants – typically, a dahl from one, the sag aloo from another, and nan bread from somewhere else, because he said each dish was the speciality of the particular house. The Baker and I went to collect his meals. We welcomed the opportunity to get out of the studio. When we delivered it, he sat back and relished every mouthful, saying, 'This is so good. You guys oughta get into this stuff!' Me and the Baker tootled off in the yellow Renault to collect the Clash's meals from McDonald's. They were gourmets too. Joe didn't have any gook on his Fish-Man burger. Mick didn't have cheese. And so we spent hour after hour – at hundreds of pounds an hour – in that sterile time capsule that was the recording studio. The musicians hiring the individual studios were just as much part of the building's machinery as the tape machines. Mick Taylor was there, two years – two years! – into his solo recording project. But the sound system was excellent. No one we knew had a stereo even remotely as good. I was amazed to hear an instrumental tune Jones had been working on come over the system with lyrics. It was only with the clarity of the system, after several plays, that I realized what, or rather, who, the song was about. Crocker! It was so tender, and so caring! We were stunned as the lyrics of 'Stay Free' came through, loud and clear. They brought a tear to the eye. After that, when the song was played live – which was rare – the Baker and I would relax our concentration on the musicians to dance feyly in the wings, pointing and making wanker signs at Crocker. His scowl would momentarily turn to a grin as he raised his can of Special Brew to his lips while waving two fingers at us.

Basing Street Studios wasn't the place for hangers-on, and very few people were invited along to the sessions. Those that were were given a beer and told to wait in reception. Dave Mingay was allotted certain times when he could film, but the sessions gave him a good opportunity to get to know the band. Joe saw the recording as something that had to be done, so he tried to make the best of it. He didn't see why he had to do the same pieces again and again, but he trusted Mick, and Mick trusted Pearlman. Topper was respected as a musician, and could be relied on to pick up the beat halfway through a song and repeat his drum rolls over and again. Getting the right sound was a different matter. It took a day and a half to get the right snare-drum sound. The drum was moved from drum mat to carpet to a different drum mat. The snare was tightened and loosened. I had to dash out to Henrit's drum shop, Soho Square, to get the complete range of drumsticks. A wallet was placed at different points around the drum rim. Topper beat the same tattoo over and again, waiting for Pearlman to say, 'That's it. Got it.' Paul enjoyed doing his bits, but this was an alien world for him. He hit on an idea, and said to Mingay, 'Here, you're into film. Get us some good films to watch.'

Mingay replied: 'Like what?'

'*Battle of the Bulge. The Battle of Stalingrad.*'

'What, from the Imperial War Museum?'

This hadn't been what Paul had in mind, but he thought it was a great idea. So we set up a projector. Paul would have had the films running all the time, but the projector's noise ruled this out. Maybe the films gave him an incentive to get his bits right, so that he could get back quicker to watching them with great enthusiasm and interest. Pearlman didn't really approve of this, although he smiled condescendingly.

Mick, however, was at home in the studio. He took note of everything that was going on. He set up shop behind the man at the control desk, spliff in hand, stubble on chin. Pearlman and his sidekick Corky Staciak didn't trouble to teach him, but he watched, asked questions, and learnt. He took tapes home and analysed them, playing them over and over.

Maybe it was the coke that made him so into it. Cocaine users can draw connections between disparate events, and give them a greater meaning. Perhaps it was the ideal drug for this sort of patchwork music-making. I came within a whisker of getting busted while scoring for Mick at a book shop in north London, the sort that stocked imports, alternative comics; generally, books which WH Smith didn't sell. But it had a greater attraction for me. It was run by a drug dealer, who was living with an old friend of mine. My friend's way of dealing with the world was to take to her bed for weeks at a time. She would hold court, propped up by pillows, in her nightdress. Mick knew I had access to these people. While Topper also used cocaine, he would go out and score for himself. But Mick wouldn't even go to the corner shop for a pint of milk for himself. One afternoon he asked me to get him some coke. 'How long you going to be?'

'Well, I'll be as quick as I can.'

'Yeah, but how long?'

'As quick as I can.'

That conversation didn't stop me from relaxing and chatting, and sampling the goods. As I left, I slipped a copy of *On the Road* in my pocket. Just then, the plate-glass shop window came in. Drunks again? A gang of men charged in.

'Freeze. Police.'

With a flick of my fingers I pulled my stash from my pocket and flipped it into a stack of books.

My friend appeared in her Chinese silk dressing-gown and said I had been chatting with her. I was nothing to do with anything else. The owner took the rap for her, and he got three years. Crunching through the smashed glass I could see the road was sealed off at both ends, and a camera crew was filming. I drove off towards Swiss Cottage, back to Basing Street, checking in my mirror for flashing blue lights. There was none. I was laughing with relief. I walked into the studio.

Mick said, 'Have you got it?'

I said, 'You won't believe this. It was like something out of *The Sweeney*.'

'Yeah, but have you got it?'

'No. I threw it away. That's how come I'm here and not down the cells.'

'Can't you go back and get it?'

I turned my back on him and walked across the shiny white floor and got a beer from the fridge, shaking my head in disbelief. And the recording process went on.

We were asked to go to the BBC's Maida Vale Studios to record a session for the John Peel show. The outing had been a shambles from the start. I had just been at Mick's flat, admiring Tony James's weekly itinerary for Generation X, neatly typed by the band's secretary, when Mick said, 'Hang on, aren't we supposed to be doing something tonight? Oh, yeah – the John Peel show.'

We had transport problems, and I had to dash around gathering up the equipment and organizing Joe, Paul and Topper. The date of the session may not have stuck in our minds, but when we arrived we were all conscious of the history behind the tiny, shabby studio – memories of the Beatles and Hendrix producing that tinny sixties radio sound in the same room. The Baker was even grumpier than usual when setting up the equipment, not welcoming the inter-ference of the studio engineers. Mick was keen to demonstrate his newly acquired knowledge of recording techniques, and Joe wanted to capture the Clash's live sound on the session, demanding a perfect balance of instruments. After Basing Street, we weren't used to recording entire tracks in half an hour. Spliffs abounded, to the growing frustration of the BBC engineers. The session was never finished, and Peely vented his anger with the Clash with some sarcastic comments on air. But the Clash were manifestly not bothered. It would have been a prestigious session – but the band had wanted to produce it themselves, and preferred not to do it at all rather than to cut corners.

8

Joe was the bag-man. He had two fistfuls of plastic bags – just from the supermarket, no designer pose – stuffed with his belongings – his clothes, books, washing stuff, tapes, Rizlas, stencils, spray cans and pens. He also had a sky-blue case, but as the flotsam and jetsam increased town by town, it contained the same as the polythene bags.

Every day, five minutes after the time we were supposed to have checked out, the entire contents of the room would be stuffed into the carriers in a frantic scramble. Strummer and I would shuffle along corridors, down lifts, across hotel lobbies, with shoulders hunched, collars up, eyes alert – past aghast bellboys and contemptuous businessmen with Samsonite luggage.

Plastic bags were not designed for stacking in the boots of motors. At the next destination the bags were yanked out, stuffed with the spilled detritus. They didn't fit the hotel trolleys and so we had to carry them to the next hotel room. Once inside, the bags – all of them – were upended on to the floor. The spewed pile was picked over by Strummer, like a tramp picking through a rubbish bin. Some things were put into place – razor in the bathroom, books near the bed – the rest stayed strewn on the floor, at hand if wanted. A home from home! But a disadvantage of the system was that items came loose. I once left a new pair of Joe's Doc Marten boots on the roof of the motor outside the Sheffield Top Rank and drove off. I still wonder who found them, and whether they realized they could have flogged them at an auction of rock memorabilia.

We were on tour – the Out on Parole tour – and it felt like we had just got out of jail after those months in the recording studio. It was great to get out on the road. It was even great to put up with Paul while travelling. He was, generally, a nuisance in the car. When he was not being beautifully languid, his curiosity knew no bounds. I was often his target, carefully chosen. He was fond of repetitive jokes, the impact increasing with their familiarity. It made for excellent company and relieved motorway tedium for the passengers. I have always found driving to be calming – a chance for reflection, even meditation, in a frantic day. Paul loved to steal my glasses, disturbing the calm, disturbing both my concentration and train of thought. It would begin gradually. A voice from the back seat as we were doing 85 m.p.h.: 'Give us your glasses, Johnny.'

I wouldn't reply.

'Oh, please, Johnny, give us your glasses.'

He'd feint with his hand, I'd twitch my head, like trying to flick away an insect while having a piss.

'I really want them, Johnny.'

I'd be annoyed and amused.

'Fuck off, Paul. I can't see without them. You know that.'

'All right.'

He'd slump back in the seat, folding his long legs. I could see in the mirror his knees through his ripped jeans. The lull was deceptive. He'd lunge with the smoothness of a snake, the deftness of a shoplifter. My glasses gone, the motorway was a big blur.

I'd roar: 'Put them back, Paul. I can't see.'

Mick, with visions of Eddie Cochran, once said: 'We'll crash. Quick. You idiot, Paul.'

Strummer would look up from his book and frown or grin, according to his mood. Topper would love it, and give a high staccato laugh. The specs would be returned. Lorries came back into focus. Calm was restored. Paul was gleeful. He'd have made his mark on the journey.

Others, from ex-Sex Pistols to the Drug Squad, were to make their mark on this tour. We had taken on Steve English, Johnny Rotten's former minder, to look after us. And since the Pistols had split, we began seeing more of the ex-Pistols – or they made a point of seeing more of us. Back in the spring of '78 Glen Matlock had asked me to go along to a rehearsal in a studio near the King's Road. Glen was a nice bloke – much too nice. No one would guess from looking at him or speaking to him that he had written 'Anarchy in the UK'. His hair always looked like it had just been washed with a mild conditioning shampoo. He was getting his new band, the Rich Kids, together, and I was offered more money to join their crew. But I turned it down. They didn't seem much fun. And the band had been dismayed at my 'unprofessionalism'.

Mick had also nipped off to join Elvis Costello in a recording session that spring. He had told me about it at Rehearsals, and asked me to pack him a Gibson, strings and plectrums. It was not exactly a secret, but he didn't want it broadcast, either, especially to Bernie. Next day he played me the tapes of 'Pump it Up' and 'Big Tears'. Was he keeping all his options open?

Then Johnny Rotten had taken a liking to Paul, or Paul had taken a liking to him. Rotten was putting together Public Image, and often asked Paul round to his place at Gunter Grove, Fulham. I usually went with him because he didn't like going on his own. In Rotten's kitchen there were crates of Guinness stacked up to the ceiling. He once pointed at them and said: 'That's success, Paul.' In the other room, there was a TV and a video recorder, which always seemed to be playing a bootleg of *A Clockwork Orange*. Rotten seemed like a recluse in a castle, although sometimes he had Keith Levene – who had been around in the early days of the Clash – Jah Wobble and other mates round. Paul was flattered by the attention (he was never flattered in the Clash camp). And the ex-Pistols always seemed to have money on them, which made him more bitter.

It became clear that Bernie and Malcolm, the old dynamic duo, were in cahoots again. Bernie's second string to his bow, the Subway Sect, were doing a short tour with another Bernie band, the Black Arabs. And the Black Arabs had started wandering in and out of Rehearsals like they had a right to, quoting Bernie's authority. They made more work for me, and the Clash didn't like them invading their home patch, but Micky Foote, who was usually with them, insisted that Bernie wanted them to rehearse. I had heard funky Sex Pistols medleys coming up through the floorboards. But they wouldn't answer any questions about what they were doing. It turned out they were rehearsing a funk section for the *Great Rock'n'Roll Swindle* film.

Also at this point Steve Jones started turning up at our gigs with black Les Paul in hand, joining in. And he was good. He crashed on to stage during encores, legs apart, like it was his show. He fitted in well, he knew the numbers. There was no looking over his shoulder for cues, and his power-chords added a new dimension to the already powerful songs. I was impressed, but concerned. It was ironic – our audiences were now largely punks with spiky hair, not street kids in leather jackets. Punk was now a 'movement', and members of the band which the Clash had grown up with, and which the movement had grown out of, were now trying to get back in on the scene via the Clash, who were now top dogs. It was, perhaps, kindness that made the Clash allow Steve Jones on-stage with them, but his presence also generated uncertainty. Sitting in my hotel room, I couldn't help wondering if the former Pistols were trying to poach Clash members to form a new band. Or was Steve Jones trying to become the Clash's fifth member? The Clash pondered the same questions, but they were never mentioned over the breakfast table.

After one gig, Mick said, 'How did he know where we were playing tonight?'

'Well, the tour dates are in the *NME*,' I said. 'And anyway, I told him last night.'

We blasted back into London to do four nights at the Music Machine, Camden. In London everyone thought they had seen it all before, everyone had seen the Pistols at the 100 Club, or so they claimed. They were too cool to get excited – the first excitement of punk had by now become a pose. But we came roaring back from the provinces, where we had found a whole country of angry dissatisfaction. We re-lit London. We left stunned, jabbering youths pouring down the steps after the gigs. The music press, which had been scornful and impatient with the Clash through the long wait for a second album, was once again eulogizing. In the car on the way back to Albany Street Joe said, 'We showed them.' He was scornful of the 'new wave' music, slick posers and bandwagon jumpers. After the afternoon soundchecks in London I'd drive him back to his flat, where he'd sit quietly on his bed, psyching himself up for that night's gig. I hung out with him, reading. I'd put a record on, and he'd whisper, 'No, take that off.' I made him lemon-and-honey drinks and we chatted. Mostly he asked me questions about myself and my life. He was interested. There were all these fashionable London kids, and excited fans who had hitched in from the suburbs queueing to see the Clash, and their lead singer was sitting on a mattress on bare floorboards in his room, browsing through his books stacked against the skirting board. Word must have got around that these shows were worth seeing. The Music Machine dressing rooms were actually across a courtyard and up three flights of steps into another building next to the hall. We were getting ready for a show when Joe spotted a row of spiky heads on the roof outside our window.

'Here, look at that!'

At the same time, one of the kids spotted his hero, and made a leap for the window, hanging on desperately. It wasn't a big leap, but his monkey-boots were hanging over a drop of three floors. Topper, who was little but strong, ran over to help haul the lad in, and these acrobats formed a monkey bridge across the gap, pulling each other over and through the window. Joe told me to make sure the bouncers didn't throw them out of the gig, and when the band went on I sneaked them through to join the crowd. We had hired a big bass rig for these shows, and every night I checked all the equipment long before the Clash took to the stage. But one evening, when the Clash launched into 'Complete Control', it was a shambles. Joe's vocals couldn't be heard till halfway through the song, and some roadies were on-stage throughout trying to sort out Paul's silent bass. (He was the last person to know how sound came out of an electric guitar.) I stood frozen, puzzling over what could be the problem. In desperation, I checked the fusebox. The fuse had gone – not blown – gone. Someone had nicked it. It was nice to know it was all friends of the band in the backstage bar. It was Agatha Christie time, but the case was never solved. I was chewed-out about it afterwards, until I explained about the sabotage. The Clash came off and another drum kit was set up on stage. Paul Cook and Steve Jones joined the band for the encore of 'Janie Jones', and Jimmy Pursey joined in with 'White Riot'. Joe, squashed into a corner of the small, crowded stage, said to the crowd, 'Don't call this a supergroup, it's a fucking awful group.'

Steve Jones had turned up in Blackburn, when we played St George's Hall, an old Victorian municipal monument in the centre of town. We enjoyed playing venues like that – they made a pleasant change to the sixties tackiness of Top Rank halls. We loved the dome roof, the entrance hall with its portraits of past aldermen in civic robes, the balcony with its polished wood rail – not that we sold balcony seats for the gig; it wasn't a spectacle, it was a participatory event. We loved the dressing rooms, built for orchestras. We fitted in very nicely.

But I knew it would be a strange day, ever since the uniformed doorman had called me over, using my real name. I was very wary. Only officialdom – bailiffs and magistrates – called me Mr Broad. Then, just before the show, a woman approached the stage door. She was smartly dressed, in a jacket with padded shoulders. She had big hair, Elsie Tanner-style, sprayed and clipped into place, and a broad Lancashire accent. It was my cousin Liz, a local headmistress. She was as out of place as one of our punters would have been at a meeting of school governors. I was pleased to see her, and gave her the five-star (cognac) backstage treatment. But her visit was an odd omen too.

It was another storming gig. The music even disturbed Crocker halfway through the set. He had stretched out on the steps at the back of the stage, designed for choirs, for a five-minute nap after a long, hard day of drinking. The cat-nap had become several hours of unconsciousness. Mick had been fretting about him. 'Where's Robin?' I could see his Doc Marten boots protruding from behind a pink flight case, but said to Mick, 'Probably out nicking.' Crocker woke and tracked down more alcohol. Steve Jones joined the Clash on-stage for the three-number encore, and we were joined by the usual gaggle of fans as we returned to the hotel, a modern, anonymous place carved into the hillside near the M6.

The manager greeted us. I had smiled at his career moustache when we booked in earlier. As usual, I had booked a block of rooms and allocated them to band and entourage myself. As usual, I asked the manager to come to me about anything – anything – concerning those rooms. Likewise, any calls to any of those rooms should come to me first. The manager didn't seem a bad bloke, and had treated us with as much respect as he gave the other guests – travelling businessmen and reps, who were dotted around the bar.

We ordered drinks and began to relax. I went to my room for some more fags, and found Steve Jones in bed with a bird.

'What the fuck are you doing?'

'What the fuck does it look like?'

Back in the bar, people were not being cool. Fans were spliffing up. They were relaxed and happy – why shouldn't they be? They probably skulked around Blackburn being stared at and abused, but suddenly with the Clash in town it was all right to be a punk – it was great to be a punk. I wandered around telling them to be a bit more discreet. I played Mick at pool. The band and punks had taken over the area around the table. Mick was an erratic pool player. Paul loved the flash trick-shots, but couldn't master them. Crocker was king of the pool table. He was pissed. It was his turn at the table. He concentrated on his game. He couldn't be bothered going to the bog. He just pulled out his plonker and pissed in the pocket of the table. Urine dripped to the floor, forming a yellow, steaming pool. The manager didn't like it. As requested earlier, he came to me to remonstrate. Crocker pushed past me, shouting at the hotel boss: 'What the fuck's it got to do with you?' He told Crocker he would have to leave the bar. Brave man. Crocker snapped the pool cue across his knee, stuffed it into the pissy pocket and stalked off. It was late, and we had places to go the next day. I went around like a sheep dog, rounding up the gang and getting them to their rooms. When I stumbled into my room, Steve Jones was in my bed with a different bird. Enough was enough. I grabbed an aerosol deodorant and sprayed it over their heads.

'What the fuck—?' (Jones' every third word was fuck.)

'Get out of my room. That's the second bird you've had in here tonight.'

As he walked out he said, 'It's the fucking third, actually.'

I collapsed on the bed, pulled off my specs and jacket and slept.

I was woken by hammering at the door. It wasn't unusual. As instructed, my door was the first point of call for hotel staff, or if any of the band or anyone else in our entourage wanted anything. Two denimed hippies stood outside.

'Drug squad.'

The manager had sent them to me first, god bless him.

I told them I was blind without my specs. 'You're not searching my room unless I can see you. You might steal something, or plant something on me. Not that I don't trust you guys ...'

They were down on their hands and knees, helping me look for my bins. Then they searched my bag – nothing; ashtrays – nothing but Rothmans stubs. I don't smoke dope. My briefcase, with its tour itineraries and road maps – nothing – except a pretty little art-deco tin, brim-full of white powder. My sulphate stash. A look of triumph. 'What's this, then?'

I took the initiative. These guys had been acting like clowns, like plodding cops in fancy dress.

'Don't you know anything?' I said scornfully. 'Haven't you the faintest clue about music? Don't you know about playing live? Do you realize how hot it gets under the stage lights?

88

Musicians sweat. How do you think they hold down guitar strings without this chalk dust on their fingers?'

One cop laughed – whether at me or his mate, I'm not sure. The other looked sheepish, closed the tin and put it back in the case.

I tried to direct every ounce of my adrenalin rush to hide the grin of triumph. 1–0 to Clash United.

'We want to do all the other rooms.'

I took them to the Baker's room next. I knew he didn't touch anything. Two halves of lager was a wild night out for him. He answered the door, grumpy and belligerent. He knew he had nothing to hide and was accordingly angry at being disturbed. While he complained bitterly and loudly to the DS, I nipped out along the corridor and drummed my fingers on the nearest door, and hissed, 'Joe, Joe, drug squad. Get up. Get busy. Joe—'

He opened the door, snapping awake. 'You and the Baker keep 'em busy.'

Joe was out the window, vaulting the parapet. Through his room door, I could see the silhouette of Joe Strummer, T-shirt and pants and quiff, running along the hillside and raising the alarm for the others. Thank god the hotel was built into the hillside. A flurry of activity descended in each room, with naked figures throwing little packages out the windows. Joe, back in his room, greeted the cops with a broad grin. 'Hallo, man. Do y'wanna come in and look around?' We had out-foxed them. All except Mick. He had missed a bit, or couldn't bear to part with all his hash. A bit of dope was stuffed down a sock. The cops seized on it. I caught Mick's eye, raised my brows and shook my head slowly. My face said, 'I despair of you.' His said, 'What made me think I'd get away with it?' He was nicked and taken down to the station. I followed behind, then came back to the hotel, rang a London brief and packed Mick's bags. His stash-bag, a green canvas satchel, was now empty and harmless.

When we checked out of the hotel Steve Jones was nowhere to be found. I asked the manager where he was. He had left much earlier – well before the bust. We met up with him the next afternoon.

'I don't know, it just didn't feel right,' he said. 'I just knew I had to get out of there, fast.' He had an uncanny sixth sense and acted on it. I had ignored the omens.

I waited outside the police station to collect Mick, out on bail. He emerged, looking tired as he slumped into the front seat. He pulled himself upright, turned and fixed me with a brooding intensity.

'Where are we playing tonight, Johnny?' he said, as we drove to pick up the others. The dawn bust was already forgotten. The show must go on. He smiled and asked, 'You haven't got any dope, have you?'

I didn't reply.

90

nd the show went on, swinging from high excitement to
tedium, viciousness to tenderness. We went to Scotland,
playing Dunfermline, Aberdeen and Glasgow. We were staying
in a dodgy TrustHouse hotel right under the Forth road bridge.
After the gig Joe spent most of the time chatting to this nice-
looking Scottish lassie. There were plenty of punks about and
plenty of stunners, but she was neither. Just a nice, ordinary
girl. I could see he was enjoying talking to her as I went
about my business – packing away the stage gear, stashing the
personal belongings away safely. We went back to the hotel
for drinks. Crocker was on the loose, playing pool, enjoying
himself. Joe was still in conversation with the fresh-faced,
dark haired, sensibly dressed young woman. Come 2.30 a.m.
he was still talking to her, then he asked me if we could run
her and her mate home. They lived in Perth, some thirty miles
away.

'Sure.'

I'd been boozing but no one then counted alcohol units. We
bundled into the Ford Granada estate. On the way Joe chatted
about the world outside Scotland. He was affectionate, gentle
even. She lived in a flat near the centre of the little Saturday-
market distillery town. Joe and the girl disappeared for a
couple of hours. I chatted to her friend, and drove Joe back
about 5.30 a.m. He'd arranged to see her at the next gig but
she didn't show, although she did come to a later gig and he
was really pleased to see her. We did the same thing again,
and I drove us back from Perth, the town of John Knox and
Scottish Puritanism, across the moors, wheeling along empty

roads as dawn approached. Joe fiddled with the car radio, then gave up.

'So what's the idea of to-ing and fro-ing to Perth? You could pull a stunner every night.'

He had put in a lot of effort with this lass. Most rock'n'rollers can't be bothered with the effort of getting on top.

'I just like her, y'know?'

He leant into me and whispered, still conserving his singing voice, 'I can't figure out why people have to pamper beautiful models, just for a shag, or to impress people. The end result is just superficial. Why do people do that?'

I knew the 'people' he meant were Mick and Paul, and said something non-committal.

He carried on. 'I mean, if you're just after sex, why not pull an ugly bird who will be so pleased to be wanted? It's the most flattering thing a human can say to another. "I find you attractive. I like you."'

Had we carried debauchery into the home of John Knox? I could imagine his sermon. 'Ye are doomed to hellfire, ye sinners.' Joe resumed fiddling with the radio: Hank Williams, 'I'm So Lonesome I Could Cry'.

Joe whispered, 'People say he was a sad man, dying so young. But the only sad thing was that he died with his slippers on. He'd taken off his cowboy boots to get into his car.'

A pink dawn illuminated the hills and heather of Perthshire. The sun came up over the Forth road bridge.

Glasgow Apollo was a big old theatre. Every band loved playing Glasgow because the crowd went mental. This was going to be a big show. When we had pulled in one of the soundcheck crew had said, 'Here, d'you know they're closing this place? This could be the last gig here.' Joe grinned. It was always a rowdy crowd at the Apollo. It was a roadies' joke that

92

a band's popularity could be judged from the bounce of the balcony. We ran a close second to Status Quo.

It was an important gig for me, too. It was at Glasgow the previous year that Roadent had walked out, giving me my place with the Clash. I set up the mikes, a job that was now second nature. I knew exactly how high to set each mike – slightly higher than mouth level, so they had to throw their heads back to sing into them. I used to get it spot on every time, make sure the guitars were tuned, so the Clash could just run on-stage and play without farting around.

There were roadie rumours that the bouncers were going to use this last gig to get their revenge on the kids, for making their lives hell over the years. It was certainly tense. We did a soundcheck and went back to the Albany Hotel where we were staying to prepare for the show. Joe used the little metal stencils he carried on the tour to spray his shirt front with car paint: GET TAE FUCK.

The band were hot from the first chords. A line of black-suited, red-necked Clydeside bouncers ringed the high stage. They were beckoning the audience of skinny little runts, pale faced like they had never seen the light of day. Ecstatic punk rockers slammed into each other in rhythm with Topper's pounding drum. Someone stumbled into a bouncer and was hurled back into the maelstrom of dancers. A lad punching the air to the beat near the black-suited ring was punched to the floor by a bouncer. He jumped up and flung himself at the man in anger, and was swatted away. Chairs were thrown. The Clash stopped playing three or four times. Jones was doing the same as Jagger at Altamont. 'Stop fighting!' It had as little effect. Joe jumped on to the raised orchestra pit to try to pull apart a bouncer and a lad. I leant from the stage trying to pull him back. 'White Riot', and the place erupted. Kids were carried out by their friends, faces and shirts spattered in blood. Never mind the Jackson Pollock splashed-paint look, this was the real thing.

After the show Warwick Nightingale – Wally of the fledgling Pistols – who was now our guitar roadie, came up to the dressing room.

'You'd better get the band out of here. The bouncers blame them for encouraging the mayhem.'

Dave Cork, the promoter, acted quickly. He produced some crates of Guinness and clanked them on to the front of the stage, telling the bouncers to help themselves. He rustled up from somewhere a large, fleshy woman who went on-stage and began an inexpert strip – not so much teasing as yanking her kit off, while Warwick played a Latin rhythm on the drums. The hall was empty apart from a pile of broken seats, the bouncers and the stripper. The punters had all limped home. A bouncer gave the woman an empty bottle saying, 'Put this to good use.' Which she did. The man-mountains began rumbling and grunting their approval.

Meanwhile, I hurried the band along and rushed them out of the side door near where my estate was parked. A half-dozen shell-shocked fans spotted us as we crossed the road. A girl shouted: 'You were fuck all use. You didn't help us, did ya?' Joe said quietly but angrily to us, 'What could we have done?' In his frustration and sadness he hurled a bottle against a wall. From nowhere a dozen cops came running full tilt, batons raised. Before anyone could move Strummer was on the deck under a cop. Paul piled in to help him, like a schoolkid sticking up for his mate in the playground. Mick ran – I don't know where. I picked Topper up in both arms and bundled him back through the stage door. Bernie was standing there, a half-smile, half-frown on his face. This was Bernie's idea of street theatre. I was back in the street in time to see Joe and Paul being bundled into a police van. I asked the cops where they were taking them but I was worried that they would arrest me too. I scooped up Topper and *NME* journo Chris Salewicz and drove them back to the hotel. My main concern then was drugs. I anticipated that the hotel would get a visit. At this point Jones arrived in the lobby, having walked across half of Glasgow to get back (very unusual for Mick). We went through everyone's room looking for their dope stashes, then Jones kept a lookout in the corridor while I hid the drugs above a panel in the false ceiling. I got on the phone to the police, and was told there was no chance of bail. They would be up before the magistrates in the morning.

We went to the court. I was worried about getting to Aberdeen for our next show. Bernie was loving it. He could imagine the headlines.

'Give the court your name.'

'John Mellor.'

'John Mellor what?'

'What?'

'Sir.'

Joe snarled. 'John Mellor, sir-r-r-r.'

They were bound over to keep the peace. In the car, Paul thought it all a huge joke. I was worried they'd hurt their hands so that they couldn't play guitar. They said the police cells had been full of kids from the gig, singing Clash songs all night. The police station had reverberated to the bellowed tune of 'The Prisoner.' Joe and Paul had been surprised and delighted that everyone knew the words.

Later, back at the hotel, as we walked through the lobby to hand in the keys, Lionel Blair walked in wearing a full-length fur coat, a suntan, wrinkles and a huge cheesy smile.

'Morning, boys!'

He had clearly heard about the previous night's escapades.

'Well, that's show business,' he smiled, flashing his teeth sympathetically. 'We're all in it together.'

We just stood and stared.

At the Holiday Inn in Bristol a mad twenty-stone rockabilly called Tiny, with a splendid quiff, donkey jacket, creepers and sideboards, had showed up one day in the foyer and asked for me. I came down to see him.

'Tiny, come for the show? Great to see ya.'

Unfortunately the flicker of his eyeballs, the cracked lips and the sweat on his brow indicated advanced amphetamine psychosis, a Tiny trait.

'More than that, Johnny. I've come to mind you and the boys.'

'Well, that's very nice of you but we've got English here.'

Steve English might have been seventeen stone, with a cropped head, dubious footwear and a strong line in sexist language, but he was doing all right. I could see there might be a problem, though.

'Hang on a minute, Tiny. I'll have a word with Strummer.'

'You do that, Johnny. Now.'

I was in the lift before you could say go, leaving behind a very nervous-looking receptionist. As soon as I hit the corridor I bumped into English. I made casual small talk: 'Tiny's downstairs, after your job.'

'Like fuck. I'll sort him out.'

He stormed off to the lift. I banged on the band's doors to announce the fight of the century: King Kong versus Godzilla. There was a scramble for front-row seats as we hit the lifts and dived behind the potted fern plants in the foyer. We peeped from behind the cover, sniggering, as these two huge guys squared up to each other in the posh hotel.

'This is fantastic!' Paul said.

Joe, while agreeing it was an amazing sight, said, 'Johnny, you've got to do something here.'

They went outside. There must have been some sort of pay-off. We didn't see Tiny again.

On a day off, Mick, Joe and me went to Eric's, Liverpool. Paul and Topper had gone back to London, along with the Baker, who had seized the chance to go back to his mum's for his

traditional Sunday lunch – roast chicken, Yorkshire pudding
and mint sauce. Even when he visited other members of his
family he was given the same Sunday fare. We knew Eric's was
where the Cavern had been, and the Clash had played there
before. I remembered the load-in was through a hatch for
beer-barrels in the pavement in Matthew Street. The sound
quality there was shit, but Eric's had a great atmosphere. We
met up with Pete Wylie, a most enthusiastic hanger-on who
had travelled around following the Clash. Mick had encouraged
him with his music, and had given him a Gibson. He later

formed Wah!. We had a good night out, relaxing in a happening place, and wandered around the docks, looking at the emptiness of what was left, before turning in for the night at the Holiday Inn. The next day, up late, I had a frantic drive down the M6 and M1 to pick up Paul from his Earls Court flat then on to Crawley for the night's show – white-line fever.

Our support for most of this tour had been the Specials, who had just changed their name from the Coventry Automatics, and had been using Rehearsals. We liked them and had asked them to join the tour. They were travelling in a big beat-up Dormobile, and also slept in it because they couldn't afford hotels. So we had given them a big Boy Scout-style tent. When we pulled into a town for a gig, we all kept a lookout for the Specials' encampment on the outskirts.

When we pulled off the motorway towards Crawley it looked like a quiet dormitory town, the sort of place where people who could afford a season ticket travelled to to get away from work. How wrong can first impressions be? Jets roared overhead to and from Gatwick, beckoning to new worlds. The venue was a big modern sports hall, anything but tailor-made for our purposes – there's something about concrete blocks that breed disrespect. Before they went on I called in to see Suicide, who were our official support band. Bernie had got them, seeing them as the cutting edge of New York art music, their lyrics of tragedy pushed out by two blokes in black wearing shades, standing behind synthesizers. Their music was OK for playing at midnight in your room, but didn't make for a riveting evening's entertainment. I knew the boys clinically knocked back a half-bottle of neat gin half an hour before going on-stage. They had made a study of the metabolic effects of different alcohols and had worked out that gin, taken in the right quantity at the right time, would give them the optimum on-stage stimulus. I wanted a slug of their gin. The Specials, looking terrifically bedraggled from their night's camping, were already on-stage. Paul, in particular, loved their style of ska music, their dynamic stage movements and cheeky grins. And so did the audiences. They were a good warm-up band.

Suicide didn't go down so well. Clash audiences wanted to see the Clash, but at least tolerated the lively Specials. They didn't tolerate Suicide at Crawley, though Suicide started their set, and I nipped back to the changing room to tell the Clash to start getting ready. There were still some fans hanging around with the band, and I started to clear them out gently. Steve English wasn't trained in diplomacy. We appreciated that he had to be tough to do his job, but didn't want him getting tough with these kids. But he did anyway. I asked a guy to get away from the guitars. He was only a little lad, and was obviously interested in what instruments the Clash used. He carried on staring at them. Then the next minute he was on the floor, with English laying into him. Mick (Mick!) leapt at him. In other circumstances it would have been amusing. His passion overcame any fear of English, the north London yob. He pulled him away, picked the lad up and told me to look after him for the rest of the night. English's days with the Clash were numbered. Mick was still panting with anger and exertion when a roadie stuck his head round the door.

'We need help! It's Suicide.'

From the back of the hall I saw skinheads climbing up the PA stack like cockroaches ascending a dinner table. A big lad just strode across the stage and whacked Martin Rev, breaking his nose. Roadies grappled with him, and he fought to free his arm so he could face the crowd and punch the air in triumph, like he'd scored a winning goal. They pulled him to the side of the stage, where English stood, legs apart, waving a knife at the baying crowd. It didn't calm anyone down. Did he really think it would? This sort of riot had happened before. At Dunstable the crowd had tried to pull over a lighting rig, which would have killed all of them if the attempt had been successful, and I'd also seen a bloke hacking at a cable with an axe. The band had gone on-stage and eventually quietened things down. Strummer knew that only he could get through to the crowd this time, and he did. To their credit, Suicide finished their set despite Rev's broken nose. Backstage, we watched him, covered in blood, leave for the hospital. We all started fiddling with the bridge of our noses. It could have been any one of us. The Clash got through their set with constant interruptions from stage invasions. It had been a riot. As they came off-stage, Paul said, 'Bit lively tonight.' He was grinning like a Vietnam vet who'd survived a fire fight.

Before the show, two old friends had presented themselves at the dressing-room door. Lisa, who had punched me out at the Pistols' gig, and Janet, who had hurled a glass at me at Lancaster. I wasn't worried about them in the rowdy crowd.

They could take the rough with the smooth. We opted for an early night at the hotel. The trouble was that I was sharing a room with Steve English, and both women wanted to sleep with me. I was in bed with Lisa, and English automatically thought Janet would sleep with him. But she called to me, 'Time to swap.'

'Come on, love, my turn,' English said. But the girls didn't want to know.

He shouted at me: 'Where'd you get these tarts?'

At the third time of asking, unsuccessfully, for a shag, he lost his temper. He picked up both naked girls and threw them in the corridor, gathered up their clothes and hurled them out the window into the main street of Crawley. They told me they had dressed at the kerbside and walked to the station to get the milk train home. Next day, the hotel manager informed us, 'Your custom will not be appreciated here in the future.'

Then as Mick got into the front seat of the car I slammed the door. He screamed. My heart sank. I had trapped his left-hand middle finger. The enormity of my deed sank in. I was supposed to be looking after him, and it seemed I had stopped him playing guitar ever again. Joe said, 'Right. Quick. Hospital.' We all went and got him into casualty. His finger had swelled and changed colour. I watched as the doctor pierced his nail and a fountain of blood pumped out. Mick came out of the hospital, as white as one of its sheets, saying, 'Right, where're we going? Southampton? Let's go.' He gave just as good a show as ever that night. I couldn't do enough for him for the next forty-eight hours.

The last night of the tour was in Bury St Edmunds. I pulled open the curtains of my hotel room the morning after and looked out over the abbey ruins. Glancing down, I saw the doorman in uniform and top hat welcoming some hotel guests. Last night's high jinks were already just a memory. It had been the end-of-tour roadies' party. The road crew, paid off for the tour of duty, had been exuberant. But for me and the band the end of the tour meant a return to humdrum life. The band had come to the party but hadn't pushed the boat out. Topper and Paul had gone back to London, and I had to drive Mick and Joe back that morning. I went to the bar to get orange juices to take to their rooms and get them going. The manager buttonholed me.

'Good morning. Would you vacate your rooms by twelve o'clock, please? And Mr Rhodes said to see you about settling the bill.'

Thanks Bernard, I thought. Bastard. I had a few quid food-and-fuel float, but that was it.

'Certainly, I'm just chivvying them along,' I said, nodding at the fruit juices in my hands and rolling my eyes in a you-know-what-pop-stars-are-like way. 'I'll be right back down.'

I woke Joe and Mick and started packing their bags as they surfaced. I said, 'Come on, we've got to get out of here.'

Mick said, 'Yeah, but where? There's nowhere to go. The tour's over.'

'Well, this place is hot. We've got to do a runner.'

They were compliant, but not even the prospect of this bit of excitement got their adrenalin going.

I went back through the bar, giving the manager a cheery wave, and pulled the car round to the rear near a fire escape. Then I walked back through the bar – 'Be with you in a minute,' to the manager – and up and down the emergency stairs with everyone's bags.

'All ready then, guys,' I announced. 'We're using the super-stars' exit to avoid all the screaming fans and cameras at the front.' And so we sneaked off, heading for London.

Mick said, 'Well, I ain't going home. I've nothing to go home to. My flat was done over this week and I don't fancy sorting that lot out.'

Joe said, 'I'm game. Where're we gonna go?'

Mick's head emerged from a newspaper to announce: 'Dylan's playing at Blackbushe.'

'Yeah? Let's do it!' said Joe.

I didn't mind, but started pointing out the problems. 'There'll be crowds of people. Loads of traffic. We've hardly any money. No backstage passes, no car parking—'

'Come on, Johnny, you can do it,' Joe taunted.

'Dylan is CBS. They owe us,' Mick said. 'Let's use them. Ellie Smith will get us in.'

Joe's words were like a challenge to me. 'Come on, Johnny. You can blag anyone.'

We motored into London and out again. As we got near the venue – a disused airfield in Hampshire – there were lines of abandoned cars at the side of the road. Joe said it was like Jean Luc Godard's *Weekend*. We bluffed our way through the first security check, but with more difficulty than I had expected. I pulled over and told Mick to sit in the back with Joe. 'Act like rock stars, you know.'

Joe, now grinning, said, 'You should have a chauffeur's cap on, Johnny.'

'Bollocks, and ruin me barnet?'

From then on it was easy. At each gate I wound down the window, jerked my thumb towards the back seat and said, 'Band,' with the arrogance that professional chauffeurs must have. Joe and Mick sprawled across the back seat, not deigning to look out the window. We breezed through to the backstage area where limos were dropping off their rock-star passengers. I parked in a corner. No one stopped me. I tracked down Ellie Smith, who was pleased to see us, and we entered the huge backstage arena full of caravans and a vast marquee with hessian matting, housing tables covered with bowls of fresh strawberries, profiteroles and champagne bottles.

'So this is what rock stars do,' said Joe.

There was a large wired-off area to the front and side of the stage. Every freeloader imaginable was there. It was near the free bar, but the view of the stage was shit, and the sound was shit; it was like being in a royal box with all the punters in the audience looking in, star-spotting. We watched a bit of Graham Parker and the Rumour's set from there, and couldn't resist meeting them as they came off-stage.

'What, playing support again?' we said, and wandered off as they responded, 'Yeah, playing support to Dylan.'

The Man himself stayed in his caravan, and I told Joe how I had missed meeting Dylan a few months earlier. I had bumped into an old girlfriend outside Dingwalls and we immediately started snogging. Ellie Smith had come across and said, 'Hi, Johnny. I would like you to meet—' 'I'm busy,' I mumbled. She said, 'Oh, pardon me,' in her polite way and walked off. I glanced up and saw her disappearing down the road, chatting to Bob Dylan. I'd missed my chance.

Mick had wandered off. Joe said we should go and watch Dylan's set from a good vantage point. We had to break out of the backstage area to join the audience by climbing over a corrugated iron fence. After a difficult climb we perched at the top of the fence and surveyed the vast crowd, then looked down, ready to jump. We looked up again, quickly, and exchanged guilty smiles. 'What a pair of pervs!' a voice said. We were overlooking the roofless ladies toilets. We shuffled away on our bottoms along the top of the corrugated iron before jumping down and joining the punters. All we could see, even from near the front of the crowd, was Dylan's top hat, reminding me of the uniformed doorman I had seen that morning. It seemed like a year ago.

The sound was better from where we stood, though, and the view was better than from the liggers' bar, but Joe, glancing round at the myriad Dylan fans passively holding their lighters aloft in the dusk, said, 'This ain't no way to experience rock'n'roll.'

10

After all that time at Basing Street Studios, CBS and Pearlman still weren't satisfied with the mix of *Give 'Em Enough Rope*. CBS had put so much money into the recording, thus were 'in for a penny, in for a pound', and asked Joe and Mick to go to San Francisco for overdubbing, and then New York for mixing. Joe asked me if I wanted to move into his room in the squat in Daventry Street while he was away, and I jumped at the chance. It was more comfortable than Rehearsals – it had a bathroom. And it got me away from Bernie's phone calls. The place was like any other squat – a terraced house with every room occupied, bikes chained to the fence, coffee cups growing mould on the table. The others who lived there were impressed that Joe had gone to America – the Clash must be moving on!

Bernie had me do some work for the Subways, but his conversations with me were getting increasingly weird. We had been seeing less and less of him, which pissed everyone off, although when we did meet there was inevitably a row. By August, even Micky Foote stopped coming round with messages from Bernie, and all contact between him and the Clash came through me. He phoned me often, at all hours: 'Johnny, it's time for a decision. Which way are you going to jump? ... Are you into the politics? ... Are you into change, or are you in this just for the money?'

It was difficult to give him a straight answer. His whole style was about keeping people guessing, keeping them on their toes. Were these straight questions he was asking me, or was it all a wind-up? Was he going to march in and announce to Joe: 'Johnny says he don't care about the politics behind the music'? Bernie had set up the whole recording deal with Sandy Pearlman. He asked mockingly, 'How's it going with the big-shot Yank producer?'

How real was all this? How much of it was part of Bernie's tactic to keep the Clash in a state of creative tension ... to force the band not to take anything at face value, to ask questions? Was this part of Bernie's daily cultural revolution? I didn't know, and I still don't, but I knew I didn't want to play these mind-games, and tried to keep Bernie at arm's length. Meanwhile, the band were getting more and more fed up. During breaks at Rehearsals, at the bar in the Caernarvon, down the café, everyone griped about Bernie.

Perhaps this rankled most with Mick, who had, with Bernie, put the band together. And Mick had a way of getting his way with the band. It could've been that Bernie had removed himself to allow the Clash to get on with it, but the band didn't want him that far removed.

Personally, I found Bernie a delightful man with outrageously fascinating ideas. But ideas are only any good if they can be communicated effectively. Bernie's way of communicating his ideas was through the Clash, but he had stopped communicating with the Clash. And as far as I was concerned, he was my employer and pay-master. No matter how fascinating his ideas of global cultural revolution were, my top priority from him was a regular, decent wage, and I hadn't been getting one.

With Mick and Joe away in America I hung out a bit with Paul and Topper, and Paul Cook, who lived round the corner and who I sometimes saw in the pub.

Cook and Steve Jones had helped get me done for drink-driving just around the corner from Speakeasy. They had been in the front seat when an unmarked cop car pulled alongside. Twice. We didn't know it was a cop. The third time, Steve Jones leant across and through the open window shouted:

'Fuck off.' He thought it was some cowboy trying to cut me up. The uniforms loved booking me.

We went to see a lot of bands, but I was generally unimpressed. In September the Ramones were in town, and Topper and I met up with their drummer, Mark Bell, at the Sherlock Holmes Hotel in Baker Street. We had met him when he was with Richard Hell, and liked him because he had really hit the drums hard – as good a reason for liking someone as any. He was dressed Ramone-style – ripped jeans, white plimsols, leather jacket and fringe – and like Topper, he looked the part, whoever he was playing for. The Ramones' management were strict. There was a curfew on the band, and fines if they were found drinking, drugging or even staying out late before a show. We had to sneak Mark past the tour manager's patrol by leaving by the fire escape. It was like he was at a public school, sneaking out after lights out. We took him to Camden to shoot pool in the Caernarvon, and went ligging down the Music Machine and Dingwalls before sneaking him back in up the fire escape. Topper and I mused on how sad it was that a band – or, rather, their management – should have to take professionalism so far. But in the Ramones' case, with DD in the band, we could understand why. I told Topper about him whispering to me behind his hand at the Bristol Top Rank: 'Got any gear?' And we had snorted heroin and cocaine in the toilets, feeling like naughty schoolboys having a crafty smoke.

Then Joe and Mick came back, filled with tales of how brilliant America was, and how it opened new horizons. They shrugged off the pain and toil that was the making of *Give 'Em Enough Rope* with enthusiasm about the power and glory of the sound of the mixed version. Mick extolled the virtues of Dr Pepper's, which I later discovered tasted like stale toothpaste. Joe's tail was up from his ride across the country to New Orleans. He had reconnoitred the place.

'They're ready for us,' he said. 'Flicking the radio dial in the car, there's so many stations – playing so much shit. Our new stuff will go down a bomb there. It's time to go.'

But first there was other business to sort out. We went to Ireland, so I couldn't appear in court on my drink-driving charge. I took Saphu with me to Belfast, to show her off. Saphu was a great looker who worked in Dingwalls' yard next door to Rehearsals. Working with the Clash was always a good pulling line, and she was the best I pulled. She had beaded hair and blue-tinged black skin – terribly exotic. I was aware of Joe and Mick seriously clocking her during a soundcheck at Ulster Hall and I was seriously warning them off with violence in my eyes. As we sat later in a beautiful bar opposite the Europa Hotel, with stained-glass windows and enclosed carved-wood booths, a group of loud anti-Brit big men gradually surrounded me. I left our drinks, and feigning a move to the bogs dropped my shoulder, doubled back for Saphu, and we were out the door.

After the Belfast gig a crowd of dozens walked back through the dark streets to our hotel, and we renewed our acquaintance with Gordy, face-to-face instead of on the phone. We played a live Gary Glitter tape I had nicked, to the delight of the band and the fans, clustered in the bar of the most bombed hotel in Europe, swilling lager, punching the air in pastiches of Paul Gadd. There had been a series of security checks just to get into the hotel lobby, let alone the bar, but there were so many kids walking in with the band, and the influx was so unexpected, that the hotel staff had just shrugged their shoulders. They lifted the car barrier to let the crowd through rather than body-search everyone. We had insisted that the crowd should come back with us, as if we were in Derby or Manchester. After all, they were only kids: no danger. But at the bar a thirteen- or fourteen-year-old opened his donkey jacket and showed me and Joe an old handgun tucked in his jeans. Gordy was called over and the youth was told to 'keep extremely cool'.

I went ahead of the band to Dublin and checked out our rooms in a hotel in Grafton Street, near the Post Office where the Irish Republic had been declared. I complained bitterly about one, and had it swapped for a big luxury suite – for myself and Saphu.

At Dun Laoghaire, we waited for ages for the local promoter and carpenters, pencils rammed behind their ears, to build what turned out to be an extremely springy stage. We drank Guinness, watching the rows of settling pints, and ate pea soup. It was debatable which was thicker. This was tourist-information-film Dublin. The Clash loved the bouncy stage and jumped and bounced like Zebedee maniacs. It compared well with some sprung Top Rank floors, which were brilliant for pogoing youth.

Back to London and to Europe the following day. I drove to Dover with Topper to make the final arrangements for transporting our equipment. Topper attracted the attention of the cops by calling the Customs men Gestapo, and I was arrested with a warrant for failing to turn up in court and spent a night in the cells.

The minibus was outside the Hotel Mondiale in a Paris cul-de-sac. The bags were already stacked in the back as the band drifted out of the hotel, bleary eyed. It had been a good start to our European jaunt. A rampaging crowd had travelled with us after the previous night's gig to help us sample the Parisian nightlife. The management of Le Palace, a swanky nightclub, had welcomed us with open arms, although they blanched at the crowd of youngsters we insisted came in with us. They obviously had trouble distinguishing who was in the band and who wasn't. The French fans inevitably moved in on Strummer, who took to them with huge enthusiasm – grunts, laughs, loads of hand-waving, *oui, non, d'accord, bien sûr*. His lack of French didn't inhibit his urge to communicate or respond to approaches. We seemed to disturb the sang-froid of the chic

109

disco crowd, however. Maybe to them punk was little more than a fashionable ripped T-shirt, but they soon thought otherwise. The live act at the club was the Village People. We were delighted! We were all out on the floor dancing, to the horror of our French punk rock fans! We were still rolling with the euphoria of our gig.

So we were bleary the next morning as I revved the engine ready to go. Crocker jumped into the front seat, with no deference to Mick, who usually sat there. The musicians folded themselves into their seats, trying to get comfortable for a kip on the run up the autoroute to Belgium. It was just another low-key day. We were ready to roll at last, but were jammed in by a cream Citroën. I sounded the horn. No response from the driver. I edged forward a metre, revving hard. No response. I shouted out the window. 'Oy! Allez. Get out the way! We've got another country to get to.' And I banged on the horn again. Nothing, not even a Gallic shrug of the shoulders. I edged forward until the motors were touching, bumper to bumper. He got out of his car, lifted a handgun and pointed it at me through the windscreen. It was a Luger – I recognized it from old war films. He was muttering darkly. I froze. I was not used to this, and certainly not paid for this sort of action. Crocker was out of the van before anyone else could take in the danger, picking up the wheelbrace from beside his seat en route, and charged at him, roaring Anglo-Saxon curses, the stolen hotel key rings jangling from his biker jacket. He didn't care about the gun. He would have reacted the same if someone had been bad-mouthing Tottenham Hotspur. The French guy looked even more worried than I was feeling. He backed off, jumped into his car, and with a hiss of the hydraulic suspension reversed into the main road. We roared in triumph and dissolved into back-patting and laughter. Crocker was supposed to be with us working as a roadie, but he never dreamed of travelling with the roadies, and I never saw him do any work. But it was at times like this that, both for protection and entertainment, it was worth having him along. As we eased along the périphérique and the euphoria quietened, we became aware of the uncomfortable silence of our two new passengers, Dave Mingay and Nick Broomfield. It gave us great pleasure to watch.

Mingay was still filming what was to become *Rude Boy*, and Broomfield, a maverick film-maker, also wanted to make a documentary. They were both insecure about their positions. The presence of each of them had been set up by Bernie – which at this stage didn't endear them with the band. It was clear to me – but apparently not to them – that the band had come to a decision about Bernard. Broomfield and Mingay were busily engaged in point-scoring over each other to get in with the band, and didn't know how to react to Crocker's handling of the gun incident. I took one hand off the wheel and pretended I was pointing a camera.

'I'd love to make a film of these two film-makers trying to make a film,' I said.

The band cracked up. Mingay and Broomfield felt they had to laugh along.

We arrived at Leuven, Belgium, in the rain, and waded through thick mud into a giant marquee. The roadies, who had got there earlier, looked like extras from *Oh What a Lovely War*. The stage had sunk in the quagmire at an angle, like a ship going down.

'You just can't play here. It can't be done,' said the roadies.

The technical problems would have made the Baker tear out his hair. But the sight of these experienced European roadies giving up made us more determined that we would do the gig. And we did. The Clash still gave it their all, although their attempts to run and leap about the stage resembled the antics of drunken ship stewards on a stormy sea. After the show Broomfield tried to chum up with Joe and played the Bernie card, not knowing it was a bad card to play. He asked, 'Will Bernard be at Amsterdam?'

'Who knows, who cares?' Joe replied, echoing one of Bernie's catchphrases.

'He won't be showing his face,' Mick muttered.

Mingay was on the phone, and beckoned to me.

'I can't get hold of Bernard. Have you got his number?'

'Why would I have it?' I said.

We drove into the Netherlands, enjoying but being slightly irritated by the hippy culture. As Holland is more liberal about dope laws than Britain, everyone we had any contact with seemed constantly stoned. The hippy stage manager at Arnhem was bumbling around. He was a walking anti-dope advert. I could see it coming. I warned the bloke to keep clear of the guitars, sitting in their supposedly heavy-duty stands, which had been welded together for us by a mate of mine in Whitechapel. The stands looked good, but they weren't. I told him again to mind the guitars, but it didn't register. I saw in slow motion Mick's prized Gibson Les Paul fall from the stand. I leapt to save it, but was too late. The guitar neck suffered multiple fractures. The hippy's nose suffered a straight fracture.

That night in the hotel's circular bar, despite Paul and me making vigorous and dramatic attempts to divert the barman's attention, Topper was caught red-handed trying to nick bottles of booze. He didn't need to nick it. We had plenty of booze with us in the van. The next morning Mick was fretting about his guitar. I told him it would be sorted out when we got to Amsterdam that afternoon. Crocker said, 'Don't worry about that, Mick, try some of this,' producing a disgusting bottle of mandarin liqueur. He'd nicked it from the bar the night before. Mick waved the bottle away, joint in hand. No words were necessary. It was a completely undrinkable, sickly thick liqueur, but since we had won it we all took a sip – then threw it out the window.

The Paradiso was something else. It is an old church with a great atmosphere. Anybody who is anybody has played there, regardless of their size. It was the home of European hippiedom. The band were really up for this gig, to turn them on with a blast of something new. The venue was entirely run by hippies, from the guy bringing cold beers to the dressing room to the person handing out the dough. It seemed like we had stepped back a decade. I had been reminded of a poem from my schooldays by the place names as we drove through Belgium, and it sprang to mind again. 'How They Brought the News from Aix to Ghent'. How the Clash brought the news from Camden to Amsterdam! And the gig was superb. Joe the showman had the audience in the palm of his hand with his mixture of scorn and encouragement. He was speaking a new language to them, and they understood. Even I, who had seen the Clash hundreds of times, was staggered at the power and channelled anger, at the sight of die-hard hippies shaking their heads and knowing, just knowing, that a whole new dimension was beginning. Joe broke so many guitar strings that night that I had to fetch more spares. I hurried down the wooden stairs to the dressing rooms. I paused there, just for a moment. I pulsed and shivered at the sheer power of the music coming down through the floorboards. I was wildly excited, yet at peace. Then I rushed to get on with my job.

After the show the dressing room filled with eager fans, wanting to get closer to the source of the energy, not wanting the buzz to stop. The band were buzzing too, and happy to share it. They knew they had hit a high note. But I wandered off into the fascinating building, through a labyrinth of staircases, and I found a bar almost in the rafters. It was tiny, but fitted with a theatre, decked in rich brocade, with seats for maybe six people. Sitting alone at the bar was a woman with a sour mouth, painted before nine o'clock in the morning. But my speed had run out and I got the chills and the shakes, and there was grass everywhere so I hit the malt whisky and I fell in love with this woman and told her I'd run away with her anywhere – to Tierra del Fuego, and I meant it.

The next morning, a bright, clear, crisp, autumnal morning, Howard Fraser arrived on the overnight ferry from Harwich. He had come for the party. Howard, an old squat mate of mine from the East End, is bald with a walrus moustache. His entry pass to any situation was to stroke the moustache away from his nostrils with forefinger and thumb while saying authoritatively, 'I'm a personal friend of the band.' He had exotic tastes. I liked him and so did Topper. I had phoned him from Antwerp, and he had come to take the damaged Les Paul back to London. I had realized that the days of relying on Bernie as a back-up were already over.

Howard was ready for a little slice of the high life and Paul in particular was delighted to see him – he loved taking the piss out of him, to the extent that he once bought a stick-on walrus moustache and tried to gatecrash a Clash gig by confronting the doorman, stroking the moustache and mumbling, 'But I'm a personal friend of the band.'

That morning saw Crocker and I in adventurous mood, and we followed the cleaner down the corridor at a healthy distance. We nipped into the empty rooms, and Crocker showed me a trick for which I have been much indebted on several occasions since. By reaching around and banging a certain point at the back, it was possible to open some sort of emergency door in hotel-room mini-bars. We couldn't believe our luck, and emptied our haul into a pillow-case which we then carried back to our rooms, Crocker skipping in his blue Doc Martens, face contorted with glee.

My room was connected to Paul's, who joined us as we started on the stolen booze – champagne first, naturally. He searched through our haul, and feigning disappointment, said: 'Couldn't you find any mandarin liqueur, Robin?' We were joined by others, and Ray Gange, along for more *Rude Boy* filming, who got stuck into the vodka. Dave Mingay came into the room. There was champagne and good-quality Amsterdam dope. Mingay was still on a high from the last night's success,

114

and his relief at still being around was evident. Broomfield had taken the hint and gone. Mingay had obviously worked out that his filming deal with Bernie now held no sway, because Bernie wasn't on the scene any more. He was now around because the Clash wanted him around – or at least were prepared to go along with his idea of the film for a bit longer.

'What a night!' Mingay announced. 'What a night to be without a film crew! What a missed opportunity! I only hope Harlesden will be as good.' He added more quietly, as if to indicate that he was now in on the secret, 'That is, if Harlesden is still on ...'

Bernie had announced that the Clash would be playing at the north London venue early in September. The gig had had to be rescheduled because Joe and Mick could not get back from New York in time. At this point the Clash, who felt they had been made to look like they didn't care about their fans, had determined to get rid of Bernie.

But Joe looked up at Mingay, surprised at the question. 'Of course,' he said. 'People have bought tickets. We owe them.' We all trooped out to look around, and found ourselves in Amsterdam's big flea market. Passers-by stared at us – drainpipe jeans stood out in European towns where flares and long hair were still the norm. Some recognized us, smiled and waved greetings. Those who had been at the Paradiso shouted: 'Great show!'

Paul stopped in front of a stall selling second-hand leathers. The stallholder's face lit up. He could see there was more chance of a bunch of strangely dressed Englishmen buying his wares than the Dutch hippies, for whom leather coats still held too many war-time connections.

'Buy us a coat, Dave ... Oh, please Dave.'

Mingay was flushed with his new relationship with the band. We all got coats. Mick's was a full-length leather. I chose an East German police coat.

We had to return to Belgium to fly back. As we drove out of Liège towards its tiny airport we saw a landmark in the town – a dummy, hanging from a gibbet outside the town hall. Topper spotted it first. 'Look at that bloke hanging.' We all looked. No one said anything. No one needed to say what we were all thinking: Bernie!

The flags were flying when we walked into the Harlesden Roxy. They formed our new backdrop – the first we had designed ourselves, without Bernie. The idea had come from Paul. We had fun with a catalogue from Black and Edginton, royal flag-makers by appointment. Everyone picked their favourite flags. We were like kids at the pick'n'mix in Woolworth's. I chose Saudi Arabia because I liked the pattern. National politics didn't come into it, although Joe quashed Topper's choice of South Africa. I had taken the order to Black and Edginton's office near Tower Bridge. The man there found it all very odd, but allowed himself to get a little excited when I explained what the flags would be used for. I wanted a Jolly Roger in one corner, but he politely stated that his company did not produce that particular flag. He was terrifically helpful. He was intrigued when I asked for the whole thing to be fire-proofed, and explained why. (The Greater London Council's safety officer would sometimes turn up half an hour before a show, whip out a cheap lighter and bend down to test the backdrop by holding a flame to the corner while looking over his shoulder, smiling, and saying, 'All right, boys?')

As we stood admiring the flags the dreadlocked figure of Don Letts, an ex-Roxy DJ, approached. 'That looks the business,' he said. I didn't see how he could tell through his trademark wrap-around shades. He said, 'Right. I've got all the cameras. We're going to do a video.'

The band started to soundcheck in the cold empty hall, still wearing their new leather coats, as Don and his crew set up their film and recording equipment. They were a pretty amateur bunch, but we figured it was better to have someone who knew what the band was about than someone with purely technical expertise. The Clash ran through a couple of numbers. Paul stopped playing. 'This ain't right. It don't feel right. We've got to have an audience for this film.'

Joe said, 'There's an audience outside the door. Get them in, Johnny.'

I invited the little crowd of London Clash fans hanging around the venue in the late afternoon to come inside. They trooped in, as the band were waltzing through 'Pressure Drop'. Their coats came off. They were already wearing their stage gear – stage gear being street gear.

A lad shouted: 'You finally turned up, then? You're going to play here at last?'

Joe said: 'Now listen, you should know that we've bust a gut to get here. If people have bought tickets – we'll play.'

Then, for the first time, in front of this makeshift audience,

117

the Clash mimed their way through 'Tommy Gun' for Don Letts' video. It took several tries. In the first couple of runs at it, the band struggled to follow the backing track. Joe stopped playing.

'How does that look?'

'Great,' I said. *'Top of the Pops* next.'

'Not very convincing,' Letts said.

'I ain't surprised.' Joe looked at Mick. 'Well, it's got to be done, hasn't it?'

Eventually the stuff was in the can.

'Thank Christ for that,' said Joe. 'Is this what it takes to turn the chart upside down?'

The Clash honoured their commitment and played the Harlesden Roxy gigs. We had flown from Liège in a small twelve-seater plane so that we could get back in time. Ray Gange had passed round a bottle of vodka on the plane but drank most of it himself, then threw up all over the floor. We flew over Heathrow with our feet up. The wind from circling Jumbo jets buffetted our tiny plane about the sky, while we waited for permission to land. It wasn't nice for any of us, particularly Topper, who hated flying – this was like one of his worst nightmares. But the Clash hadn't let their fans down.

11

*T*here are those who would say that the introduction of order, moderation and self control into one's life constitutes the framework for progress and happiness. Caroline Coon seemed to subscribe to this philosophy. Mick Jones himself was a very neat man: wherever he ensconced himself, his possessions and artefacts were laid out in a tidy and accessible way. But this was not reflected in the Clash's daily demeanour, and certainly not in their affairs. Almost overnight, Bernie had become merely a memory. In the aftermath of this there was an atmosphere of teenagers leaving home, of freedom, of independence. But Coon, like a clucking hen, with a scrawny neck to match, soon set to work to make sense of the chaos. However, when it came to the Clash, Coon could not juggle. Bernie specialised in keeping balls in the air and if one dropped, then so what?

Give 'Em Enough Rope was released in Clash style. A place had been booked near Wardour Street for the press launch, and the Baker and I dropped the band off outside. We had been told we weren't invited, and were going to push off to the Ship for a beer when Crocker loomed up from behind a huge cardboard cut-out of the album cover.

'Hang around a minute, we might need the wheels,' he said. We sat in the van and watched the suits – journos and record company executives – file in. Then Crocker and Topper appeared with arm loads of boxes of records and piled them in the back.

'So that's it, then?' I said. 'Let's have a look.'

'No time for that. Get going.'

'Where?'

'Cheapo's. Where else?'

So with a screech of tyres I drove the few streets to the shop, and we unloaded the albums into the basement. Before we could drive away, the owner already had a copy of *Give 'Em Enough Rope* displayed in his window. The album was on sale at a second-hand record shop before the first reviewers had even heard it. Topper stood the drinks in the Ship, delighted. Paul grinned from ear to ear, and Joe was amused. Even Mick, trying to disapprove, had to smile.

Then came the Sid Vicious benefit gig at the Music Machine. The Clash had been asked by Sid's mum to help with his legal fees after he had murdered his girlfriend Nancy Spungen.

We had all gone to Sid's farewell show at the Electric Ballroom that summer to pay for his fare to America. Everyone had pitched in. We'd all loved Sid, no matter what state he was in. He could be forgiven for anything, almost. I was stage manager, and although I had thought everything had been arranged, I ended up spending the day going backwards and forwards from Rehearsals for stage equipment. After a low-key shambolic start to the day, with punk musos drifting in and around, no one quite sure who was doing what, I asserted myself in Clash manner and started getting the stage prepared as I would for a Clash gig. But I gradually realized that other musicians were totally unused to this way of working. Sid had been magnificent at the soundcheck, realizing that this was his day. Then I relaxed. After all, I didn't have to be a perfectionist there. Sid was all right, but he wasn't the Clash. I'd watched Nancy muscle on-stage to the side mike, and laughed as it wasn't turned on. But she had to be on-stage – it was entirely and utterly appropriate – because the whole occasion wasn't in the least about music. And in that, McLaren had been inadvertently vindicated.

I had been with Sid at the Speakeasy watching Johnny Thunders earlier that summer. He had tried to join in on-stage, falling over and knocking over the bass amp. I had nodded out while chatting at a table with Vic Goddard of the Subways and Sid and Nancy – some conversation! I had slept while a cigarette burnt through the flesh of my right-hand middle finger. I'd been smacked out.

Topper had taken over Sid and Nancy's flat in Maida Vale. The Baker and I went to help him move. There was a bit of cleaning needed doing. In this case, blood off the bathroom walls. Sid had lain in the bath, graffitiing the walls with blood, as though icing a cake, with a syringe. I set to with a bottle of Jif and a scrubbing brush. The Baker refused to help.

'I ain't having nothing to do with that junkie nonsense. You do it. You'll end up like that anyway, Topper.'

'Leave it out, Barry.'

Topper had moved in. Battersea, the dog, moved too. But his wife didn't. Wendy stayed in Finsbury Park. Topper had moved on.

And now Sid had moved on – to a murder charge.

Just before Christmas that year, we spent a weekend at the Bell Inn, Aston Clinton, Aylesbury. It was a treat from Coon, who had drooled about it in advance.

'You'll love it. It's fantastic. Marvellous.'

It was as if she was Mary Poppins taking little wide-eyed guttersnipes to a plush country hotel with suites in converted stables. I found it culturally patronizing. Coon had always seemed to treat Paul as Pygmalion. She stopped short of elocution lessons, but introduced him to the delights of opera, took him to a black-tie Frank Sinatra concert – he wore his Doc Martens beneath his dinner-jacket. She took him to the USSR to 'civilize' him, like Rousseau's noble savage. He brought some great badges back from Russia. And now she was trying it on with us.

Mick was beaming as I unpacked him at the hotel. The rest of us nicked the fancy soaps, gels and shower hats. I made an effort to hit the gourmet dining room. I ordered an alarm call in order to go down for my breakfast, except of course it was lunchtime, and I was all alone apart from eight trainee French waiters in ankle-length white aprons. I had the venison and Cumberland sauce. I had never been treated with this much respect, but then, I hadn't wanted to be. I mused on the rich, while picking deer meat from my teeth. I told Joe about the feast he had missed when I woke him up, but he was unimpressed. There was a feeling that a new broom was about in the Bernie-less Clash camp. But no Bernie had meant no one to field the bills and sort out the finances. Caroline had been given the job of facilitating the day-to-day administrative side of things, but one of the first things we had done was to give ourselves a pay rise of another tenner a week. We soon realized, though, that the Clash coffers weren't overflowing. In fact they had been frozen.

With Coon's encouragement we had brought in the Derek Block Agency for the optimistically titled Sort it Out tour. I went to court and lost my licence just before the tour, but it didn't matter. We had a proper driver, Andrew Bond, who had given up motor racing for a quieter life. He wore pastel jumpers, and went out in the mornings and cleaned the car.

The tour manager, Steve Lindley, was known to us as Andy Pandy because of his permed long hair and habit of wearing striped dungarees. He just didn't understand. I was in a sandwich bar with him, Robin and Paul. I'd given our order, opening my pink flight case to get the food-float, and I could see Paul nudging Crocker from the corner of my eye. When I went to return the cash-bag, my case was shut. I opened it to find it now contained a cheesecake. I knew Crocker had done it because he was licking his fingers, but I knew Paul had put him up to it, and lashed out at them with my feet. They skipped out of reach, grinning, while the owner said, 'Who's paying for that?'

'But it's inedible,' I said.

122

Andy Pandy stood aghast. I had been trying to boot one of my employers in the nuts? One of the band had got up to such a childish trick?

He carried a briefcase, but it wasn't Clash atomic pink. It was black shiny leather.

The Derek Block Agency had offices in Oxford Street. Bernie's office had mostly been his home, or he had me do his calls for him from the pay-phone at Rehearsals. The agency issued proper backstage passes, tour itineraries, held proper meetings, discussing with the band which venues would be played, and when. Joe put in a plea for the Cardiff Top Rank to be included, and mine and the Baker's hearts sank. We loved to hate that venue. All the Top Ranks seemed to have low ceilings, which played havoc with the sound and made it difficult to raise lighting rigs away from skin-scorching proximity on the stage. But these weren't the main problems at Cardiff. The hall was in a basement, with a set of double steps so steep we couldn't believe how we didn't fall and break our backs carrying the cabinets up and down. There was no lift.

But a little entourage of Joe's friends from his earlier days always turned up there, politely asking if they could see Woody. I made sure they were on the guest list. They were mostly studenty types, and would sit and chat nicely with Joe after the show: 'So how's it going, Woody?' He always treated them well. And he was always Woody to us for at least twenty-four hours afterwards. Me, Crocker and Paul would phone him in his hotel room, putting on Welsh accents and asking if Woody wanted to come to the Students' Union bar.

And on a previous tour we had been turned away from a hotel we had been booked into at Cardiff. The manager had taken one look and said: 'Oh no. You're the Clash. No.' He held up his hand like a traffic cop, stopping the procession. 'Not after last time. All those kids all over the hotel. I don't need that sort of clientele. No.'

123

We couldn't really argue, and had to return to the Bristol hotel where we had stayed the night before, which meant a long drive after the gig, followed by Woody's mates in an array of vehicles. But I couldn't understand how the Cardiff manager hadn't known the Clash had been booked in at his hotel. I later found out that Dave Cork had been booking our block of rooms under a variety of names as a joke: we were the Hackney Footwear Company, the Tolletian Leather Workers' Association, even a ballet company. I couldn't imagine Derek Block doing that sort of thing, and I was right.

Topper loved martial arts, and even wore an incongruous yellow bodysuit. On tour, he loved to get up early and work out and he asked the agency to make sure our hotels had gyms. But he also insisted on acting just as he always had. Topper and girlfriend Dee once disappeared on to the beach when we stayed in a cliff-top hotel at Bournemouth. The bar was packed with businessmen, couples, elderly winter-breakers, when they re-appeared with big grins, goose pimples, shivering and dripping, stark naked, with Robin behind them carrying their clothes. They walked to the bar and ordered large brandies.

In the Piccadilly Hotel, Manchester, Topper went to the basement and collected a box of metal cruet sets. Back in his room on the eighth floor he started throwing the salt and pepper pots on to car roofs in the car park, and was caught doing it. But with Topper, it often seemed like getting caught was almost part of the fun. Andy Pandy had plenty to say to him about it, and made Topper pay for the damage. I mused about the incident: it had been a stupid thing to do, but I loved the way it wound up the tour manager. Was this the price the Clash had to pay for having a great drummer? Was this the sort of thing Matt Busby had to put up with from George Best?

On-stage, the Clash were magnificent as ever. Behind the scenes, everything was costed. In hotels, no one was allowed room service. There was no bar bill: everyone had to pay for their own drinks. But everything was organized. The musicians were asked what pre-gig drinks they wanted. There had always been beer backstage, but now it was iced. There had always been bread and cheese, but now it was a selection of continental cheeses, not just cheddar. Our roadies had largely been friends of friends – I had once taken on Roland Gift, later of the Fine Young Cannibals (who I had known when he was a kid in Hull), for a few days' work, not because we needed a roadie, but because he looked the part, all studs and black leather. Now we had professional crews, with seen-it-all-before attitudes.

We had always refused to play student gigs unless they were open to all. At one venue in Glasgow a kid complained to us that he hadn't been allowed a ticket. Joe asked, 'Well, what are we doing about this?' As far as we were concerned the usual rule still applied. Joe put on the guy's spare bike helmet and went with him to the ticket office, where he too was refused a ticket because he wasn't a student. Joe said, 'Don't you know I'm in the band? And we ain't playing the gig.' And we didn't.

The situation wouldn't have arisen with Dave Cork and Bernie.

One consolation was that the tour did not include venues like the Hastings Pier Pavilion. There are some places that no matter how hard a band tries, how much they give, it ain't going to cut it. Our 42ft low loaders had parked on the esplanade in lashing rain, there were roadies hanging around the ramps in unfamiliar cagoules and waterproofs, reluctantly waiting to push the gear through the chicane of the bingo parlour and slot-machine arcade. We had been grateful for the backdrop, for once. We used the black polythene to protect the equipment from the waves crashing over the pier. The audience also looked like they had been wrapped in plastic and lugged up the pier. Backstage, the band tried to keep warm, huddled round a small gas fire. The result: cold band, cold audience, hard work. But on this tour we didn't meet as many characters like Hastings' legendary one-armed humper man, who worked for the pier theatre. He could lift cabinets that would usually take two men to carry.

Derek Block provided better sound, better lights and looked after the band better. It was good for the fans; it took away a lot of the worries of the tour. But it took away a lot of the tension the band fed on. It was more and more incumbent on me and the Baker to prick the cosy bubble. Derek Block took away a lot of the incidental fun. Town maps were issued, with venues highlighted. Previously, we enjoyed pulling into town and asking directions. We always asked three people, reckoning that one was probably a visitor himself, one was likely to be crazy or on drugs, and one would actually know the way.

A highlight of this tour was playing at Canterbury Odeon. Paul had said his dad was coming up from Ramsgate to see the band, and Topper said his mum and dad were coming from Dover. I had met them before. His dad was a headmaster. Topper had invited me to Dover for a weekend, and he had loved being the local boy made good. We had gone to see Bill Barnacle's jazz band playing in a pub, and Topper had sat in on drums, then we took in a band at the Leas Cliff Hall, Folkestone, Topper skipping about like a pixie, drumming rhythms on every surface. It had been lovely to see. So I asked my parents along too. They drove down from Gillingham, and stopped to ask the way from some King's schoolboys, dressed in their boaters and winged collars. They were stunned.

'Do you know who's playing there tonight?'

'Yes, the Clash,' my dad said breezily.

There was a little box at the venue, and I got the roadies to build a barrier with some flight cases. The three sets of parents stared at their sons and the punks happily slamming into each other with some pride. They didn't understand what

126

was going off, but they could see it was being done extremely well. That's showbusiness. I brought them a tray of brandies, carried above my shoulder, Martini-advert-style, through the crowd.

On the last night of the Sort it Out tour we stayed at a hotel in a castle fifteen miles out of Newcastle. The band had baronial suites, with four-poster beds. I was in the converted stables. Derek Block didn't try, and anyway couldn't have stopped, the practice of having kids back at the hotel after a gig, and as usual Joe and Mick were concerned about the kids' safety. After all, it was not so long ago that Mick had been in the same boat as the fans, following Mott the Hoople around the country.

I had five people staying in my room in the stables that night, including Citizen Smith, named after his characteristic beret, who had arrived to follow the tour in his black Mercedes. He was insidiously nice, and always had a stash of cannabis – he wasn't much use to me. He had baked a dope cake in the shape of a guitar for Mick to mark the end of the tour, and everyone was eating it in the dressing room. I nearly took a piece, but Mick warned me of its content. It just so happened that I had pulled that night, and I wasn't going to let my lodgers get in my way. So they slept on the floor and I shagged in the bed. They complained about the noise, and I told them to keep their eyes shut.

The band had had enough of long hauls by road, and caught a train back to London the next day. For them, the thrill of the tour was over, and they just wanted to get the come-down over with. I cadged a lift off Citizen Smith. We drove the whole way in pouring rain, the grey day matching my dampened spirits, that awful end-of-a-tour feeling. As we approached London he asked where I wanted dropping off. I didn't know what to answer. I didn't know what to do with myself. Suddenly I had no one to look after but myself. I said, 'Camden,' – I don't know why, because I no longer had any links with the area, but it was all I could think of, all that I knew. I found myself alone in the Caernarvon Castle on a rainy Sunday night. No fun. At the end of other tours I would at least have shared the anticlimax with the band until I dropped them off at their flats, and I would have had tasks to busy myself with – stashing the guitars and amps. Now all that was done by the Derek Block Agency. Who was this Derek Block anyway? I never saw him on the tour. I even started feeling sorry for myself. I phoned a woman I had met a few weeks earlier. I asked Lindy to come and pick me up and be nice to me. She drove down the hill from Hampstead and took me back to her place. I later married her.

Bus boredom....

12

We sat in a jumbo jet, breathing deeply in relief as we got stuck into the miniatures (so little in them for the long haul to Vancouver). Joe was buried deep in *The Executioner's Song*, Mailer's ode to Gary Gilmore. It was a heavy book that pushed him up towards the excess baggage level. Seeing a common interest I sat next to him. We spoke about killers and their psyches. We were talking about alienation and disaffection. We knew all about these concepts – they were what we had in common with our audience – but serial killing seemed a drastic way of dealing with them.

In an interim stop at Edmonton we both stared over the frozen wasteland that is the prairies in winter. We watched the baggage handlers on the tarmac wrapped in mountaineering duvets.

'Remember seeing *Badlands* at the Screen on the Hill? This was the very spot,' said Joe. Charlie Starkweather. It was cheerful stuff, appropriate on our inaugural flight to the national home of murder.

For Topper, the eternity of the long-haul flight meant that he had to be sedated, legally. Even the stewardess's nod towards the first-class cabin as she brought us a note didn't interest him. It was from Phil Collins – a class drummer in Topper's book. Phil's message said: 'Hi'. I knew we were high – we were in the same plane. But we were coming from very different places, both called London.

Excitement grew as we crossed the Rockies, and I ran through a mental checklist: endless Coon-calls at all hours, crisp efficient lists of dates, numbers and people; hours of

transatlantic calls, hiring stage gear, booking hotels, rehearsal rooms, buses and dope ... it was like shopping by phone. But it was all sorted out. It seemed like the perfect moment to get togged up. I reached into the overhead locker and yanked out a black bin-liner packed with twenty-four Pearl Harbor T-shirts. Joe had come up with the name for the tour, and there was no contest once the suggestion had been made. It said it all perfectly. The T-shirts had been knocked up at the last minute by Fifth Column, a Camden collective of young Clash fans, and delivered to my flat at midnight the night before. I had stayed up late ironing each one to heat-seal the screen printing. The design, which took up the full length of the shirt, was very bright and featured a kamikaze pilot's face on the front, with a bombed American battleship in flames on the back. The writing was Japanese. Balanced on a seat, I pulled off my old shirt, and pulled on the new look. The shout went up: 'Cor, give us one, Johnny.' Hands grabbed at the bag. I noticed three horrified Japanese businessmen sitting behind

Simonon. Laughter got the better of my footing and I slipped from the chair across the aisle.

We settled into the Inn on Denham Place, Vancouver, but jet-lag and adrenalin is an unsettling cocktail. Sitting with the Baker in the empty rooftop bar on the nineteenth floor, slugging Michelob for breakfast, we watched the sunrise over snowy mountains: proper mountains. One stood out.

'What's that one called, mate?' I asked the cleaner.

'Mount Baker.'

'No thanks.'

So what to do? A swim in the basement pool? Hotels in London had underground car parks, not pools.

Baker said, 'I don't swim.'

I said, 'I don't not do anything. Fear only exists to be confronted.'

We decided to just get out there.

The cab driver asked, 'Where to, buddies?'

As I was lighting a duty-free, I offered him one. 'D'you want a fag, mate?'

No answer.

'Take us somewhere to get cowboy hats – the real McCoy.'

He did a double-take at my shades, leather coat and silver earring. YMCA? With a frozen smile he edged away.

Suitably sorted out in the hat department, we walked the edge of the Pacific Ocean. After Cardiff and Stoke, we'd forgotten the world could look beautiful – but on tour it was only a snatched moment. As we rounded a full-size totem pole in the park by the hotel we saw Topper running, full of energy and enthusiasm, champing at the bit. And there in the clear blue morning, with the snow caps of Grouse Mountain behind, the plan was in place: a training camp in the Rockies followed by a few days rehearsal and a warm-up gig, and we'd be ready to hit the States proper.

•

As we pulled in at US Immigration I hoped there would be no more problems. I'd already had three days of hassle over work permits before we left Britain, trying to talk away busts and subversion with 'We're just a rock'n'roll band.'

'But you're not just a band.' The issuing officer spread a collection of Clash newspaper cuttings that I would have been proud of all over his Grosvenor Square desk.

We sensed the border crossing was a significant moment. Bob Gruen, New York photographer and personal friend of the band, put his finger on it and took a photo of the team line-up. 'One for the history books,' he said.

A Canadian in uniform approached us. What now? He handed over a parcel containing our studded belts, arm-bands, pocket knives and combs that looked like flick-knives. They

had been confiscated on entering Canada. Customs had been looking for drugs, but all they got were harmless accessories and smug grins. Joe had said, 'If I'd known they wanted drugs so much I'd have brought them some.'

Back on the bus, bigger and better than a British model, naturally, the band made a beeline for the front lounge with its sound system and video player. It also had a kitchen, shower and tiny bunks stacked like coffins. Mick tried sleeping in one, endured half a night, and never tried again. The back room – a smoking room – became his state room and bedroom.

We motored down the coast. Everyone was asleep but me and the driver. We were pulled over for speeding. The driver – a good old boy from down south (as every driver turned out to be) – said, 'Leave this to me. Sit tight. Stay quiet.'

He spoke to the cops, who looked like Gestapo. He then climbed back in and drove away.

'Didn't we get nicked?' I asked.

'No sir. This is now Dolly Parton's bus and she is asleep in the back.'

As we drove around Seattle, Topper felt it appropriate, as a devotee of the martial arts, to pay his respects at the grave of Bruce Lee.

'What about Jimi Hendrix?' someone said.

'He's dead.'

So we looked for Bruce Lee's grave.

'It's up a hill,' said Topper. 'Next right.'

Topper had never been to Seattle. He had no map. But he had the authority of someone who knows the way to a party. We blindly followed his directions, the driver steering the Greyhound round housing estates, until we realized that Topper was off his head. We booked into a cheap motel and a welcome bed that didn't move. The usual early morning call was not the one I was expecting. It was Bob Gruen.

'Sid's dead,' he said.

A bleary awakening of Joe in a daze. 'Sid's dead.'

133

Sid had said it often enough, but it was still a shock. Joe threw an empty coffee cup across the room. He was furious with Sid. 'Fucking idiot.'

As we headed for San Francisco the talk was all of Sid – fond memories of a nice bloke. They were sobering thoughts. Paul, with a gap-toothed grin, raised a toast to drink his health. But there was a stealing realization that this was the city where the Pistols hit the buffers, and now they really were gone for good, leaving us. If this country could do that to something as powerful— The ghost of Sid, the ghost of the Pistols, opened a door for us but also sat heavily.

The spectre of Alcatraz hung across the bay from our hotel at Fisherman's Wharf – a circular hotel around a courtyard, like Alcatraz. Lindy flew in from London to meet me. The circus began, as we knew it would. Fans round the foyer, and Strummer holding court in the hotel bar, delighted that the grand piano had a built-in ashtray for lounge crooners. Joe really got into the role, confusing guests, record company executives and journalists by tinkling out sleazy standards. But Mikal Gilmore understood. He had come to interview the band and he quietly revealed, as if naming his favourite cigarette brand, that he was Gary's brother. Strummer was far more impressed with this than the fact he wrote for *Rolling Stone*.

We strolled along the front, but the circus never sleeps. It was full of street performers. The greatest of them drew Paul straight away. It was a brightly coloured Punch and Judy-style tent: The Human Jukebox. Paul's eyes lit up. 'Joe, Get some of this ...'

Inside was a bloke, just his head visible, singing. Shout him a song and he would sing it.

Paul said: 'He ain't gonna know no reggae – give us Eddie Cochran.' And he did.

'Whew, I know how that guy feels,' Joe said.

We were whisked off to Tower Records for a personal appearance, courtesy of CBS. The record store was bigger than a Tesco's. The manager was ingratiating as we arrived, walking past a big cardboard cut-out of the Clash in the foyer. *Give 'Em Enough Rope* was blaring out. Strummer grimaced, grabbed me and said, 'Get that shit off.'

He sat at a table, and the manager was flabbergasted.

'But this is your record. This is how to shift product. This is what you're here to sell.'

Joe said, 'No, we're not. We're here to meet people. Put something else on.'

There was a long, orderly line of American youths clutching their *Give 'Em Enough Rope* albums for signing.

'What shall I put on?'

'You've got a shop full of records. What do you recommend?'

'Joe Ely,' I said.

Strummer, knowing my love of Country and Western, looked at me and said quietly, 'Is it any good?'

'Sure.'

The manager scurried off and soon, to the strains of Texan steel guitar, the Clash started chatting to the fans, while the manager tried to hurry the boys and girls along. I could have told him he had no chance. I had tried to clear people like this out of dressing rooms night after night, and the Clash didn't finish until the fans were finished. Afterwards, Joe and Mick were in arm-in-arm agreement. 'We ain't ever doing that again.'

'If that's what it takes to make it in America, forget it. I ain't no product.'

We eventually walked out with a good handful of free records each.

'Anyone know the nearest Cheapo's?' Paul said.

Mo Armstrong did. Bald and bearded, with a 'haw' of a laugh that was mimicked endlessly, he had the credentials of a beat poet. He worked in Leopold's, a tiny independent record shop not much bigger than a broom cupboard. Mo had been around the Bay since the days of Kerouac, and was waiting for a change. He had been waiting for the Clash. The fact that he had been sprayed with Agent Orange in Vietnam made him doubly cool – he was the kind of maverick we loved. He didn't want a cardboard cut-out in his shop. For his enthusiasm, he got Strummer's white stencilled jacket to decorate his store.

Mo clicked with my love of Country music and gave me some fifties tapes: Willy, George Jones, Guy Clark. I had to fight in the free-for-all to collar the bus's sound system, but once successful, Jones and Strummer nodded approval.

In the Californian sunshine we strolled round a flea market, the size of three football pitches, in Sacramento. We hit a stall selling uniforms like bees round honey. Joe spotted a blue and grey Sear's Security uniform. I bought it for him, just for those get-away-from-it-all moments. It was a bit over the top, but the cap stayed perched on his quiff till we hit the Atlantic.

The hotel lounge was a hive of media activity organized by queen Coon. I was up and down the lifts ferrying journalists clutching typed invitations to meet the band, and ferrying the band with typed schedules of who to talk to and when. Meanwhile Mo was hitting Joe: 'There's another way of doing this. This ain't the home of alternative culture for nothing.'

'What, hippy shit?'

'No, it's moved on. There's an underground press, alternative radio.'

Joe tuned in. Mo went off, and other, stranger people soon started drifting into the foyer. The dual cultures, cheek by jowl, didn't mix. A dodgy Mexican, Rudi Fernandez, with an evil eye, the head of a toad, and charming packages of free cocaine, just turned up and shared a lift with a suit. Strummer played the piano. Howard Fraser showed up from England, shooing away the hotel manager: 'I'm a personal friend of the band.' Roadies, only there for the live shows, worked on getting out of it on speed and booze and held sprint races around the circular boundaries on the fourth floor, jostling the visitors and guests. The Baker had gone down with a mystery bug and taken to his bed. His appetite seemed healthy. He asked in a weak voice for pizzas the size of truck wheels. 'And if you're passing a porn stand, get us a few mags.'

I needed air. Fernandez had a car, and said he'd show me the sights.

Coon said, 'Johnny, there's work to be done.'

'Let them sort it out. They'll be all right,' I snapped
impatiently. On the grassy slopes of Mount Tamalpais,
overlooking the Golden Gate Bridge, I hit a rare moment of
romantic tranquillity with Lindy and a bottle of Tequila Gold.
On the way back we argued and I kicked her out of the car
with no money. I was driven back to the maelstrom. She
hitched back.

Our first gig in the USA was at the Berkeley Community
Centre, with an audience of toe-tapping, hand-clapping,
smiling, scrubbed faces, which reminded us that in California
being laid-back is a virtue. The energy went one-way, with
Strummer striving to push it into their faces and Jones and
Simonon working up into sprints across the huge stage.

Mick asked me, 'How was that, then?'

'You should know. It was a good show.'

Joe said, 'Nice. But nice ain't good enough. Who put us
here with this bunch of dozeys?'

I pointed at the backstage pass. 'Bill Graham Presents.'

Joe said, 'How come we're with Bill Graham, Caroline?'

Stern-chinned, she stuttered: 'If you're not with him you
don't play the Bay. You don't play San Francisco. You don't
play California.'

'Who says?' Joe turned to Mo. 'Is that right, Mo?'

He shrugged. 'He's not a man to mess with.'

I knew what he meant. I'd read *Hammer* of th*e Gods*, where
Zeppelin's minders did over Graham's dearest with baseball
bats over a money matter. They didn't do California for a while
after that.

'Well, it's just as well he's out of town,' Joe said.

Outside the door was a mixed bag of people in tie-dyed
sarongs and saris, pestering me to get them in.

'No. Bill Graham,' I said, using his clout, but they were
pleading with me.

'We'll give you our hats if you let us in,' they said. They

were wearing coloured baseball hats with animals and propellers on top. They were so weird they were straight out of a Paul Simonon tall story. So they were in, straight into the dressing room. I walked ahead of them, wearing a hat with a propeller-carrying crocodile. The band saw me.

'Give us that hat!' Hands flashed out to snatch my new headgear.

I was sent out to get Sandy Pearlman, in the audience in baseball cap and capped teeth to see his protégés in America. The Clash lined up to shake hands, roaring with laughter, in their new hats.

Joe asked, 'What does a band have to do round here to get an audience going?'

'Play to the right audience,' said the now hatless visitors, who then told us about a benefit gig the following night for a bunch trying to break the stranglehold of big business.

'Can we do it, Johnny?' said Joe.

The American crew was consulted. 'We've got to be in Los Angeles in forty-eight hours,' they muttered miserably. Joe and Mick pleaded with them. I'd heard a story about Abba's roadies, who had been offered the choice of a cash bonus or a snog with Agnetha and Anni-Frid. To a man they chose the snog. But it didn't work here. They were given a bung. I was all for doing the gig, even without any extra pay.

We turned up the following night and Mick was delighted to find we were playing at the old Filmore West, a fine, ramshackle wooden building. The people running it were ramshackle as well. I warned the band about the Acid Test. Who better for a spiker than a star catch? The stage would not have passed our London health and safety man. Who cared? The joint was jumping as Coon muttered darkly about the 'ramifications'. The lack of organization was made up for by enthusiasm. It was a storming gig from the second the band ran on to the disintegrating stage. The Clash rocked out and the crowd was with them. Joe's delirium showed. He climbed from the stage into an opera box, waving and twitching.

Wheeling down the freeway later, we agreed we had done it right, happily discussing our free show.

Coon looked up from the open briefcase on her lap. 'These are important company people we're meeting in LA.'

We hit Santa Monica Civic Centre, a concrete barn of a place by the ocean. There were promenades and what looked like a job lot of palm trees. We found an empty stage. We had got there in time for a quick soundcheck by the skin of our teeth. But the gear truck hadn't. The roadies were sitting about smoking. But this was the home of the music business, and we were able to hire emergency sound, lights – everything – from SIR. The band ran through 'Protex Blue' at the belated soundcheck while a stagehand showed me how the angle of the floor – the entire floor – could be raised and lowered.

Bloody hippy audience! WHERE'S THE GAFFER TAPE?!!

'Oy, cop this,' I shouted.

'Yeah, but can you dance on it, Johnny?'

Backstage some dangerous-looking people appeared, sharp calico suits, razor-cut hair. Their cocaine was uncut, straight from Bogotá.

'Hour and a half to show-time,' came the call.

Our missing truck arrived. The crew unanimously pointed at the set-up equipment: 'Leave it there.' But Mick was having none of it. He wanted his tried and tested equipment on-stage with him.

'If you won't do it we will,' he said, and the band started dismantling the hired gear. With a fresh snort all round, we pitched in, and the doors had to be held closed until we were ready. Topper put his own kit up, but didn't make such a good job of it as the Baker would have.

The show went well, and Bo Diddley was a revelation. Playing support, he came out with all guns ablaze, resplendent in a wide-brimmed hat and a gut to match. He overwhelmed us. He wasn't there as a rock'n'roll relic, but we were disappointed the audience seemed largely unaware of their own rock'n'roll past.

Backstage, it was clear that the Pearl Harbor tour didn't fit into the plans of the men in suits, the CBS executives brought in on the gravy train to 'assess the band's marketability'. The Pearl Harbor T-shirts looked cool. But the suits weren't interested in cool. CBS issued laminated passes to their own people with *Give 'Em Enough Rope Tour 1979* on them, which we refused to acknowledge, and which left the professional US crews using two sets of passes, just to be safe. CBS T-shirts for the tour were cheap, instant and throwaway.

A sleazeball sidled up to Mick, drawling: 'I've got the album. My daughter thinks it's great.'

'Good for her,' Mick grunted.

The high point for these guys was a group photograph, painstakingly assembled by the promoters, ordering any drifters back into the line-up. 'And ... ready ... smile!' I was standing behind the photographer, looking at the set-up, realizing how appropriate the band's name was. Joe looked at Topper; Paul looked at Mick. Not a word was said. They walked away before the camera could click. The gasps of amusement at 'English eccentricity' turned to heartfelt grumbles when they realized they would have no commemorative snaps for their mantelpiece or to plug their egos in trade magazines. I laughed as I joined the band and said to Joe, 'Smart career move.'

'I ain't gonna be no trophy on their wall,' he replied.

Back in my hotel room, drink and cocaine flowed. Later, in bed, the room began pressing against my head.

Lindy and I walked on the beach, wide and very black with the roar of breakers. I became aware of dots of light and low voices: 'Hey. Over here. D'you want some of this?' I saw no one in this Mansonesque territory. Frozen with fear and cocaine, I was out of my depth. Gingerly I edged back, eyes widened to catch any movement. Back to the dimly lit boulevard. No recovery. Two figures in black approached and we hid behind a palm tree. I pulled a penknife with an inch blade and felt pathetic, but I was going to fight. A clump of boots across the road and I was ready to spring.

'Oy, Johnny. What you doing? Having a piss?'

It was Joe and Mick having a stroll. Funny place to write a song.

In the morning the paranoia was still with me and an unspeakable horror lurked on the balcony. I flashed to Mal Evans, big and bespectacled like me, shot through his hotel door by the LA police having survived after all those years as the Beatles' road manager. With great relief we escaped from LA.

With all the liggers and hangers-on left behind it was down to the hardcore on the bus, and Bo Diddley; especially Bo Diddley.

BO - DA. DA. DA
DA - DA. DVM
DVM
Diddley

Joe said, 'You can't have too much Bo Diddley.'

Mick set up camp in his state room in the back of the bus, laying out his belongings: scarves, books, tapes, dope, each in their rightful place. We visited him individually, to peep out the back windows as the Arizona desert passed, but he always had the curtains closed. The driver pointed out a road-runner. 'Nothing like the cartoon,' said Paul. 'Beep, beep.'

We stocked up at supermarkets: crisps and beers, tortillas, Dr Pepper's. The video machine was a hit: *Blood for Dracula*, *King Creole*, *Star Wars*, *Heaven Can Wait* (crap film, but Julie Christie ...). Bo Diddley and Topper preferred *Behind the Green Door*, which featured Marilyn Chambers and a particularly fine ending of multiple ejaculation in psychedelic colours. Bo ran the sequence again and again, laughing his long, rumbling laugh that came from deep inside his barrel-chest, slugging Rock on Rye straight out the neck: 'Haw, haw, this keeps the cold outta ya chest, boy.' Topper and I matched him. Come bedtime, if there was such a thing, we never saw Bo

143

attempting to squeeze his impressive girth into a bunk slot. He preferred to give his bed to his guitar. I watched him gently put the guitar-case between the sheets, tucking it in, then open the case quietly and check the distinctive square instrument was snug, stroking it like it was his child. Miles passed. Bo was persuaded to tell of the pioneer years. He had done this ride with the young Rolling Stones – and he seemed to rate us. He told of pride and Buddy Holly. He spoke of magnificence and Little Richard. He talked of rip-offs and double-dealing.

" If my bRAIN huRts
"this bAd it must
bE AMARiLLo..."

'God knows I'm not a rich man but I got a Cadillac in my drive and a bomb shelter.'

'A what?'

'Sure have, boy, and it's full of tinned peaches. Tinned peaches to help me fight off the holocaust.'

144

Strummer's 'electric leg' trips me up on stage (*Pennie Smith*)

Joe's Fender is coming my way again (*Pennie Smith*)

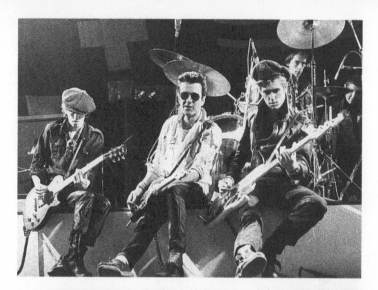

Top: Time is Tight – so get there early for the soundcheck (*Pennie Smith*)
Above: The winner by a knockout is Topper Headon (*Pennie Smith*)

Left: The Baker relaxes – Topper doesn't (*Pennie Smith*)

Below: I gaffer up Joe's arm to stop self-mutilation from manic strumming (*Pennie Smith*)

Joe's lost pints of sweat; I fix the drinks (*Pennie Smith*)

Joe basks in the after-show glow (*Pennie Smith*)

Mick tunes up, turns on, drops fag ash (*Pennie Smith*)

Me 'n' Paul strap in for lift-off (*Pennie Smith*)

Left: Sound check's best for special requests: '"Protex", please, Mick' (*Pennie Smith*)

Below: Joe full on (*Pennie Smith*)

Top: I'm up with the driver – you can't have too much desert (*Barry Myers*)
Middle: Paul and me grab a kip in the sky as guardian angel Ray Lowry watches over us (*Barry Myers*)
Above: Clash city rockers roll up at the gig (*Barry Myers*)

Top: Me flat out on the tour bus Arpeggio (*Barry Myers*)
Middle: The romance of rock'n'roll – I'm so bored . . . (*Barry Myers*)
Above: Some team – me and Baker on the ball (*Barry Myers*)

Paul Simonon, the epitome of cool from his barnet to his boots (*Mark Rusher*)

Mick calls for a nice cuppa and a clean shirt (*Mark Rusher*)

Joe's just got back from the boot fair (*Mark Rusher*)

Top: Strummer's on top of the game with the set list sorted (*Mark Rusher*)
Above: Some frontman (*Mark Rusher*)

Top: Camden Town reunited – Joe and me put the squeeze on Bernie Rhodes (*Pennie Smith*)
Above: Back from New York with the trophy (*Polly Broad*)

At 4 a.m. we pulled into a floodlit oasis to refuel. Me and the driver were the only ones awake. With the tank filled, we left. Out of the corner of my eye I saw a flash of movement. Bob Gruen, in his boxer shorts, ran barefoot across the dirt, arms waving frantically. We hadn't seen him get off, and he had been within an ace of getting marooned in the desert. He owes me one.

Ace Penna was the American tour liaison officer. He was the better side of even-keeled. He thought and moved quickly, which seemed unusual for an American, but suited us a treat. He knew how to lay his hands on good gear in the most obscure of places, which in his position was a more useful talent than an intimate knowledge of the American freeway system. At the point that he turned on the radio we were travelling up Route 66 from Amarillo – the wrong way. The weather forecast was grim. The worst blizzards for years were already gripping the Midwest.

Ace started shouting: 'Abort, abort. Red lights flashing. We ain't gonna get there. The crew and the gear won't get to Cleveland. The roads'll be blocked. Abort!' It seemed that his natural reaction to imminent disaster was to give up. But not in our book.

Mick said, 'We'll surf the snow. We'll fly in.'

We all shouted: 'Driver! Airport.'

Ace panicked. 'I can't just get you all on a plane.'

'Get the agency to pay. Get them to dip into the bucks they're making out of us.'

We boarded the only flight out to St Louis – not quite the right direction, but as some Zen bloke says, the journey of a thousand miles starts with but a single step. Topper was curled up in his seat in a terrified ball. I shouted to Mick: 'It was Clear Lake, Iowa, wasn't it?'

'What? Oh, yeah, Buddy Holly.'

Paul picked up on wind-ups quickly. 'No, Reading, weren't it?'

'No, that was Glenn Miller.'

'Big Bopper?'

Joe countered, 'Patsy Cline.'

I added, '1958, Busby Babes.'

I said to the stewardess, 'An extremely large brandy for my friend here,' pointing at the quivering Topper. The routine became a running joke.

At St Louis we ground to a halt waiting for the Cleveland connection, and we holed up in the airport hotel bar, which was as if we had walked into the bar scene we knew off by heart in *Star Wars*. Livened by stimulants and the absence of the bus, we noticed a small band playing in a corner. The end of each standard was met by tumultuous applause, whoops and hollers – but from our tables only. The combo were suspicious, but pleased to get some response.

Topper, delighted to have his feet on the ground, said, 'It's jamming time,' and strode across the bar to sit in. He didn't quite fit in with their lime-green spangled tuxedos, but went straight into a slick version of 'New York, New York'. To everyone's astonishment but his own, he slotted spot-on into the combo, sounding like he'd just finished seven days' rehearsal with the outfit. Joe was still roaring for the Midwest anthem, 'What Made Milwaukee Famous', when Topper returned to us in triumph.

Paul said, 'That's showbusiness, eh?'

Next day, we beat the fog into Cleveland. Amazingly, the Baker and crew had beaten us there.

'How'd you manage that, Barry?' I said.

'You wouldn't want to hang around in Salt Lake City. No booze.'

He regaled us with tales of Mormon restaurants, terrifying Rocky passes and dazzling Soul radio channels.

Joe had raging toothache. I was surprised it didn't strike more often considering the blackened, rotting stumps in his mouth. I asked for the nearest dentist at the hotel reception, and was about to set off when the doorman stopped us in horror.

'You won't make it to the end of the block,' he said. 'They're mean streets out there.'

Joe said, 'Sounds good.' But we jumped in a cab. The dentist did something – I didn't ask what; I'm terrified of them – but said the shot would take twenty-four hours to work. His advice was to cancel the gig. Coon was sympathetic. Joe said, 'I ain't No-Show Strummer.' The show went on to a wildly lively crowd and we sussed that the industrial heartland of America was more Clash than California. It had the familiar hard and desperate edge. And then we had Manhattan in our sights.

Joe Strummer... highly advanced

...No stranger to dental decay...

DALLAS 1979..

147

We knew New York was important. New York claimed to have invented punk. We would show them. The bus pulled up at a brownstone house. We stared up. Mick said, 'Where's the hotel?' 'This is it,' said Coon. 'Isn't it charming?'

'Looks like a fucking rat-hole to me,' said Mick, as we entered the lobby.

'It's a period building. Larry always stays here,' said Coon.

'Larry who? Where's the bar?'

'There isn't one. But there's a delightful Indian restaurant through there – so unusual.'

'Fuck this. Get us into a proper hotel. Did you book this?'

'It's so hard to get in here.'

'Get us out of here. Get us into a proper hotel.'

People walked by carefully when Mick was riled. But we didn't move until the next day. We couldn't. Coon had booked the Indian restaurant for a meet-the-glitterati party. It was all Tandoori bullshit, canapés and gushy talk. I went to an Irish bar down the block. After a bit of low life I returned refreshed. I got up early next morning to see the sights. A brief whirl round an outdoor skating rink and the Chrysler building in the frosty clear air made the city almost attractive. I caught a cab with Lindy to the Chelsea Hotel, put the cab on hold and went in to look at the strange ceramic lobby, the marble stairs and wrought iron, the paintings on the wall and general artistic seediness – and then got back in the cab. I had paid my respects to Sid. Back in my room, the phone rang. It was Joe.

'Johnny, can you come down? Now. I've done something terrible. Awful. So awful I've got to tell you.'

My mind raced. I was worried.

'I shouldn't have done it.'

'Done what?'

'I went out with Andy Warhol last night to Studio 54.'

That afternoon in the Palladium we did a soundcheck and a half. Every light was focused, every speaker double-checked,

A StaRRy, StaRRy Night in old New York town...

every spare guitar tuned, every drumstick sanded. That night the Clash looked hard and ripped the joint apart. After I stuffed the sweat-soaked stage gear into holdalls the famous came to back-slap, joined by a chunk of streetlife I had brought in through the stage door – there was no 'élite only' here.

'Studio 54 tonight, lads?' I shouted. It's hard to have secrets on the road.

We shot off in a bunch of cabs, but not before I had

grabbed the band's special gift from Ron Delsner, the promoter – a jeroboam of Dom Perignon. Studio 54 was a hard gaffe to crack, but that night we had the keys to the city and smoothed our way in past the drooling, star-spotting crowd. The floor was sand. There was a stuffed polar bear in the corner. The venue breathed decadence. I was amused to hear over my shoulder a scuffle and 'I'm a personal friend of the band.' The place heaved. A massive dance hall, a huge backdrop of lights, a crescent moon came up with a face and hands, the hands pulled up a spoon of cocaine, the moon snorted it and the whole backdrop went 'zing' and 'YMCA' came on and we hit the dancefloor. The Clash had cracked New York. A lackey arrived to invite us to the balcony VIP room. Mick went. I made my excuses and left. It was terrific to have a look, but I had no desire to join that élite scene. I had the Dom Perignon for breakfast. I had tied the bottle out the window with gaffer tape, and it was covered in snow. The city had ground to a halt, but they had cleared the airport and we flew out northwards to play the last date of the tour.

13

The cold and damp familiarity of London in February jolted us out of the triumph, the strangeness, the freshness, the space that we had tasted briefly in the US. It had felt terrific to break into the huge inertia that was America, but we all knew that the places we had played had been selected because they were rock'n'roll cities, at the nerve ends of America's otherwise static body. *Give 'Em Enough Rope* was also near the top of the American album charts, and had been voted second best album in the *NME* readers' poll, which also made the Clash the best band of 1978, and 'White Man in Hammersmith Palais' the best single. The Clash were at the top of the tree. We had hammered that home to London and the music press at the Lyceum before we left for America. Tickets had been at a premium for the dates. These were among the rare gigs when we couldn't let the faithful dispossessed in through the stage door, although many tried. I was very apologetic to them, but it couldn't be done, with all the slick West End security and the people and paraphernalia of the augmented *Rude Boy* film crew. I was called to the back door for about the fifteenth time, and once again was wary when I heard someone use my real name. It was a freezing night and huddled into the door was my ex-wife and a suit, looking as though he hoped no one he knew would see him, like he was at the door of a seedy strip-joint.

'Now, about this maintenance that you owe ...'

I got two of the theatre bouncers to get rid of them.

Backstage, on-stage and out front were awash with technicians. The multi-core cable ran from all over the building to the mobile recording studio parked up off the Strand. This was to be Dave Mingay's big night. We were impressed with the set-up.

Mick said, 'About time you got round to doing it properly, Dave.'

Mingay's partner, Jack Hazan, muttered, 'You shut up. What do you know?'

This was to be the last piece of filming, and I got the impression Hazan couldn't wait to get it over with. I began clearing the dressing room, when Mingay returned, as nonchalantly as his nerves would allow, to ask where 'I Fought the Law' came in the set.

'See Johnny,' said Joe. I had huddled in a corner with him earlier and took down the set list, then copied it on to small strips of paper to be gaffer-taped to the tops of their guitars. Mingay had asked the Clash to all wear black shirts for the filmed gig.

'Trust me, it'll be wonderful,' he'd said. Dave was nervous but looking forward to his big night. He had always claimed he didn't know the plot to *Rude Boy* until it was all in the can, but 'I Fought the Law' fitted into it somewhere. Come the song, Joe sang that he'd killed his baby, not that he'd left her. Mingay's knees sagged as he heard the words and he held his head in his hands.

'He's ruined the storyline,' he wailed.

'What storyline's that, then, David?' I said. 'I didn't think you'd worked out the plot yet.'

It had taken this last, high-tech day of shooting for it to finally sink in that a film was being made about us. Dave Mingay and his crew had been following us around since Victoria Park, but Mingay's words then had proved true: it *was* amazing how quickly we had got used to being filmed. From the start, Mingay had been boyish, enthusiastic and charming. There had been no script or storyboard, no continuity woman with a clipboard, just Mingay with his little Woolworth's notebook and his smile, and a skeleton crew designed to fit into any cupboard. I had enjoyed the project. I'd enjoyed watching Dave and Hazan arguing about how to do the next scene – it broke up my hectic days. Dave and Jack were opposites. David was golden, Jack was dark and lean, mean, tense and impatient, often clad in an expensive biker's jacket. He was the eye. He moaned and swore a lot, and as the project wore on so did he.

Mingay was also good for a tap. He must have got up in the morning and crumpled notes into various pockets, which he could pull out in response to a request for a loan later in the day. And he must have known he wouldn't get it back. We once filmed a scene in the early hours on a roundabout at Aldgate, near Tower Bridge, when I asked Dave if he couldn't bung me twenty quid.

He said, 'What on earth do you want twenty pounds for at two in the morning?'

I said, 'Well, taxis are expensive round here.' But after I got the cash I nipped round to a nearby dealer for half an hour.

Bernie had told Mingay to work with me on the day-to-day details of filming. Although Bernie had neglected to tell me of this arrangement, it worked out well. Mingay hired Drury Lane Theatre to re-create the scenes of Glasgow bouncers beating up Clash fans. I earned myself free entry to Dingwalls for life by hiring its entire complement of bouncers for the shots. They got into their roles so much that two kids had to be taken to hospital. One of the detectives in the film was someone I knew who was actually awaiting trial for armed robbery. The Camden Ferrets had played a gang of punk girls. A friend, Liz Young, is the girl on the film who gives Ray Gange a blow-job in the toilets. After filming, Ray said to her, 'How about doing it for real?' She said, 'You must be joking.' Even Paul and Topper earned themselves some extra cash for being filmed throwing Gange into a bath. Joe and Mick wouldn't do it.

Gange was the rude boy of the film. He was with the film crew, but he got into the Clash way of life. He had great hair for a start – a good, full-bodied quiff – and he was much better informed than anyone first thought. He was a partici- pant, not just an observer and actor. At a meeting between Mingay, the Clash and CBS in Paris he had been told politely and very firmly to leave after throwing food at other diners. Ray's was a strange position. Mingay could say to me: 'Johnny, could you go out and come in again so I can film it?' And I could say, 'No, I'm busy.' But Ray was with the film crew – he always had to do it. He could only show dissatisfaction with a petulant stamp of his young foot. Continuity may be about wearing the same shirt for different filmings, but Mingay's continuity problem with Ray was filming him at the same level of intoxication. He didn't know the film's plot any more than any of us.

Mingay says he had a tough time making the film. He had soon learnt how difficult it was to communicate with Bernie, and to rely on me as his middle-man with the Clash. Mingay, always a good listener, was caught between both sides of the power struggle between Bernie and Mick. He heard Bernie constantly sniping to the other band members about Mick: that he was going off the rails, taking too many drugs, getting too big for his boots in a classic rock'n'roll style. Mingay says: 'Bernie was interested in having a band, but not in the least interested in the personalities of the members of the band. I told him he should spend more time on psychology, rather than attempting amputation.'

But Bernie's chaos was preferable to Caroline Coon's hostility to the film project. She restricted filming and wanted editorial control.

But the band made no concession to the filming either. The crew had tried doing close-up shots at the Glasgow Apollo gig, and Mick had quickly waved at me to get them off the stage. By doing so he inadvertently did the film a favour. The cameraman had to pitch in with the fans down the front, and got much better shots.

Whenever I was in the West End I called at Mingay's Marshall Street offices and asked to see the rushes. They were very cagey, but perhaps appreciated my interest, showing me carefully selected snatches and turning off the tiny viewer immediately afterwards.

Mingay was disappointed to find the sound quality of the live sets was duff and seemingly couldn't be improved. It was a drawback of using such a minimal crew. The Clash agreed to dub over them, using George Martin's gaff, Air Studios. The sessions were done at night, with the film projected on a big screen so the band could play in synch. The rhythm section was looped, and Joe went through the same vocals over and over again. Kate Bush was recording in another studio, and Mingay said he noticed how she whispered into the microphone, but played back, her voice would sound big. Joe sang full blast, and engineer Bill Price had to turn the vocals right down to mix with the backing track.

The studio had a communal canteen, but at night you had to rely on the self-service machines. I was there when the phone rang, and a little girl's voice asked for four cups of tea.

'Who'd you think I am? Get it yourself,' I said.

'Oh, sorry,' said the voice, and minutes later Kate Bush came in and walked to the drinks machine in the tightest jeans. I went back to our studio full of it, and everyone beetled up to the canteen to admire her arse. There was no privacy in these studios. Kate Bush couldn't get a cup of tea without people ogling her, and Mick needed the space to get his thoughts and his music together. I found a toilet window that opened on to a concrete balcony five floors up, looking down on to Oxford Street. Mick liked it out there, and Joe joined him sometimes. There was more action on Oxford Street than there had been on the Harrow Road below Mick's gran's flat. I left them there, keeping watch so no one shut the window and shut them out.

155

We weren't used to all that 'all musicians together' chummi-ness. George Martin was producing America. When they came into the canteen, all smooth, long blond hair in ponytails, we roared with laughter. I met Hugh Cornwell of the Stranglers, making his solo album, *Nosferatu*. It takes one to know one, and pretty soon I was scoring for him.

And so I amused myself, while in the studio the work was intense. Mick and Joe weren't fazed at all at coming face-to-face with their own giant moving image, re-played over and over again, while they attempted to reproduce the urgency and excitement of a roaring Friday night in Glasgow in the sterile cell of the studio. In their effort to be realistic they were alert to every detail of the film – re-enacting their stage movements, pulling the mikes away from their mouths in time with their image on screen, doing it so well that they became marionettes, with the celluloid Mick and Joe pulling the strings. Italian meals in plastic boxes were sent in in order not to disturb the concentration and to save wasting valuable time in the expensive studio.

And so with the Clash's role in *Rude Boy* finished, Mingay began the long process of editing the many hours of footage. Dave Mingay came from a completely different cultural direction to the Clash camp. His door into the Clash was via Bob Dylan, Woody Guthrie and folk protest. But our paths ran together for a while.

Air Studios were plush. We were now out in the cold. We were back in England, top of the tree, with nowhere to rehearse. We had been on the run since leaving Bernie, and nothing was in place to support us. While Caroline had helped out with the administrative side of things through a rocky period, she had been only a stop-gap, not an executive decision-maker. Almost inevitably, she and the band drifted apart. The Clash had no manager, no secretary, no office, no way of getting money for petrol, guitar strings, egg mayonnaise sandwiches, drumsticks or grass. And we didn't have a base, or even a phone number, only my home number in Hampstead. The band were itching to rehearse and get on with it. This was top priority. The Baker and I were put to it. We started, as befits a top-of-the-poll band, at Nomis, behind Earls Court. It had a series of deluxe soundproof rooms, once you got past the high-profile security and a little peg board (Room Seven: Dire Straits). It was soulless and, anyway, we didn't have the money. We looked at Eel Pie, the Who's gaff at Shepperton, but that was built for stadium rehearsals and was too far out of town. Having drawn blanks at the top end of the market, we started at the bottom, sitting in a café with a Biro and a copy of *Melody Maker* on a Thursday afternoon. We didn't even look in Camden. That was Bernie's territory, and we had moved on. We made a list, and went to look at the options. The Baker had bought a second-hand Transit van and done it up (or done it down) in matt camouflage paint. The Baker had The Knowledge (he could have been a cabbie) and he had all the lip, usually out of the open window at other drivers.

He had a ghettoblaster hung behind our heads, often with the O'Jays blasting out, the Baker singing along like a falsetto choirboy, much to my disgust. As we drove around, studios were delighted to see us when we rolled up. They saw my pink case and they thought: the Clash – big prestige, big money. They were disappointed. We tried a lot, and they all felt wrong: there was either no privacy, or they were really expensive, or they were shit-holes. We were renting space by the day, persevering, stacking the gear in corners so that other bands could come in. We knew we'd had enough when we played at a place that at least had the honesty to be named the Black Hole, just across Tower Bridge. A band meeting was called there and the six of us sat down round a table.

Mick said, 'The trouble is that we're rootless. We've got all these ideas and we can't relax into it to produce them, we have to up and move, and there's all these people wandering around all the time. I feel like Greta Garbo.'

I knew what Mick was on about. When people thought he was throwing a moody and staying in his room, I knew he was being creative, getting his thoughts and his music together. He was ready to take the next step, to produce the music, but we still needed to work without distractions. We needed Rehearsals, but that door was closed to us now.

The Baker and I scratched our heads. Maybe we needed to go about this in a different way. We even considered using the Pistols' old place in Denmark Street, but the thought of going cap in hand to Malcolm was too much like humble pie.

Then we struck lucky. It was called Vanilla, and it came from just another small-ad. It was in Causton Street, down by the river, near Vauxhall Bridge.

The Baker and I went down a ramp into an indoor courtyard, where there were a couple of Rollers parked.

'Puts a different twist on garageland,' I said, and we were going to walk out. But we had to give it a try.

There was a glass cubicle, and everything was a seedy cream. It looked like they'd got a job lot of magnolia and painted everything they could see. A youth showed us to a door at the far end, unlocked it, and took us up stairs with no banisters to a long and low-ceilinged, rectangular, bare cream room. There was a carpet, but no windows. It also had a six-inch platform running down one side and across the far end.

The Baker was aghast, but I said, 'Yeah, it's got a stage! Perfect! Can we have this for a chunk of time? I don't want to share it, and I want the key to it. I don't want anyone else in here.'

The lad said he'd have to ask his boss, and re-appeared with a Maltese guy, camel coat over his suit. All he wanted to know was whether we could pay up front. This was a worry to me. The people we called at CBS were always in meetings. When we turned up there, the people we wanted to see were always just off to meetings. We had a go-between accountant (who we called Mr Quister the Twister), brought in by Caroline Coon to sort out our finances with Bernard. Our assets were still frozen, and CBS was reluctant to invest any more cash into the Clash. Quister wasn't his real name, and he wasn't a twister. He turned out to be a good guy. He had an office in Baker Street – very handy because it was three doors from McDonald's. When we first met him he sat up straight in his chair, in a neat pale blue shirt, tie and suit. We had very formal meetings with him. He'd say things like, 'Could you bring me Mr Jones's accounts, please.' It was like being in the headmaster's study, and we expected his disapproval when Mick would roll up late. We always needed cash, and, after logging everything in his books, Quister would reluctantly send his assistant to the bank over the road. But gradually we started popping in there if we needed a sub. Quister became Peter.

He OK-ed a cheque, and we were in Vanilla. The band turned up daily, promptly, even early, with a spring in their step. Jones would be the last, of course, but it didn't matter because Topper was always early, and the others started playing, and mucked about playing each other's instruments – something I had never seen them do before. The Baker picked Mick up, and he would ask to be taken straight to Vanilla – and then send out for an egg mayo sandwich when he arrived. The rehearsal room also had the vital requirement – a good café round the corner, where we became fixtures. It had the added advantage of not looking like a rehearsal studio. It was a garage. Out front, smart cars were being resprayed. We asked no questions, nor did the mechanics. We left instructions: 'We ain't here.' We were not disturbed.

The only disturbance we had during those long rehearsals was when we nipped up to Newcastle. The show was *Alright Now*, for Tyne Tees telly; it was one of the few that fulfilled the

Clash's TV criteria: live and in front of an audience. Me and the Baker went up the night before, staying at a cheap bed and breakfast where we were made to feel part of the family. The Baker loved it.

The TV studio was cold and bleak, full of technicians scurrying around with clipboards. A woman floor manager said, 'I've got you over here. Which side does the bass player stand?'

'Stage left.'

'Well, this podium is perfect, then.'

And we clocked four little round podiums, laid out as if for Herman's Hermits. The band came up by train on cheap Awayday tickets. The producers kept trying to stop the Clash mid-song as they ran through 'English Civil War', running round the little stage before the little crowd. A quick glance, and Paul and Mick dashed across to switch positions as Strummer dropped to one knee, pulling the mike down with him. The camera men couldn't keep up. There were too many interruptions, and we all trooped over the pub, saying we'd be back when they were ready to shoot. The studio audience came with us, pushing past the stage manager's outstretched arms. The Clash eventually played as loud as ever, giving the TV soundmen huge problems.

Filming over, we went back to Vanilla. Mick brought in folders and notebooks, which he stuck on top of his Boogie amp, a relic of the exotic days of Sandy Pearlman. ('You must have a peach daiquiri in Atlanta! You must have a Boogie amp.')

The gear was set up at one end of the room, as if the band were playing a small show, like at Rehearsals. But the only audience was the Baker and me. Joe lay on his stomach on the floor, writing songs like a kid concentrating, doing drawings on the living-room carpet. New material came in quick bursts. It was worked up from Mick's chords. Topper tried them against different rhythms. Bass was added, then finally Joe's words. The new songs were pursued up to a point, and then dropped or put on hold if they weren't working. Then they would run through an old song. 'Protex' never sounded fresher. Each one of the band walked in to rehearsals with ghettoblasters blaring with music from all over the globe. Paul showed enormous confidence, playing reggae tapes, and leaving them running while he picked up his bass to play along. He'd come a long way from learning his notes by rote on tape at Rehearsals. He'd pick up Joe's guitar and start bashing out Eddie Cochran chords.

Vanilla began to feel like home. I bought an electric kettle, some mugs from a cheap mini-mart and a tin tray with a picture of the Lake District on it. I was still banned from driving, and usually took the Tube to Pimlico. The first thing I'd do in a morning would be to run a Hoover over the fag-ash on the carpet. I'd check through all the gear, switch it on, tune the guitars, put the fires on – even in early summer it was cold – while the Baker picked the band up. We had swapped jobs for a while. We acquired some chairs and put up little tables to put cups of tea on, but the room was always sparse and functional. It was a room to work in.

Topper also blossomed. Always a terrific musician, he was no longer the new boy. He could play guitar, and watched Mick's fingers intently as he tried out tunes. Topper had found his own way of expressing himself, putting his ideas into the band's music. He had found his feet at Wessex Studio, an old converted church between Islington and Stoke Newington, which we'd used to record the 'Cost of Living' single in January. He had turned 'Capital Radio' into the funk song that can be heard on the EP. The others had listened to what he was doing, and agreed to go with it, scrapping earlier rocked-up versions.

And all the time, they were swapping music. 'What d'you think of this?' Paul would play a reggae song, Joe some hillbilly, Mick some rock. I was playing a Hank Williams tape when Mick came in one day, picked up his guitar and launched into 'Oh Lonesome Me'. I was stunned: Joe, perhaps, but Mick playing Country was unheard of. All the band were opening their ears to any and all musical forms. Their dope smoking was also prolific, but, like back in Rehearsals, it seemed to lift them and focus them on the music. There was no sitting around stoned. I never touched it, except when Joe shouted: 'Who's got the jazz? Skin up, Johnny.' I still rolled the best joints. It was cups of tea rather than pints down the boozer or even cans of lager; herbs, not powders.

We didn't give people the Vanilla phone number, and it was rare that the mechanic downstairs came and knocked. We had withdrawn, on our terms. There was another tiny rehearsal room downstairs, but it was hardly ever used and we rarely saw anyone there. But one day I'd gone down across the drive and caught Annie Lennox, then of the Tourists, halfway up the stairs, bending an ear towards the music, and I chucked her out. We had gone to Vanilla to get away from people, especially other musicians. Even friends were discouraged from visiting until late in the afternoon. But there were a few distractions. The Tate Gallery was nearby and Paul sometimes called in there. One day the Baker came in excited, and took us to a church hall a couple of streets away, saying, 'Look at this. Wow.'

And there was plenty to wow about. It was the annual show of the British Cacti and Succulent Society. 'Member B35439, B. Auguste – plus guests' was on his invite. The hall was full of these most amazing things, the sort of plants not normally seen outside of the Kalahari Desert. The Baker grew cacti in his shower. It would take him half an hour to clear the plants out if he wanted to use it.

Paul said to him, 'They say people look like their dogs. You look like one of them cactuses, with your prickly hair.'

But we were touched. The Baker was a private person. He was showing us a part of himself.

162

There was no street life round Pimlico, which was strange to us, coming from Camden and Portobello, where people just hang out on the street. Just at the time when the regular world was returning to its low-rise flats, people scurrying to close their front doors, we emerged into the daylight with a football. It had started when the Baker produced a ball from his van and was tapping it against a wall. I joined him to play headers, then Paul came down and just started whamming the ball round the place, off the walls and into the cars, and the mechanic came and threw us out.

'Well, is there a park round here?' we asked.

'Eh?'

Opposite was a school playground with a high fence – and an open gate. From then on, kickabouts became regular, and if mates wanted to visit, it was always, 'Come down for a match' – never, 'Come and see us rehearse.' When a deputation of CBS men came to see how their investment was coming along they found they had timed it wrong and were soon on the receiving end of knee-taps and crocodile tackles on their ankles. Their suit jackets were hanging off the wire fence. One of Joe's maxims was: 'Always wear shoes that are good for running or fighting.' Our clomping boots were ideal for fearsome tackling. Their leather slip-ons weren't so good.

The Baker had some deft touches, and for a short, tubby bloke he was quick on the ball. And he laughed a lot while he played little flicks, little caresses with the outside of his foot. Half of them didn't come off, but he fancied himself.

Joe was everywhere on the pitch, like a terrier after the ball. Battersea played as well, and it was a race between Joe and Topper's dog for every stray ball. Joe always went straight for goal. Paul was lethal: if he was coming at you, you got rid of the ball fast. He was hugely enthusiastic, prone to big hoofs and long shots.

Topper was good too. Well coordinated, he could show people the ball, drag it away, go both ways round them then look up before playing the ball on a sixpence. He spotted openings. He was the first to be picked every time – followed by Paul: no one wanted to play against Paul.

Everyone took the piss out of Mick's football style, running up the wing with his arm in the air shouting, 'To me! To me!' He tried to do intricate things with the ball. He could dribble and played a passing game. But Paul thought a pass was something he received with a charming smile from women.

While Robin was a good player in any position – a ruthless defender or a forward with the finishing power and class of Denis Law – I was a clogger. I had played one game in the North Wales League Division Two for Cerrigydrudion, when I had been instructed to hurt the bloke with ginger hair on the other side, which I did.

Non-sportsmen were also persuaded to play. If Howard Fraser turned up in his big bulbous sixties Volvo (good for getting a lift home) Joe would shout: 'Come on, Howard, you're a good personal friend of ours, get stuck in.'

After the football we went back to work, and opposing teams were packed off to a nearby boozer to wait. The Clash didn't rush to join them. At the end of each day Vanilla was a mess of apple cores, drink tins, newspapers and magazines, which I'd clear up the following morning. A night out was to meet up at the pictures.

All the time the work went on and the music was honed. This routine became daily life for us for nearly three months. We'd occasionally have a bit of madness, though. I once let off the fire extinguisher downstairs. Paul had been joking about doing it, but I ended up letting it off. A huge cloud of powder filled the workshop, covering the cars as it settled. Paul danced across the dust, leaving footsteps, a sort of step-by-step guide to the samba. Then we got a bill for £120 next time I went to re-book the room.

I took it down to Quister. He'd mellowed since our first meeting. I found him with his feet up on the desk, tie

164

loosened, with music playing in his office.

'What are you doing down there?' he said. 'CBS cannot understand why it's taking so long to rehearse.'

'It's going really well,' I said, slipping the bill in with the rent invoice. But he spotted it.

'Topper?' he asked, shaking his head sadly.

'Me.'

He looked at me as if I should have known better. But he came up with a cheque.

CBS weren't really interested in another Clash album at that time. They were releasing a revised version of *The Clash* album in America, and didn't really want another Clash product muddying the waters. But it had found a Clash manager that it liked in Caroline Coon. For the Clash, the music they were making at that point was the way forward. For Coon, America was the way forward. She was always formulating action plans, targets, setting agendas; and the Clash let her get on with it. It was nothing to do with what they were doing. She went spinning off to New York. CBS had hooked someone from the Clash camp they could do business with, but when they reeled in the line, all they found was Coon on the end. The Clash had unhitched.

It soon became apparent that the new material was taking shape so fast that we needed to slap it down on tape. The Baker and I realized we had to do it, but neither of us had a clue of how to go about it. Bobby Pridden of the Who helped us enormously. We had used ML Executives, a rental company set up with the Who's millions, for hiring stage gear in the past. Pridden, a small, bearded and balding bloke with smiling eyes, who resembled a pot-bellied garden gnome, was happy to share his expertise, which was rare in the roadie world. He came in one morning from Shepperton to take a look and was appalled at the seediness. But he told us what we needed. Over a weekend me and the Baker went in and set up a Teac four-track reel-to-reel with a portastudio. The Baker learnt how to get the sound balanced, and spent a lot of time with a cheap notebook, studying the tapes, working on the equipment.

Up to this point the Baker, me and Battersea had been the only audience for this material. Only we knew how good this music was. But with the tapes, the Clash were able to sit back with a spliff and listen to themselves, confirming what they had felt while playing it – that it was good. They knew it had to be put on to record urgently.

Joe wanted to do it at Vanilla. 'Let's do it ourselves. Fuck CBS if they don't like it. Here, it's got rawness. We want the dynamism, the vibrancy.'

But try as the Baker might, we were never going to get a good enough sound there to make an album.

Mick said, 'We'll get as close as possible. We'll use Wessex.'

We had liked Wessex, it had the right rough feel, and the right privacy. Only one band at a time could use it. For us it was perfect. Mick was aware he knew enough to produce an album himself, but we knew CBS would not buy it. They needed to have someone in charge, someone responsible for the budget, someone to put his neck on the line. They didn't trust the Clash because the Clash didn't play ball with them. CBS wanted a big-name, big-budget producer. But when Mick named Guy Stevens, there was no contest in the Clash camp. When talking about ambience, feel, greatness, as opposed to the technical nuts and bolts, there was only Guy Stevens, who Bernie had got in to do the first Clash demos, pre-CBS. But Guy was off the musical scene and supposedly off the rails. Joe said he would track him down, and went off in search.

'I found him in a boozer in Soho,' he announced three days later. 'He was interested, but he wants to hear what we're doing first. Make him a tape, Barry. And, Johnny, get him a cassette player. He ain't got one.'

I hadn't met Guy Stevens, but I'd heard of him. I couldn't believe a record producer didn't have a tape deck. I went off on the Tube to Tottenham Court Road and bought a little mono player. It was all we could afford. That night we were delighted. The Clash were producing the music they wanted. We had the man we wanted, and the studio we wanted. We had a few beers. On the way home I had a kip on the Victoria line and ended up in Seven Sisters. It wasn't till I reached home that I realized I had left the cassette player and the tape on the Tube. Unfortunately for bootleggers, the Baker had labelled the tape 'Val Doonican'. I phoned left luggage the next morning, but no joy. There was nothing for it but to own up. All I got for my confession was 'wanker', and the band made Guy another tape. He loved it.

We were ready to record, but first the Clash wanted to road-test the new material. It was mid-summer. They had missed playing live, and were also conscious of sniping in the music press regarding the fact that they hadn't played in Britain since the beginning of the year. But there hadn't been time. The new material was flooding out and had to be recorded. There had been no time to set up gigs, nor to even talk to Ian Flooks at the agency, so now we did it all ourselves. We all took an afternoon trip to Leicester Square. Paul had remembered the Pistols playing the Notre Dame Hall, and it looked and felt ideal for our purposes. We set it all up ourselves, hiring the PA and lights from the Who, and Bobby Pridden did us a favour coming down from Shepperton to help set it up and do the sound. He came over afterwards and said, 'That was a bit good, weren't it?' This was a man who had seen the Who since their pub-band days; in his understated way he confirmed what I already knew. Joe had made some surreal posters with umbrellas and trumpets, and I had them photocopied in an office-equipment shop. We'd all trucked around putting them up in Camden and Ladbroke Grove. Joe invited his mate Kate from his squat days and her girls' band, the Mo-dettes to play; Terry McQuayde and his mates' band,

Low Numbers, made up the bill. The new material went down well, but loading the gear away by a big stack of chairs at the back of the hall, I became aware of *Sounds* journos Garry Bushell and Dave McCullough hanging around, determinedly grim-faced.

'Oi! Joe! Can we have an interview?'

It had been a small-scale, intimate gig, and many old friends of the band were there. The Clash wandered about the hall chatting, and kids who hadn't been able to get in came in from the street asking for autographs. There were also lads wanting interviews for fanzines. Joe told the *Sounds* men it wasn't the right time for a formal interview, but they were welcome to chat. And it developed into a great debate on the state of punk: what is punk? Where is it going? It reminded me of naff conversations about the meaning of art. Voices were raised and it developed into a long, heated debate, but it wasn't like the David Frost show. People wandered up, put in their four-penn'orth, and wandered off again.

The Clash had always been aware of the usefulness of the press, and scrutinized the music papers every week. The band made sure that any journalist covering them was always looked after. This could involve anything from providing beer in the dressing room for a kid from a shabby fanzine in Portsmouth to sending up bottles to unsympathetic journos like Paul Morley in America. His favourite drink was Liebfraumilch. But it worked. He gave us a page spread. The Clash – Joe in particular – were always keen to get over their point of view and knew the ordinary fan could only get information from what they read. They were always keen to get their column inches. But Bushell and McCullough seemed to want punk to stay the same, for the Clash to stay the same, to look and sound the same, to sing about the same topics, and take it with them to the grave.

Joe said, 'There is no promised land. Take it and throw it in the air and follow it and see where it goes.'

14

We set up the equipment at Wessex, still messing around with the drum sound, and setting up little separation panels to stop the sound of one instrument spilling into another. We employed all the little recording tricks of the trade that Mick had picked up from Pearlman. Bill Price, the resident sound engineer, was all energy and efficiency, bustling around with instructions. He had a good head of hair – the makings of a Bobby Charlton comb-over – and late-night eyes. He clicked with the Baker, who responded well to the crisp commands, handing over the technical reins to Price, the master of the faders. Price was on home ground, and everyone plays well at home. He knew the big, high hall inside out. Jeremy Green, the second engineer, was tall and gangly, and moved and spoke slowly and surely. He was methodical, and appeared unflappable. He was also proud of his shoulder-length permed hair.

The Clash arrived, dressed for the job, a little nervous and excited, like it was the first day at a new school. They entered the studio as if they were going to do a gig – pacing around, cracking jokes, feeling the floor beneath their feet, and each of them had a plink on the black grand piano in the middle of the room. Topper put his coffee mug on the top and Price bawled him out for it. Me and the Baker knew how the band wanted their equipment set up, neat and tidy, from the height of the high-hat to the turned-up flight cases used as tables. We had had two new atomic pink cases built for all of our bits and pieces. The Baker's was squat, square and wide, opening from the top to reveal an array of neat compartments. Mine was six-foot tall and thin, and the moment I opened a drawer or moved it it fell over. Mick carried out his routine, walking around, touching the red-eyed amps and guitars on their stands, making sure everything was in its right place, then got into a groove on the drums, which he played with subtlety and a confident look in his eye.

The hall, decorated with wooden slats, was in half-light. The ceiling, high above, could hardly be seen. The control room was full of machinery – a mixing desk the length of the room, padded at knee-height, with a couple of big office chairs on castors. The front wall was glass, looking over the studio. The back wall was lined with massive spools of two-inch tape. All the level faders were set at zero, ready for a fresh start. I was sitting in there on a deckchair of blue canvas and chrome when Guy Stevens whirled in.

'Right, are we ready?'

I had to do a double-take. He was scruffy. He looked like a tramp. I thought he'd come from Green Lanes, just up the road. Price was giving orders, Green was adjusting microphones.

Price muttered, 'We're working on the snare.'

'No, no, no, stuff all that. Are we Ready? Is it Happening? Mick, how are you? Joe! Joe! Fantastic!'

He hurled a bag towards my chair and I heard a familiar clink. 'Whoa, tequila!' I said, and the bottle was in my hand, top unscrewed, in one fluid movement.

Guy swung away from Joe and swung at me, and I pressed into the back of the chair so his fist just scraped my chin and I laughed. But he didn't: 'Get your hands off my stuff.'

After that first day I never nicked his booze again: not out of fear, but out of respect.

He led the Clash into the studio: 'Let's hear it! Let's hear it!' I immediately knew why Guy Stevens was there. The Clash were enthusiastic about their new material – there was no doubt in their minds about it – yet this bloke had even more enthusiasm. They went straight into 'Brand New Cadillac'.

Guy said, 'Wow. Vince Taylor!'

Paul had dug out the song and brought it into the Clash repertoire. He was into maverick rockabilly, and Taylor was one of the few British rockabillies who cut the ice.

Guy wanted to get it straight down, then and there. He wanted it all now. He was hungry. Price attempted to obey while struggling to explain that it was impossible, but his and Mick's technical knowledge was overwhelmed by Guy's tidal wave. The traditional recording studio delineation of roles, with producer and band divided by the glass window, didn't last long. The band had brought in about a dozen songs in a more or less ready-to-record state, and Guy, shouting over the intercom, heard them through a few times each.

Between songs, Paul's voice came over the speakers, nodding towards Guy's bearded, tousle-haired figure in the mixing room. 'Are you going in there with him?'

'Yeah, why?' said Mick.

'We rarely mix with people with beards,' said Paul, trying to stay deadpan, but his face cracked into laughter.

The red and green lights (Enter; Do Not Enter) meant nothing to Guy. Guy was a man who drove the wrong way up one-way streets. If he spotted something sub-standard, something not being delivered at the maximum, he shouted over the intercom, never caring if the tape was running, or ran into the studio, shouting, arms waving. I'd read music-press accounts of Guy and had heard stories of him and Mott the Hoople from Mick, but it still didn't prepare me for the real thing. He muttered to himself constantly, shaking his head, then he'd be off, flying into the studio while me and the Baker sat stunned in the control room. All the band's eyes would widen as he'd sprint in, dash past them and hit a stack of chairs at the back, kick them over and hurl them about, arms whirling. He'd pick up flight cases and slam them down. He'd run up behind the band, push and shake them. I once

171

saw Paul tense and I thought he was going to whack him. But the Clash played on, and started to grin. 'Everything. It's got to come out. Everything,' Guy would shout.

The rhythm tracks were laid down first. Topper's fitness programme paid off and he played with a focused energy, gelling with Paul's bass. Topper was ready to do it again and again, but he rarely needed to, and Guy didn't want him to. Paul once hit some duff notes and sloped into the mixing room, looking cheekily sheepish. 'Sorry about that.'

'What? It was great!' yelled Guy.

'But I hit a couple of duff notes.'

'Fuck that! It doesn't matter. It was coming from the heart and that's what's important.'

This was music to Paul's ears. This was always his style of playing. He was aware that every note is usually scrutinized in recording studios, but that wasn't important to Guy, and he relaxed and enjoyed himself.

A guide vocal was added, intended just to let all the musicians get the feel of a song, where to ease down and where to hit crescendos. Joe didn't care if it was a guide or the real thing, he put everything into it. And Guy was ecstatic.

'That's terrific; that's it! That's it!'

He wanted to make the guides into masters. He didn't want to lose the spontaneity by doing them again, and the Clash had to gently put the brakes on. Joe knew he could do better, and had to point out that he was still tinkering with the words, and tidying up the songs. And he was. Even while some tunes were being recorded, more were being written. Strummer could be found perched on a stool, lying down behind flight cases or stuck away in a dark corner, shining a torch on to little scraps of paper and different notebooks, scratching things out, jotting down words and phrases. Throughout these sessions the Clash were coming in early and using the time for full band rehearsals, trying out new material.

When they got on to doing the guitar dubs Mick was very precise and self-critical. He didn't need asking to do it over and over again. He wanted to meet his own standards of perfection. Guy's response, listening to these endless takes, was, 'For fuck's sake, Jerry Lee Lewis would have this in the can and be round the boozer by now.' He once picked up an aluminium ladder and charged at Mick with it, whirling it round his head. Besides almost knocking over every bit of equipment in the studio he could have put Jones in the casualty ward. Mick moved on to the next track, making a mental note to try the last one again when he was on his own.

Guy often rang me at home early in the mornings, asking for an early start to recording. I had to point out that none of us had got home till half-four, but had to admire his keenness and complete lack of understanding that anyone else could need sleep when he wanted to work. His world was on fire and he wanted to fan the flames.

Guy always made an early start. One day he had walked in and said to everyone and no one: 'Pay him.' I went out and found a minicab driver with his hand out, and this seemed like a sensible plan for the future, so I set up an account and arranged a standing minicab order to bring Guy up from Clapham. We didn't really want him wandering around on the Circle Line on his own. The cab driver said one morning, 'It's going to cost more than usual because I had to keep the meter running at Highbury.'

'What, did he stop at the offie?'

'No, the football. He wandered off into the stadium.'

I asked Guy about it later. 'What's with the Arsenal?'

'Royal Arsenal, Johnny.'

I understood. He was a hardened Gunners fan. But we didn't hold it against him. I managed to make a deal: someone in the Arsenal office must have liked the Clash.

'We've got a bloke who wants to kneel on the centre spot each morning.'

173

'Clash, eh? All right. Couldn't send us a T-shirt, could you?'

Guy was delighted. 'It's wonderful to walk through the marble entrance gates, past the bust of Herbert Chapman and out on to the pitch. It's uplifting.'

Guy turned up with another bloke one day. Jeremy Green enquired who he was. Guy just said, 'He's with me.' The bloke was tapping his toes, fetched himself a cup of tea, and sat down again. He was really interested, passing comments on the songs. He took a spliff, had a draw on it, accepted a can of lager. At the end of the day he asked for £67.

'Eh?'

'My cab meter's still running,' he said.

•

Guy at the Controls - London Calling

Joe was trying to put some piano on to a track and Guy had his hands in his hair. Joe stood away as Guy strode purposefully, beer in hand, into the studio. He ignored Strummer and emptied the beer into the grand piano.

'This'll help the sound.'

But it didn't. Price was furious. It wasn't a hired piano, it was his. The problem hadn't been the piano, it was the player. Eventually Micky Gallagher came in on keyboards. He struck up a musical rapport with the Clash. Session men had come and gone, but Gallagher stayed longer, and his skill added the missing ingredient to songs like 'Clampdown', which had been worked through and through at Vanilla. Gallagher hadn't come from a musicians' directory. He had been with Ian Dury's Blockheads, along with Kosmo Vinyl, who was an occasional visitor, and whose brash Cockney tones would reach us before he did. Vinyl loved the Clash. He told us so all the time with over-the-top *bonhomie*. I'd first become aware of him at a do that Paul McCartney had thrown to launch *The Buddy Holly Story*, and Topper and I had gone for the free cocktails. As the rock aristocracy climbed into their stretch limos for the 200-yard journey from Peppermint Park to Leicester Square, Kosmo had grabbed the helmet from the head of a genial copper outside and rugby-kicked it up the road with a loud hooray. He'd have got a kicking and a night in the cells for that in Camden.

Bill Price had carefully adjusted each fader with hair's breadth precision, his ear cocked to the giant speakers on the wall. Guy leant over and said, 'Stop fiddling around like a girl's blouse,' then whacked a fader up to maximum, yelling, 'Into the red! Into the red!' They both put their hands on the mixing desk, gradually increasing the strength of their grips, before ending up with their arms round each other's neck, and falling to the floor sending the chair spinning into my shins. I thought, So this is why the front of the mixing desk is padded. The Clash loved the scrap – 'Who's in charge here? They are.'

They were recording far too many tracks, but Guy was unrepentant. No thought went into selection, there was never a thought of keeping a song up the sleeve to be a single in six months' time.

I enjoyed sitting in the mixing room and hearing the clarity and power of the music – and the lyrics. People always said they couldn't hear the words of Clash songs, and I was the same, even though I heard them again and again at rehearsals. At Vanilla, Joe told me 'Clampdown' was about parking clamps. Hearing Mick's soft voice over the studio speakers singing 'Lost in a Supermarket', and its story of high-rise walls, I turned to Joe and said, 'He's got that right, ain't he?'

Joe smiled. 'I wrote that. It's like a present to him.'

But there was only so much a person could take in the control room. It was like having a tightening metal ring around my head. We spent long hours in the studio, and the band needed breaks, even if Guy didn't. Upstairs at Wessex was a lounge with a pool table, telly and little open-plan kitchen. Upstairs was for talking, reading, taking in all sorts of influences from books and magazines. I talked to Joe at length about the political chaos of the Spanish civil war when he was writing 'Spanish Bombs'. We watched the TV news, observing the down-turn to the right, shouting at the screen.

Joe said, 'This place is moving right but people can't see it, like they can't see their hair growing from a Sunday to a Monday.'

We needed a lot of food breaks. At first Lindy, a pro chef, brought over meat and vegetarian meals that she heated in the studio oven in the early evening. We nibbled at it, but all our attention was on the music and the band were just as happy with a bag of chips from the local kebab shop, which was what we lived on when Lindy realized her efforts weren't being appreciated. Guy didn't eat. I never saw him do speed, but I knew he did. The speed fed the alcohol and the alcohol smoothed the speed and I knew where that road led and tried

176

to get him to eat something. But he was adamant. 'No time for that'.

People occasionally dropped by via a fire escape to the first-floor lounge. Like at Vanilla, visitors would rarely be allowed downstairs to the recording rooms. Crocker gave master-classes in pool. Barry Myers came with records and tapes for the band, which were eagerly seized and squabbled over; nothing was rejected out of hand. Max from EFR Guitars sometimes came by with van-loads of classy, rare second-hand instruments, including Gibsons, Les Pauls, Juniors, Flying Vs, and a white Phantom which Mick purred over, and topped up his collection with, whacking it down on the recording costs.

Guy said, 'Yeah, very nice, but really you can do it on that,' pointing at Joe's battered Telecaster. 'It's what you play, not what you play it on. Mott the Hoople had three hundred and twenty guitars, but they could only play one at a time.'

CBS men came round from time to time. They praised everything. (They would have applauded a fart down a flute.) But they never really committed themselves. Muff Winwood from CBS A&R would drop by and get dropped in it. He only ever heard one track from the Clash – a stuck record: 'It's got to be a double album. There's no song that's second rate. To speak like you do, we can't prioritize customer-friendly tracks. We're working at double speed – you can put out a double album.'

'I hear what you say ...' he always said, like a mum in a toy shop saying, 'We'll see.'

CBS boss Maurice Oberstein paid a personal visit with his chauffeur and his pet dog, which went everywhere with him. Guy trod on it by accident. The Clash asked for a double album. Maurice was pleasantly non-committal. As he was leaving, Guy laid beneath the front wheels of his car.

Maurice said with a false chuckle, 'Good old Guy. Come on, Guy. I've got to get going. Come on, get up.'

'What do you think of this music? Isn't it magnificent?'

'Yes, it's great. It's really good.'

'It's magnificent. I'm not moving until you say it's magnificent.'

Oberstein had saved Stevens from obscurity and the gutter by agreeing to let him do this job. But Guy didn't give a damn about being polite.

The girlfriends popped in occasionally. Joe was living with Gaby in her mum's high-rise council flat at World's End, Chelsea. Gaby was not long out of school, intelligent and good company. It was always worth pulling up a chair for a chat with her. But she didn't go to the studio to chat with me. If you haven't got a function in the recording rooms you have to learn to kill time. It seemed whenever she started spending some time with Joe he was off to do more work, and she was left to moon around. It was no surprise that it brought conflicts. I once stood on the top of the fire escape watching her read the riot act to Joe. Strummer, the most articulate man in rock'n'roll, was unable to explain himself to her. He was good at words about war, poverty and politics, but he never sang, 'Baby, baby, I love you'. His inability to express himself had him in tears. He was crying his eyes out. I was the only witness. It was so touching I went and got a camera and took a photo.

The lounge had a big set of stairs and a phone link with the studio and an internal window. When the phone rang it would usually be a call for guitar strings, pens, Rizlas or plectrums. I got fit on those stairs.

Paul had been touting round a reggae bass riff for weeks, playing it first thing in the morning as a warm-up exercise. Soon the others got to know it, and when they arrived in the mornings they'd pick up their guitars and join in, inventing chords.

One day Paul said, 'It's got words an' all, you know? You want to have a go at them?' He fished out a sheet of paper for Joe, who said, 'No, you do it.'

'But I can't sing.'

'You do it, go on.'

And the others encouraged him, refusing to do the song unless Paul sang it. Paul practised repeatedly in private, headphones on. Joe and Mick watched with pride. Me and the Baker listened, cajoling and encouraging him. And eventually 'Guns of Brixton' made it on to the album.

Guy rummaged in his bag and pulled out a battered biography of the film star Montgomery Clift. Drunk, he spoke with irrefutable conviction: 'Here's a story of greatness and tragedy. It uplifts you through your tears. Here is a man that never took his foot off the gas.'

I reached for the book, but with a snatch Strummer got there first. I borrowed it next, passed it on to Mick, who passed it to Paul, then Topper. By the time it reached Crocker 'The Right Profile' was already beyond the demo stage. As Joe shouted his tribute to the dead man into the mike, Guy beamed at him through the window, raising his bottle in a toast of celebration. 'I've made it ma – top of the world.' As I heard the words, loud and clear, I knew the song was about Guy as much as about the actor.

At Vanilla, me and the Baker were the Clash's audience. Here, the Clash were playing for Guy. He was a one-man audience, as rowdy as a thousand young punks. He was big enough to complete the circuit and create a charge. And the Clash knew he was only interested in greatness.

I lit a fag in the control room, and idly played with the flame of my Zippo. Paul started nudging my elbow, pushing the lighter closer to the back of Jeremy Green's head. Guy Stevens looked round from the mixing desk, saw what was going on, and we all grinned mischievously. It had to be done. The crackling was like the Black Forest going up on a hot summer's day. The stench of burnt hair was overpowering. Green swivelled round, looked stunned, and touched the now bald

THE GUNS OF BRIXTON

patch at the back of his head. I saw in slow motion his expression change as the red mist descended. I sprang for the open doorway as Paul rolled on to the floor, laughing, and Green tripped over him, landing in Guy's lap. Everything stopped, and everyone roared with laughter, and there wasn't much then that Green could do. I got away with it.

We took Jeremy Green to Finland with us, which helped to make amends. Ian Flooks, who had left Derek Block and was just setting up his own Wasted Talent agency, phoned out of the blue.

'I suppose you're too busy, and I told them you were tied up recording,' he said. 'But there's still a spot going, and they want the Clash to play.'

I passed this on to the band in the upstairs lounge. Despite their worries over disturbing the recording, instant cash was very attractive.

Guy said, 'Do it,' but he hadn't needed asking. His reaction could have been predicted. The Clash welcomed a chance to flex their muscles, feed off an audience, and take a short break.

We went to Finland of course, but we were back in the studio, charged up and quids in, by Monday morning. We worked into the early hours until everyone had run out of steam for the day. When Guy ran out of steam, he just passed out wherever he was, which was when Mick would step over him to the desk and start tinkering with the precise technical details that Guy found irrelevant; dropping in the little phrases and overdubs that he felt enhanced the texture of the work. These became moments of quiet, pensive deliberation in contrast to the raucous, if productive chaos when Guy was awake. Sometimes Guy woke like a startled animal, and Mick caught my eye and glanced at the door. Mick didn't want to argue or fight him, but he knew more had to be added to the music's energy. I'd use various devices to persuade Guy to join me for a walk. Something like, 'Come and help me sort out the jukebox round the corner,' and we'd go off for a pint, Guy regaling me with tales of Chuck Berry, James Brown, the sixties mod and R&B scene. I tried to throw my Bo Diddley stories in but they were pathetic in comparison to his tales of glory. There were nights when he and I just walked the dark, empty streets.

Late one night, Duff Windbag had dropped in unannounced to check on progress, only to see me carrying Guy like a baby to the waiting minicab. The driver knew where to take him. Guy was long gone. Winwood just shook his head despairingly, muttering about wasted talent.

'You wouldn't know magnificence if it kicked you in the balls,' I just stopped myself from yelling.

Mick's knowledge of studio techniques came to the fore, channelling the whirlwind that Guy was whipping up. His snatched hours at the mixing desk became days at a stretch, and Mick's single-mindedness saw the project home. On those days, it was my unenviable job to ring Guy and tell him we were taking the day off, and I had to bring the Wessex receptionist into the conspiracy. I felt awful doing it, but I understood why it had to be done. I felt awful lying to someone who was so brutally honest, especially to himself. One night we had walked round Clissold Park nearby, burning off excess energy, and watching the dossers getting ready for the long night outdoors with their bottles of cheap sherry. Guy stopped thoughtfully and said softly, 'Some of us are looking at the stars.'

Calls had started coming through from the outside world. If I was called down to the phone while the band were recording I had to come down the fire escape and through the control room into the corridor. We had several regular callers. Vanessa Redgrave had been given the Wessex number by Ellie Smith at CBS. Redgrave was always on at us to do a benefit for the Revolutionary Communist Party. It became a running joke. I had to keep stalling her on the band's behalf. The Clash respected her for being someone famous who was not afraid to nail her colours to a radical mast, and liked her for phoning personally and persistently, but they didn't want to get involved with party politics. And it was difficult to get an instant yes or no decision on anything – one of the drawbacks of having a democratic band.

Mo said Cuba. He had flown in from San Francisco and laid out the plans on the floor of my flat. He'd been to Cuba a couple of times and told us the government there was mustard to have us go play. Joe was up for it. Dates were floated, and I talked to Mo's connections in Havana about hiring equipment. Flights were examined. Topper worried about American immigration.

'Fuck 'em,' said Joe. 'We played Belfast when no one else would.'

Paul took it further, 'Oy, Mick. You know part of the deal is working on a farming collective. All visitors have to spend a day in the fields – show they're at one with the workers. Everyone has to get their hands dirty.'

Mick scowled. 'I'm a musician.'

Despite our detailed planning, we never went.

A woman from Gingerbread, the single parents' group, was another persistent caller: 'Hello, Veronica here. Remember me?' I stalled her, too. All sorts of right-on groups wanted the Clash to do benefits for them. We could have done a full-scale tour, playing for a different cause each night. We had discussed doing a benefit with Feargal Sharkey and the Undertones' management, who were pressing for English bands to play in Derry. The plan had progressed far enough for the date and venue to be publicized in the music press. Then a letter came by courier. It had a note paperclipped to it: 'I don't know if this is serious, but you should have it.' I was with Joe in the corridor when he opened it. He froze and his face turned white. He was silent when he handed it to me. It was badly written on cheap paper: 'Dear *NME* ...' I scanned through it, and couldn't believe what I was reading. '... if he sets foot on the free soil of loyal Ulster the scum Strummer will be shot dead and left like a rat in the gutter ...' It continued in that vein. It was signed 'Red Hand Commando'.

Recording stopped as Joe showed the letter to the others, still without speaking a word. They immediately said the Clash couldn't do the gig. We rang Neil Spencer at the *NME*, who said he didn't know what to make of it. 'Could be some nutter. But if it's not ... I should get it checked out.'

We didn't know where to start. We didn't know much about that side of law and order. But after going through briefs, a man from the security forces turned up at Wessex. We sat in the upstairs lounge to talk to him, and he pronounced the letter genuine.

'These blokes don't make idle threats,' he said.

We took him at his word, but Strummer did not want to pull the show.

'Can you get me on that stage and out of there again safely?' he asked. I set to it with the Irish show organizers. I looked at ferries into Eire, hire cars and a drive to the north with disguises. I looked at helicopters landing backstage – like Woodstock – but there was no space to land. I got a diagram of the sports stadium venue, with a series of high-rise buildings around it, offering clear views of the centre microphone. We had taken it as far as we could. I had to tell Strummer his safety couldn't be guaranteed. It put Joe in a terrible spot. Was he prepared to risk his life? The band were adamant that they would not do it, and at that point Joe accepted that decision. The gig was cancelled, as the music press reported, because of recording commitments.

Trying to arrange a tour on the Wessex telephone, wall-mounted in the corridor near the toilets, juggling the

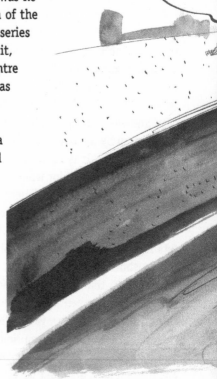

receiver with scraps of paper on my raised knee was getting ridiculous. Every outside call had to go through the reception. It was just unworkable. Peter Jenner and Andrew King of the Blackhill Agency had been sniffing around the later recording sessions. They were proper managers, with secretaries and cash-flow, and they offered their services eagerly. To them was handed the task of organizing a seven-week tour of the USA.

15

We were right up against the clock when Ray Lowry walked in. We knew we were going to America – Topper had his spurs on. But deadlines had come and gone and still the music was rolling on to the tape. Lowry curled his angular frame into a corner. He didn't speak for an hour, just stared through the window on to the studio floor, quiff bobbing with the music as he watched Joe's vocals and Mick's guitar overdubs in the half-light. He whipped out a notebook and started sketching. We knew his black humour from his *NME* cartoons. Nothing was sacred to him, not even the pure essence of rock'n'roll, which he loved with his whole soul. He loved the Clash. We had talked to this shy figure when he came backstage at a gig in his native Lancashire, and it seemed sensible for me to suggest that we take him along on the second American tour – the big one.

Joe had said, 'Yeah! Like those blokes who go with the army to the battle zone. Their canvases are in the war museum. Great idea, Johnny. Do it.'

But CBS didn't think it was so great. They were already griping about the cost of us taking our own lighting and sound engineers. So Ray paid his own air fare.

I went over to Ray. 'Passport? Money?'

He replied: 'Have you heard the news?'

'What you on about?'

'The news ... there's good rocking tonight.'

At the airport Ray already had some drawings of the band looking smart and cool, almost chic, in overcoats and trilbys.

Mick even had a tie on and a handkerchief in his breast pocket. Just as the public thought they'd sussed the Clash's style, they had made a shift. Unlike in Britain, the Clash were not recognizable faces in America, but it didn't mean they didn't have to look sharp. Joe always had a rough edge, but he was doing his best. He had a gold lamé jacket (shades of Elvis), though he hardly ever wore it. Mick looked terrific, but you couldn't imagine him on the back of a motorbike.

There were two massive nineteen-twenties trunks, the sort of thing people took with them for a three-month cruise on the *Queen Mary*. Paul grinned. 'What d'you reckon? Picked them up cheap at Camden market.'

I loaded them on to the conveyor belt.

'Wait till you see inside them, Johnny.'

Yeah, I couldn't wait.

On the jumbo I put Ray next to Topper so they could console each other in their terror. 'Big Bopper ...' The band had brought along the girls. Joe had Gaby; Topper had Dee. Paul was with Debbie, a New York model. She had the soft eyes of Bambi.

I said, 'Oy, Paul. Imagine a deer with the eyes of Christie.'

Paul had lived briefly with Coon in a new town house on the site of 10 Rillington Place and had relished the notoriety of the address. But he chose to be obscure and sweet. 'What, Julie Christie?'

Joe was huddled into a book and Gaby. Mick was full of joy, floating up and down the aisles, elegant in his white shirt-sleeves, indulging in badinage with the entourage, free as a bird. He didn't have a bird with him, though. Topper followed him up the aisle and was immediately run down by the drinks trolley. The Baker passed him a drink and dropped it all over him. He blew the short fuse he was on, so to cheer him up I bunged the stewardess for the use of their rest-room and him and Dee later joined the Mile High Club.

We were met at San Francisco by a fleet of four-wheel drives, the tour manager, representatives of William Morris agency and the record company West Coast area manager. This was the official business reception; there was also our own reception party. Rudi Fernandez was there with his battered Buick and Mexican face grinning ear to ear. Mick had appointed Rory, an old mate from London, as his own official tour manager. No one else had agreed the appointment, but Mick treated him as the official tour manager. Rory in turn

188

had to get on with the official official tour manager, Mark Wissing, a pleasant, amicable professional, who no doubt had pictures of his kids on his desk. Wissing said, 'Hi, guys,' with hand outstretched. Mick walked straight past him to Rory, who said, 'I got it, Mick.' Mick was gasping for a spliff.

Mo blustered his way into the throng. He drove me with my knees under my jaw in his tiny Fiat along the coastal road to Monterey. I made him stop and buy me three avocado pears for the journey. I wanted to be in America, not just in an American hotel room with a rock'n'roll band, and Mo regaled me with refreshing tales of Kerouac and Vietnam.

The Clash were due to play the resurrected Monterey pop festival. The hotel, Mission Ranch, had wooden bungalows dotted around a sandy compound. I set up home with Lowry and some tequila. He was enthusiastic, shuffling around with his sketch book, quietly poking into all corners. The Baker would never share with me. He hated to be disturbed by the personal needs of band members, although he fussed and disapproved like a good mum about Topper.

We spent a day on the beach at Carmel. It was blisteringly hot and Topper was very enthusiastic. He tried to charge into the ocean, only to be repulsed by waves the size of a house – good for surfing; lousy for a skinny drummer wanting a quick dip. I had to pull him into the shade.

'We can't have a drummer with sunstroke. Amuse yourself quietly. Look at Clint Eastwood's house up there.'

Paul looked made for the place. He had the right girl, the right body. Even the surfer boys cast admiring glances at him. Mick had stayed in his room with his curtains drawn. When he as self-absorbed he didn't want the world to intrude. The California sunshine bored the daylights out of Mick, who was listening to music, writing music and generally preparing himself.

Over shots of tequila one night, Ray shook his head and said, 'Who are these lunk-heads?' He had been driving with

Andrew King and Kosmo Vinyl that afternoon. 'I spotted Cannery Row. Steinbeck, you know. Not in a book. Here. I was met by two pairs of blank eyes. They hadn't a fucking clue, Johnny. Because it's not rock'n'roll, they don't know it.'

Chet Helms of Family Dog had decided to re-do Monterey, revive the legend of Janis, Jimi and the flowering of the West Coast. The line-up included Robert Frith, Maria Muldaur, the Mighty Diamonds and Earl Zero from Jamaica. I was delighted to find Joe Ely on the bill. He came to see us one sunny afternoon at the Ranch, attracting admiring glances with collar tips, 'gator skin boots and a terrific white ten-gallon hat. The Clash were into his music by now and we spent a while talking Texas and looking forward to seeing him there. He said he would have some surprises lined up. We went to visit Earl Zero and the Jamaican boys who were staying in a house down the road. We zeroed in on them as we figured they must have the best grass around. As we came round the corner we knew it was true. They were all sitting up a tree like crows, dreadlocks dangling. Mick said, 'Drive on.'

The gig took place in what Americans call a 'fairground', but there weren't any ferris wheels. We went straight into a trailer as hippy staff laid out rows of seats. Paul put a little cross of lighter fuel on the stage. 'Look, this is where Hendrix set fire to his guitar. It's still burning.' Cheap joke, but it broke the nervous tension. This gig had assumed a lot more importance than just another show. In fact, more importance than it deserved. The Clash were playing the afternoon shift in the sunshine, but after Finland we knew we could do it. I didn't need to gee up the band for this one. Every West Coast hippy had crawled out of the woodwork for the festival. It was Haight Ashbury revisited. Lowry wandered into the caravan to grab another beer. 'They're mad. They've missed the point. They think it's a fancy-dress party. There's a guy dressed like Santa Claus. There's a bloke in full angel gear with wings.

There's Wavy Gravy in full rainbow flares like nothing's changed.'

A girl showed the band two oil paintings she had done of the Clash circa 1977. Her art looked nothing like the greasy quiffed characters who now emerged to sign the canvas. The Clash constantly changed and updated their look. These people hadn't changed their T-shirts in ten years. I dashed frantically to and from the stage. Even the backstage crowd was so laid-back it was like swimming through mud. Close to the changeover of acts, the Clash were pushing to get out of the caravan, bursting to get on-stage. I shouted, like I was stopping a child dashing across the road, 'Stay there,' until I had made sure everything was ready. A black woman in a domino catsuit pinned a badge on me then yanked me four yards into the wooden toilets near the stage. She stuffed an inhaler full of cocaine in my nostril and dropped to the floor unzipping my flies. I said, 'It's very nice of you, but ...' and had to step over her to get out. Strummer screamed at me: 'Where've you been?' and I cleared the way for the band to run on-stage.

Strummer barked out the first line then careered backwards as if he'd been shot, slamming into the drum kit and wedging

Don't touch the BROWN Acid, MAN..

.. I'M SO BORED With the U.S.A.!!..

MONTEREY · September 1979.

his shoulders between the tom-toms and bass drum. Topper's face showed stunned shock, but he kept beating the rhythm. The whole crowd stood. In my wired concentration I sprinted instinctively to protect Joe. He stared menacingly at the crowd, not moving. He whispered, 'Fuck off, Johnny. I'm all right.' I had a head full of cocaine, and he gave me a heart full of adrenalin. The show was full adrenalin until the end. As we quit the stage Joe shouted, 'See you in a month.'

We had fixed up Monterey ourselves, through Mo Armstrong. The tour itself was vast, and we brought our own sprawling entourage with us at great expense. We wanted to do it properly, but on our own terms, with our own trusted road crew. Warren Steadman was terrific. He played the lighting as if he was a keyboard player on the stage. The lights weren't pre-set for smooth changes but were manually operated, dramatic and at one with the music.

The tour proper started in Minneapolis. I pointed at a woman in the hotel lobby. 'Elizabeth Taylor!'

Mick said, 'It's my mum,' as the elegant and voluptuous woman walked over. Mick told her where the gig was to be.

She said, 'Wow! I saw Elvis play there.'

Lowry was impressed, muttering, 'You're right, she's left, I'm gone.'

Mick said, 'I've got you a room, Mum.'

He had wanted the best, and had I sorted it out for him, on the second floor, with a connecting door to his room.

Mick took me to one side. 'What? I didn't mean that close.'

So I took Mick's room next to his mum, and he had a room two floors up. His mum and her husband were good company.

St Paul Civic Auditorium, Minneapolis, was a huge concrete barn, with an artificial floor which allowed it to be used as an ice rink. The stage moved on wheels towards the back of the hall, depending on how many seats had been sold.

I said to the stage manager, 'That's a lot of empty seats.'

He said, 'Not as many as for Abba.'

'I bet that was a great night.'

He just looked blank. Abba were touring America at the same time but our paths never crossed, to my disappointment.

New heads and fresh hearts waited for us. The Undertones joined us for the first chunk of the tour. We liked their music and loved their attitude. One day we walked past a journalist interviewing Feargal Sharkey, and overheard, 'I'm not English and I'm proud of it.' Joe zoomed straight in on that and talked to him about Irish republicanism and terrorism. He was always keen to find out the details from the man on the street on the spot.

The American sound crew awaited us, looking like they were ready to go to bed. Their gear looked as though it had come from a flea market. They were a bunch of burnt-out hippies. As I put my fags on the monitor desk on the first night I was astonished to see the soundman with hair to his waist, reading a book. He was wearing headphones – not plugged into the music but unplugged to block out the noise. We crossed from the dressing room to the stage, which seemed like a five-minute jog, and Joe said, grinning, 'Are you sure Hank done it this way?'

The set was OK, but the best sound was probably way up in the roof. 'Good night' echoed round the stadium. As the Clash bounced off-stage, Strummer grabbed me.

AMERICAN
STAGE HAND
1979..

193

'The candelabra. Quick. Now.'

I knew what he meant. In the dressing room he had spotted a huge candelabra. Liberace must have left it behind, with all twenty candles intact. I sprinted across, grabbed it and ran back to where the band were slugging a quick drink behind the stage. Joe said, 'Zippo,' and he lit the candles. With the stage lights down, the band eased into the gloom, and started the chords of 'Armagideon Time'. I guided Joe as he crept behind the drum riser, candelabra in hand. It looked loads better than a bunch of weedy lighters held above heads in a crowd.

After the encore Mick said, 'That was brilliant, just brilliant – improvised theatre. Keep that. We'll keep that in the set.'

I put the candelabra straight in the flight case, but the manager copped me. 'I'll have that back.'

Mick said, 'Pay him. Buy it.'

And I pointed the manager to our man with the calculator.

In Chicago we found the shop underneath the loop railway. We had been told Wax Trax specialized in unusual records. The most unusual thing we found was a big stack of bootleg *Capital Radio* EPs. It reminded me of Bernie's flat. I finally got a copy.

'We'll have them, thank you very much. This stuff is illegal,' said Mick, picking up a great wodge of them. Not that we minded the shop having them – they had been freebies in the first place. The EP had never been released in the States, and we handed copies out to all and sundry, like we had done with Bernie's free badges.

When I picked up the driver from his room to take us to the show he was strapping on a shoulder holster. 'What you doing?'

'Well, this is Chicago.'

'Oh, right ...'

He didn't need to use it, but we could have done with him around after the show. Joe, Lowry and a bunch of us wanted to see some blues. Our cabbie had drawn a blank at a couple of clubs when I had a better idea. Guns were still on my mind.

'Do you know the Biograph Cinema?' Blank look. 'The place where John Dillinger got shot? Public Enemy Number One?'

He dumped us outside the renamed theatre, but I wasn't looking to see what was playing. It was the alley down the side, where Melvin Purvis of the FBI had gunned down our man forty-odd years before, that I wanted to see. Bullet holes were still in the wall. Strummer fingered them, thinking of the bank robber. On to another club and we struck gold, with a Big Mama Thornton lookalike belting out blues standing on a table. We sat on a long trestle table as the audience burst into 'Happy Birthday' to Sunnyland Slim. We couldn't have been in a better place. We had inadvertently crashed a blues birthday party. We tried to get Joe on-stage, but it wasn't his style to do so.

I went in search of more action with Lowry. Staggering across a busy intersection in central Chicago, Ray announced he needed a piss. The most obvious place for him to do it was down the leg of the jackbooted traffic cop on the central plinth. Before the cop could reach for his gun I smiled weakly. 'He's English. He's a cartoonist. He's mad and I'm taking him straight home.'

Detroit was next for the Clash attack. We had badges from CBS – well, buttons, which were so awful that we all wore them. They were little stars, each with a band member's face on it, so that fans could collect a Clash set. They had 'Clash Attack' written underneath. Detroit, the Motor City, had great radio stations – the band loved doing radio interviews. And the place loved the Clash. We could tell there was a buzz. People were sitting on the edge of their seats taking notice. I rushed around ferrying the band in different combinations to different radio stations. We taped the music and interviews on ghettoblasters we carried into hotel rooms every night, and played the heavy funk back on the bus, where it blended

195

nicely with the demented hillbilly wailings that Joe had picked up from K-FAT on the coast.

It took a lot of smooth talking for anyone to get backstage before we went on. It took someone special. Ted Nugent – local boy makes rock god – thought he was, but he'd reckoned without us. I answered the knock on the dressing-room door to find the local promoter and a bloke with long frizzy hair shuffling next to him.

'This is Ted Nugent. He wants to jam with you guys.'

"Ang on." I went and told the band how lucky they were.

Joe said, 'Tell him yeah, Johnny.'

I scratched my head. 'Eh?' He handed me a pair of scissors. I timed it perfectly.

'The band are looking forward to it, but could you cut your hair first?' I said, reaching for his locks.

'The hell—' he said, jerking his head away and pulling back a fist before storming off.

It was our second time in Cleveland, Ohio, and we had been busy with press and radio interviews, which had swelled the crowd this time around. But Joe was suffering his eternal problem of a croaky throat. He had tried lozenges, medicines on prescription, and a worrying piece of apparatus with a long tube that had made him gag, which went straight into the dumper, so I was kept busy with the electric kettle making honey-and-lemon drinks.

Lowry and I decided to have a quiet night with Wild Turkey and the telly. He put down his doodlings of ideas for the cover of *London Calling*, always trying to make the connection with Elvis, the Beatles, the flame-carriers of rock'n'roll.

Ray said, 'Joe's a madman on-stage, you know. He's demented, possessed. He came roaring over to me tonight, screaming and pointing his fingers down his throat, his face right up against mine.'

I grinned at what he must have faced – an apparition of

open mouth, wired eyes and broken teeth.

'He only wanted a drink to gargle, Ray,' I said.

We watched a documentary. Americans do the most fucking stupid things as loudly and badly as possible. Some geezer lay in a chest with a device that exploded. The bloke was revived with oxygen, then pow! he did it again!

We talked about explosions and fireworks. Ray remembered kids throwing bangers in back alleys in Cadishead, the little town in Lancashire where he'd grown up. Twenty years later and eight thousand miles from there we made the connection. My dad was from Cadishead. I'd visited him and thrown bangers on bonfire night with my cousin's gang.

'I'm fucking hallucinating,' said Ray, next morning. 'That whiskey is evil.'

I knew what he meant because I was too. I struggled to get everyone together and pulled out a camera as Ray sat on the windowsill in front of a great view of some Cleveland skyscrapers. I was worried he'd fall backwards he looked so wobbly. I took his photo. It was the only photo I took in two months in America. I wasn't a tourist. It wasn't even my camera – I'd 'found' it at Heathrow. I left the camera-work to Pennie Smith.

New York brought its own special brand of intensity. It was always special. Lindy had flown in with the English music papers, and a bag of London heroin in her knickers. With her was Howard Fraser, who marched into the lobby of the Statler Hilton. 'Is there a room booked for me? I'm a personal friend of ....'

Paul called me on the hotel phone. 'This room ain't no good.'

'Well, it's a room, ain't it?' But I went along to have a look. It was a small room, tucked behind the lift system, the sort of place a cleaner might be put up in if she missed the last bus. Paul had added to its individuality by turning it upside down.

Debbie looked impressed. I said he could have my room, but added, 'Oy, give us a hand first to clear up this mess you've made.'

As we finished the soundcheck, crowds were gathering tight around the stage door despite the pouring rain. I took Joe back to the hotel. He wanted to be on his own. He sat quietly in his room, drawn into himself, in the eye of the hurricane, experiencing a moment of serious stillness. We got a yellow cab back to the hall, and I carried his stage gear in a brown deli carrier bag. He was still a bag-man. Joe had a big hat on (it's now in his garage, covered in cobwebs) and was hunched against the driving rain. The security man wouldn't let us in. Neither of us had stage passes.

'Fair enough, mate,' I said. 'But you ain't got a singer tonight.'

Backstage there were people treating the show like the social occasion of the autumn season. I was more interested in the few street kids who were there, rather than Robert de Niro having a drink in the corner. I made a point of barging into the glitterati, spilling their drinks, as I tried to clear the dressing room. Harley sat grim-faced. He wasn't the glitterati – he was gutterati. He looked like he wasn't moving anywhere. He looked like he was in the band. He looked like it was his dressing room, his theatre. He didn't respond to pleasantness or threats. So for sheer bottle he was allowed to stay. He was thirteen, more streetwise than the whole of Glasgow.

Joe sang 'Garageland' – 'I don't give a flying fuck what the rich are doing' – while I stood next to Debbie Harry at the side of the stage. I saw Bianca Jagger dancing on the opposite side. I hared around behind the backdrop and told her to get off. I didn't like any clique getting on-stage, but the combination of the song words and the rich woman hit me. I looked back on-stage to see Simonon clutch his bass by the neck and start smashing it on the floor like he was chopping wood. I ran on stage. 'What you doing?' It was so unlike him.

198

He said, calmly, 'Fuck off, Johnny, I know what I'm doing.' And his eyes were composed. Paul had kept this card up his sleeve for New York – Debbie's home town. She was impressed. When I went to call them back for the encore Paul grinned as I handed him a towel. 'Got a spare bass, Johnny?'

I went for a walk next morning. Leaving the lobby, there were roadies everywhere – all looking like typical roadies. I saw a bloke I knew from London. 'Who're you with?' I asked.

'Jackson Browne.'

He didn't bother asking me – he knew. 'We're playing a No Nukes thing over the road – Madison Square Gardens.'

I strolled over. Backstage, I asked, 'Can I have a look?'

'Who are you?'

'I'm Johnny Green. I'm in town with the Clash.'

'The Clash? You'll be here in a year.'

'I can't see that happening.'

He was keen to let me look around, and put me in a lift with a security man. Bruce Springsteen was soundchecking. I was impressed with his care, singing a Buddy Holly song into a radio mike from all corners of the stage and checking with roadies for the sound quality in each part of the auditorium. But it was big, flash and soulless. I wouldn't want to watch rock'n'roll in there. I like to see the reds and whites of the band's eyes, to feel the flecks of spittle from the singer's lips on my face.

We were still reading the rave reviews of our gig as we headed north. The Clash were elated. They knew they'd done good, but it's still nice to be told and given respect. And from the bus speakers were the first takes of *London Calling*. Bill Price had flown in with them, and they were good too. We were not given to playing Clash songs to ourselves, but we were delighted with this.

We appreciated the musical worth of Micky Gallagher on keyboards. Gallagher was known as Gluggo for his alleged

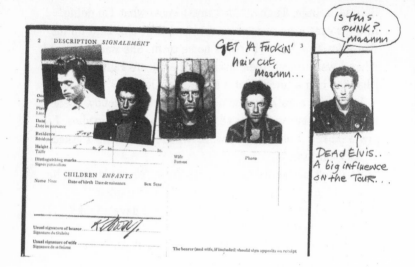

DESCRIPTION *SIGNALEMENT* 3

GET YA FUCKIN'
hair cut,
Maannn...

Is this
PUNK?..
Maannn

DEAd Elvis..
A big influence
on the Tour...

The bearer (and wife, if included) should sign opposite on receipt

enjoyment of a beverage, although I never called him that – I
thought he was a dilettante. He had the wife and kids along
for the tour. He was a jobbing muso with a taste for the
tackier end of Ted fashion, but we didn't mind that because
he was stuck behind the keyboards at the edge of the stage.
To me he was an extra, and came as part of the package with
Andrew King and Peter Jenner, whose company, which had
handled Pink Floyd and free concerts in the park in the
sixties, had stepped in to take care of the business side of
things in the absence of any other Clash management.
Someone had to do it, someone had to deal with the cor-
porations. Their idea was to make everything as smooth and
as calm and efficient as possible. It felt uncomfortable.
Jenner was the sort of person for whom rock'n'roll was an
intellectual, cerebral exercise. King was the kind of dad you'd
leave home for. Kosmo Vinyl was their front man, bringing
his professional Cockney knockabout attitude to bear on all.
He was brighter and brasher than a second-rate English music-
hall comedian.

God knows what they thought when we hit a college gig in Worcester, Massachusetts. As we pulled into the leaf-strewn campus avenue the riot cops were three-deep. Students strolled past looking curious, and a bunch of young punk rockers from the nearby town hung around. There was no action, but the cops seemed to want some now they had turned out in their kit, slapping their night-sticks in their hands.

Joe went up to a rather sad looking bunch of young punks and they told him their woes – the cops wouldn't let them in for the show.

Joe insisted on talking to the student organizers and the chief cop. The kids watched the show from the front row that night.

Ray Lowry had been glad to get out of New York. He had spent two days running from art loft to art loft. He was supposed to be doing a new Clash backdrop but as soon as he had explained why he wanted studio space everyone bumped up the hire price. It left him with a jaundiced view of the New York art scene. It became a running saga, Ray lugging a huge rolled-up canvas and cans of paint everywhere by cab. He ended up with the canvas stretched across the flat roof of a tower block, then eventually gave up on the project.

He asked, 'What happened to the other backdrop?'

As far as I knew it was still in its aluminium case. It had been flown to New York, and is probably still there somewhere now. We had commissioned it from a designer in Islington, and Paul and I had gone several times to his studio, checking on its progress. We had sat carefully choosing the picture around a table at Wessex Studios. It was designed in long vertical strips, and in its full glory showed B-52s in blue and grey with strips of bombs falling behind the amps and drums. It cost about £1500. It made its first appearance at a soundcheck. Mick took one look.

'No,' he said. 'I don't think we should be seen to be encouraging violence.'

And it went back in its case, not to be seen again. The Clash had always used a lot of military imagery, but it had always been the deal that if one of the band said no, it was no.

On the bus, there was a scramble for a look at Pennie Smith's contact sheets from the films she'd had developed. Ray, humming, 'There's good rocking tonight,' seized on them. 'That's the one for the cover,' he said, pointing to the photo of Paul smashing his bass. Everyone agreed.

Heading for the Canadian border, Mick summoned me to the backroom of the bus. He handed me a lozenge tin. 'Look after this,' he said.

I didn't have to take the lid off to know what was in it – Mick's grass. I took it, went back to my seat and bounced straight back up.

'Carry it yourself, I'm not going to.'

Eventually, and to Mick's reluctance, it went out the window.

Toronto is a rock'n'roll city, as Mick knew well. It did not pass his scrutiny that we were playing the O'Keefe Centre. It was here that Keith Richards had suffered his monumental heroin bust not long before, and it was here that Mick Jones ran out of dope. The tour ground to a halt.

A bunch of fans in the lobby were dispatched to the four corners of the city to score, but we were still waiting for one of them to return when departure time came and we were booted out of the hotel on to the kerbside. We boarded the bus.

'Let's go!' said Joe.

'I ain't getting on that bus,' said Mick.

He had dressed for the occasion in a straw boater, black suit, tie and gold tie-pin. He plonked himself next to his trunk in the bus's cargo bay.

'I need a joint, Johnny.'

THE First thing that you LEARN is that you Always..

..hAve to wAit. BoRedom and pARANOiA ... ToRoNtO.

Communications with the rest of the party were conducted through me or Kosmo. It felt like a hostage negotiation.

'He says he ain't going nowhere without a joint.'

'Tell him he's a selfish bastard.'

'You're a selfish bastard, Mick.'

I knew chemical dependency, when every nerve of the body screams for a fix, and I knew marijuana didn't do that. No one needs a joint that much. I did my best to persuade him.

'It's only a short run back to the USA and marijuana aplenty.'

'Yeah, but I want it now. I can't face that bus without a joint.'

I had to admire his nerve. No matter what the pressure from everyone else, he wouldn't move. We continued to wait. Mick's emissaries didn't show. Paranoia crackled in the air. Anyone who came near looked like a nark. It felt like a heavy-duty stakeout. Pennie photographed it. Lowry lay on the sidewalk and sketched it.

A cab pulled up. I paid the cabbie. A fan gave some dope to Mick. I paid the fan. The cab pulled off. We pulled off with a screech. Mick was at the Rizlas.

An hour later we hit Niagara Falls and the band posed for Pennie's photos as if nothing had happened, as if it was just a gang's day out.

In Quebec the hotel receptionist proudly informed me I would have an emperor-sized bed for the night. Even with Lindy in it, I had to crawl across it to get to the phone. No one needs a bed that size.

I was still struggling at each stop with the trunks Paul had bought. When the lift broke I sweated with a hotel porter for the best part of an hour to get them upstairs. Mick swung his trunk open in his room. The trunks opened into mini-wardrobes, with drawers, tie racks, even little pull-out mirrors. 'Got any socks?' Mick asked.

'Got any socks! You've got this fucking great trunk and you haven't got any socks! Wash yourself a pair!' was what I wanted to say. He'd asked me to wash out his socks before – and I'd done it. Then I went down to Islington and bought a big box of socks and took them on tour in a flight case. I knew Pete Townshend's roadie carried vintage clarets in his case. I carried socks. I fetched a new pair.

I dropped Paul's trunk off. He asked me for two Brandy Alexanders in special cocktail glasses. Was he taking the piss?

The tour was structured so that the band had nothing to do except rehearse, turn up and play. It was designed to make life pleasant and smooth for them. It was fast becoming the norm.

We threw a party to say goodbye to the Undertones before we headed south. Kosmo stacked the fridge and cracked the jokes. We had treated them well, but the crowds hadn't. I had watched them every night, as I always watched the support bands. Feargal had been taking notes from Joe, prowling the stage and talking to the audience, not at them. But it hadn't seemed to make much difference.

We also met up again with Bo Diddley in Chicago. And we had Sam and Dave along on the tour. I loved the soul veterans more than the American audiences did; more than the record company did. CBS couldn't figure out why we didn't have a whole clutch of English punk bands with us, but they'd reckoned without the Clash's depth of knowledge and love for American music.

The four Clash members formed a tight unit. But Sam and Dave were fractured. Getting them out on-stage was the high spot of the night backstage because they had separate dressing rooms and never spoke to each other.

I'd go to get Sam. 'Is Dave ready?' he'd ask.

I'd say, 'Yeah.'

'Tell him we're starting with "Soul Man" tonight.'

But I never saw anyone go down as badly as Screamin' Jay Hawkins, being carried on to stage in a coffin with his voodoo sticks to do 'I Put a Spell on You'. Generally the audiences gave the support acts hell. It had taken a lot of effort to put them on the bill – the record company didn't want them, the promoters didn't want them. But the Clash did.

Strummer described the tour bus as a submarine. There were only so many permutations of things a person could do on it: eat, drink, walk three yards, watch videos, play cards, shag with difficulty and no privacy. One of Kosmo's great talents was to find places to go in the mornings before we hit the road – usually shopping for novelties to keep boredom at bay, buying hats (stylish or silly), magazines and toy guns. Dee collected anything pink. 'Nicky, buy it me,' she'd say, and

Topper would always be tapping me for money.

'What do you want it for?' I'd ask.

'There's this pink thing I want to buy for Dee.'

Joe's creativity went into the bus's CB radio. Joe's conversations with truckers and housewives about Hitler, Elvis, the Pope and American policy interested Lowry enormously. Miles passed.

The corporate wrath of CBS hit us in Atlanta. The money dried up. Someone was sent to New York to plead with them for more cash for tour support. They said we had too many people with us. The Clash said they wanted to do it right. Meanwhile, unpaid rowdy roadies in their dirtiest, filthiest road gear lined up at the cocktail bar of the flash Atlanta hotel.

'We'll have the money soon,' they were told, but these boys worked simply for money – they had no commitment to the Clash. We were strangers in their midst. The centre of the hotel had a sliding glass roof with a swimming pool in the middle, big palm trees and ferns around the sides. The bar was doing a special deal: if you ordered a cocktail you got to keep the glass. The roadies were lined up, knocking back big, sickly cocktails in one. Then one would peel off from the line, run through the indoor tropical garden and hurl himself into the pool fully clothed, great greasy boots and all, then climb out, leaving big puddles of greasy water. It was all chalked down to room-service because they had no money. It caused chaos. Good old southern hospitality only went so far. Kosmo was sent by King and Jenner to calm them, but as far as these tough pros were concerned, he was just the bloke in the suit that danced on the side of the stage. I went over.

'Point taken, lads. Why don't you go to someone's room and have a drink? Get some bottles in. The money will follow you up as soon as it gets here.'

They eventually got paid in the hotel. I didn't.

The Baker lingered at the bar. 'They were in a tough mood

last night as well,' he said. And he told me with some relish how a girl had asked for a lift. They had said, 'No ass, no pass,' and she had gone along with it as the roadies unzipped themselves while queueing down the aisle of the bus to screw her. Every one of them had a go, then they said she couldn't have a lift after all, and booted her out.

'That's bad sex, Barry, and no way to treat a fan,' I said.

'That's abuse. Keep that story under your flight case.'

Hot shows and a poor diet leave a person feeling run down. King and Jenner decided the band would have Vitamin B-12 shots to keep them chipper. The rest of us were left to look after ourselves, but I took the band down to the room with a doctor and no one wanted to be the first one in. So I went first to check it out and got a free vitamin shot in the arse. I went out crying in agony, although it hadn't hurt at all. Then I had to convince the band I had only been kidding.

By the time we were heading for Texas, bus travel had become a survival game. Joe, Paul and Topper retreated into their girlfriends. Mick retreated into the back room. We hibernated uncomfortably on the bus, waking up irritably when it stopped. We pulled into a motel at night. Its floodlit pool was a radioactive green, with the monster of the swamp lurking beneath the surface. We piled blinking off the bus. I pressed my face to the glass motel door to see the porter look up from his porn mag and firmly shake his head. I swung my pink flight case at the window, which cracked top to bottom. 'Open up, mate, and give us a hand with these bags.'

A bung saw him all right and the window went on the insurance. We trooped in to dream and sleep.

Tom, the driver, was hungry and stopped at a steak-house he knew on the road. He either didn't know or didn't care that Joe and Mick didn't eat meat. At this place customers could survey the quality of the meat while it still moved. There was a corral right by the entrance, packed with beefalos, a cross between buffalo and cattle. You could admire the beast before eating the back legs off its brother or sister. Mick stared at these things like they were from the Andromeda galaxy. He had an omelette.

But we enjoyed Texas, especially with the Joe Ely band playing support, and lively audiences in Austin, Houston and Dallas. Ely went down well on his home territory, and he liked where the Clash were coming from. We liked his music and we got on great. He invited us to play in his home town, Lubbock, Texas. We were all up for it. It was a great idea. It was one thing to play in a club down the road in Britain, another to divert our big American tour machine hundreds of miles off the planned route, but the Clash wanted to do it and so we did. I was so keen on the plan that I jumped on to Ely's Winnebago to get there first, missing a band trip to Dealey Plaza to see where JFK was killed. Ray told me Kosmo lay down in the road on the very spot, pretending he was dead. Mick thought this was terrific.

"..CAN it EVER bE bettER to tRAvel hopelessly tHAN to ARRIVE.?"

We were surprised to find that the Clash's reputation was so big in such a small place. Ely had lined us up a night at Rock's Club, built for two-bit bar bands, and judging from the crowd in the parking lot we could have filled it ten times over. In a raw place like that, the Clash shrugged off their road-weariness and played like they were fresh from rehearsals, raring to go. They were all terrific, Strummer better than ever, and probably every person in the place left feeling he had touched them personally. The Clash were exhilarated, and arm in arm with Ely's band headed for his spread out in the cotton fields, making a slight detour to pay our respects at the grave of Buddy Holly. It was corny, but we had to have Buddy's music blaring from the bus. Strummer did a little jig in the cemetery, careful not to tread on the graves. I left my own tribute – the top of a Seagram's whisky bottle, next to an arrow arrangement of plectrums from each of the band members. We hit Ely's. Topper had done too much of some kind Texan's gift. To stop him turning blue the Baker and I walked him up and down the dirt road, keeping him conscious, keeping him moving, stopping him from OD-ing, stopping him from dying.

The band flew to LA. They wanted a couple of days off in the city, and the bus had lost the last of whatever seedy attraction it had once held for them. Ely had marked my card that there were such places as dry counties, and I had wheedled a large bottle of rot-gut tequila from the barman at the Rock's Club. I'd dropped it and it smashed as we walked from the Holiday Inn to the bus, but the hotel manager was a nice man and slid me a replacement bottle. It kept us going across the desert; Barry Myers, Lowry and me in the once-packed tour bus. I was also keen to use up the last of the cocaine. I had had enough of that cocaine paranoia in LA last time.

In a truck-stop the waitress said, 'How are you?'

The correct southern response is 'I'm fine, how're you?' but since she'd asked me, I told her exactly how I felt: I had a head with a sledgehammer inside, I was trembly, I hadn't slept decently, eaten or washed for days. I was fucked off.

We ate and made a mess of the table with fag-butts, food, ketchup and coffee, then we walked out. It had been thoughtless, not vindictive, but Lowry was appalled.

He stopped me outside: 'That was awful, what you did to that woman.'

'What?'

'Treated her like shit. And she's got to clear up after you. It was unnecessary. She'd done you no wrong.' But what really hurt me was: 'The Clash wouldn't have done it. They don't treat people like that.'

San Diego Zoo is world famous. We never saw it. I stayed and helped the Baker with the stage gear that night instead of driving back to Los Angeles with the band. In London, I spent all day every day with the Baker. Here, I bumped into him now and again, and I had missed his good-natured grumbling and English sense of humour. I missed sharing his deep concern with all things Clash. He was one of the family, and this was a good opportunity to pick up the threads and muse. Loading up the drum kit with the Baker was a brief return to 'normality', a respite from the madness of bus, boredom and booze, cocaine, concert halls and hotels. The organization of the tour, with every job pigeon-holed, was separating us; there wasn't enough of the friction and tension which the Clash thrived on, and which pulled us all together. The respite didn't last long. A woman photographer ran us back to LA. Baker sat in the front; I was in the back with her mate, snorting her cocaine. She gave me a blow-job. Baker kept turning round. 'What you doing, Green?'

'Keep looking at the road,' I replied.

The hotel in LA was the Sunset Marquis. Breakfast was delivered to the door – a plate of fresh pineapple and Danish pastries. This was no way to start a day: what I needed was a large expresso and a quarter-bottle of Jim Beam. Once that had kicked in, I strolled to the nearest 7–Eleven for a litre of Tanqueray gin. There was no point mucking about with bar measures.

The hotel was built around an outdoor pool. Paul had metamorphosed into a Hollywood film star, an Adonis on a lounger. 'There's a bag of washing in my room, Johnny,' he shouted. 'Mick's got one an' all.'

I numbly collected their dirty clothes and headed for the windowless launderette in the basement. The drier whirled noisily, and a hunched figure stared at it, clutching a beer bottle. Lowry said, 'It's hypnotic. I can't stop watching it.'

'You missed a great show last night, Ray.'

'I was burnt out. I couldn't cross the road.'

I loaded clothes in the machine, then stopped. 'I'm here for the music, not their dirty fucking socks.' I hurled the laundry bags away from me, and stalked out purposefully to a liquor store.

The gig in LA was at the Palladium. LA's idea of punk was the Addams family. Its idea of dancing was to cram in as much angel dust as possible and do The Worm across the stage. It was like being invaded by giant slugs, but they had the strength of three people and it took a lot of strength and muscle to yank them off the stage and lead them back into the audience, where they did it all over again. We had a rule: three times across the stage and out. The Clash had gone on late that night. Paul had gone missing. He had asked to be run back to the hotel with Debbie after the soundcheck and had not reappeared. I got a lift. I rang him from the lobby. No reply. I ran up to his room. No reply. I kicked at the door. He must have made his own way to the hall. I hared back. He wasn't there. He showed up when the Clash were over an hour late on-stage.

He got a right bollocking from Joe and Mick after the show. He took a stab at an excuse, like a kid late for school. 'Well, no one came to get me.'

AUTHOR to ILLUSTRATOR... WHERE IN FUCK ARE YOU??.. GROAN.... HAVE I MISSED THE MANCHESTER TRAIN?

PUGET SOUND..... FRANCES FARMER WILL HAVE HER REVENGE ON SEATTLE — KURT COBAIN.

'Bollocks. I was banging on your door.'

The Clash were fined that night by the local promoter for being on-stage late. It was the only time that had ever happened. But the money wasn't what upset Joe and Mick. The Clash had let people down. The Clash didn't treat people like that.

The band flew on to San Francisco to avoid travelling in the bus, but I was so frayed at the edges I stayed on the thing. It had become the only home I could remember. I shared the ride with Ray Gange, latterly a sometime resident of Los Angeles. He had moved there after *Rude Boy*, taking two cases with him: one containing his clothes, the other containing Carlsberg Special Brew. American beer was too watery. He asked me if the film was finished, if I'd seen it.

'Are you relying on it to make your name, Ray? Is that what you're doing in Tinsel Town?' I replied.

Old friends met us in San Francisco. By now I was so warped that Rudi's Mexican face looked the same as everyone else's. He did the usual honours, ferrying me around. In a state of burnt-out exhaustion I saw Bill Graham's swarthy glaring face backstage at the Kezar Pavilion. He betrayed his hippy mafia roots when he snarled: 'Punk rock ain't music. It's shit.' Usually I was all for a bit of constructive criticism, but not that night. I leapt to the defence of the band with both fists, which never hit their mark. Two giant minders, either side of him, picked me up and carried me away. I got off very lightly.

We'd nearly finished this tour, and I hadn't been paid. I didn't know if it was a cash-flow problem or a wind up. I was struggling to keep a rational hold. I confronted Jenner and King in their hotel room. Jenner sat on the bed, wizened behind his wired glasses, looking up at me.

'Cool vibes, Johnny. We haven't got the cash. We can't pay you. But we will.'

'You've been saying that for weeks. I want some readies in my pocket. I want to buy my mum a present.'

'Trust me, Johnny.'

I didn't trust myself, let alone anyone else. I switched on the table lamp, took off the shade, calmly smashed the lightbulb and held it to Jenner's face.

Andrew King had an actor's fruity voice, but he didn't speak as he opened a suitcase full of notes and paid me the several thousand dollars I was due.

Seattle was next up the coast. Each room of the Edgewater Inn, famous in rock lore for Led Zeppelin's antics with a groupie and the live mud sharks, had a balcony over Puget Sound. Lowry and I strolled along the Sound, which we immediately re-named Nancy Spungen Sound. Sprawled on every corner, in every gutter, was an American Indian, asleep or talking incoherently and clutching a bottle in a brown paper bag. I knew how they felt. I was gripped with agonizing

213

stomach pains, and despite lying on the vibrating hotel bed, operated by a coin slot in the wall, I had to be rushed to hospital. I missed my first and only gig. The doctors told me to eat. I had forgotten about eating for the last four days. I left the hospital and dressed for dinner in Texan black jeans, black shirt with silver buckles, buttons and studs and ordered lobster thermidor from the hotel restaurant. I ate it and threw up. I should have had something less rich. Barry Myers came back to the hotel to see how I was.

'I caught the guitar, Johnny!' he said.

I was past caring. 'Good for you.'

But I did care. It was mine and Joe's game. As he worked up into a crescendo at the end of the set he would slip his Fender Telecaster on to one shoulder, then behind his back, then shift it into his hands and with a huge shove hurl it in vaguely my direction. I was always able to catch the glint in the eye as he peeped to see where I was. It was our little game and one that I had never lost, although there had been nights when I had dived full-length like a goalie to stop the treasured instrument smashing to the floor. It must have looked terrific from out front. Free of the guitar and lead Joe bounded like a devil, flexing his shoulders, free of the umbilical cord of the guitar lead.

I awoke refreshed from my night off. I must have retained some nutrition from the lobster, as I noticed how burnt-out everyone else around me looked. Of course it wasn't just me. This long tour had taken its toll on everyone. I had been so intent on doing my job, fulfilling my role in the band, I hadn't seen how it was affecting everyone else.

As the Clash prepared to go on for the last show of the tour in Vancouver, the American soundcrew felt compelled to pull a similar stunt to the roadies in Atlanta and my own showdown with Jenner and King. They shut down the PA rig, pulling the fuses, until they were paid. Pleading with them was a waste of time. 'Money or nothing.'

Me and the Baker took the crew boss to a back boiler room. The Baker had a length of tube from a cymbal stand as a cosh. The boss was threatened. I gaffer-taped him to a chair, and we took the fuses from him. We would have hit him, but were pleased we didn't have to. Our purpose in life was to get the Clash out front, in the finest possible way.

We locked the crew boss in the room and started up the system. There was just time to run to the dressing room and put on Joe's strum guard – old towels cut into strips wrapped round his right wrist and forearm to stop his arm being cut to ribbons while he manically played his guitar. We drew up the set-list at a speed that gave me cramp, pausing only to think that I hadn't heard 'City of the Dead' on the whole tour. It was one of mine and the Baker's favourites, and as a treat to ourselves I added it to the top of the list Joe had given me. We led the band through the system of backstage tunnels and got lost, going round in circles trying to find the door to the stage. We were running late because of the problem with the PA, and the crowd was ripping up the theatre to give themselves something to do while they waited. A mighty roar eventually welcomed the Clash on to the stage. The band went straight into 'City of the Dead', which the Vancouver crowd took to be a massive insult to themselves and proceeded to prove they were very much alive by hurling everything they had trashed – lumps of wood, bottles and metal – at the band in a full-scale riot. The riot cops were called. The Clash looked at each other quizzically. How did 'City of the Dead' get into the set? Joe looked at me. I stood at the side of the stage, smiling. I raised both thumbs. What a wonderful way to wind up the tour.

Next morning I went to wake the band. It was the usual round of morning calls, with air tickets in my hand as a bonus. I went into each of their rooms, stepping over the jumbled debris of clothing. I woke Joe, and he told me he was leaving the band. So did Paul when I woke him. So did Topper.

Mick said, 'They're leaving? They can't. I am.'

The bus driver out the front wanted paying and I knew he had a gun. I tried again to wake the band.

'Come on, get on the plane. Let's go.'

No one moved.

I went back to my room and picked up my bag and ran through the lobby. The hotel manager said, 'Oh, Mr Green.' I stopped. 'And you can fuck off as well,' I said. 'They think they're quitting – I fucking quit.' I threw the plane tickets in his face and marched off to a taxi, leaving him scratching his head. Ray Lowry came running after me. The Baker told me later that all the road crew knew something was up when they saw me pacing up and down swearing. The moment I got in the cab, the roadies had grabbed their bags and run out of the hotel like rats off a sinking ship. I had just left them to it. I picked up a bottle of champagne at the airport, boarded the plane and slumped low in my chair, holding the bottle by the neck, and watching the doorway. I was convinced the band would get on the plane and do me over.

As we took off into the clear air above British Columbia, I opened the bottle and toasted their very best health.

The Baker said they had got their acts together pretty sharpish after I'd left and reached the airport just after the plane had finished boarding. Mick had pleaded to be allowed on to the plane.

'Oh please let me on. Just for a moment. I just want to hit someone.'

Lowry and I were met at Heathrow by a uniformed chauffeur holding a little sign: 'The Clash'.

'Yeah, that's us mate.'

We were driven in a huge Daimler limo that CBS had sent to welcome the band home. With some style and amusement we pulled up outside mine and Lindy's council flat. After a nap I hired a car, picked up our dogs from Devizes. Lindy and I drove straight to the Scottish Highlands for ten days, where I

Philadelphia - Weirdness City

insisted that our hotel rooms had no music, no television, and especially no telephone. I cut a strange figure, tramping the hills: big Doc Marten boots, Clash trousers, a Western shirt and my cowboy hat, with the dogs, Smack and Cherry, running rings around me.

For the first time I was having serious doubts about why I was involved in all this. I still liked the music – live, the Clash were magnificent. Every night, about halfway through a gig, I'd lean against the mixing desk, light a Rothmans and have a slug of brandy. This was the moment I'd fight to reach every day. I'd started out as a fan, and this was the ultimate place any fan wanted to be at. But the balance was wrong. I had a vision of myself as a wizened rheumatic retainer bowing to pampered and isolated, once-great recluses.

I had never been in it for the money (what money?), and if something was getting in the way of the crack, what was left?

Peace and quiet, tranquillity and reflection halfway up big snowy mountains was all very well, but there was still just enough of the buzz to pull me back ...

16

I was apprehensive as I walked into Wessex. I didn't know if I still had a job. I didn't know if there was still a band. I put my head cautiously round the control-room door.

'Ah! Put the kettle on, Johnny,' said Mick. 'How was your holiday?'

'We're too loud,' I said.

'What you on about?'

'I've been to hospital. Doctor said he'd never seen such compacted wax as in my lugs.'

'You've been to an ear hospital? I thought you were talking about a clap clinic,' said Paul.

'No, listen. That bloke from the 'Oo told me at Notre Dame Hall. It don't have to be so loud through the monitors on-stage.'

'Bollocks.'

And I wandered off to make the tea.

The band were still putting the finishing touches to the recording. 'Armagideon Time', a favourite since the American tour, was slapped down very easily after I had scoured north London for an electric sitar. They recorded various versions, with a break to watch the fireworks on Bonfire Night. Someone suggested recording the firework explosions, and me and Joe wandered around the car park with mikes on long leads, trying to capture the sounds from the nearby garden bonfire parties.

Ray Lowry had returned to darkest Lancashire to de-tox after the tour and work on the cover of *London Calling*. I had watched the marriage made across the States in his feverish mind, from humming songs from the Sun sessions to staring at that Elvis sleeve to mirroring the lettering. There had been no question about the photo as soon as we saw Pennie Smith's contacts. Joe said to Ray, 'That's it,' and it was. Joe gave Ray the lyrics, and Ray wrote them out in his own hand (for the inner sleeve) on the kitchen table at my gaff and round at Joe's at World's End.

Ray came back one night. 'They're arseholes at CBS,' he said. 'We are reinventing rock'n'roll, but they stuck me in some corner while they raved about Shakin' bloody Stevens. And they've got access to all this new music, yet they had the radio on!'

Joe had given Ray complete control of the design, and Ray made lightning raids on the printers from Lancashire. Beer always made him miss the last train back.

And 'Train in Vain' never made it on to the cover. The song was whacked out at the last minute. Mick had arrived with the song on the day that the Baker and I were packing up the equipment.

'Hold it. Don't move that stuff,' he said. We were surprised. The song was taught, learnt and recorded there and then.

A New Year tour was well into the planning stage, but couldn't come quickly enough for me or the band. I was tired of slapping around the recording studio. The Clash wanted to play their new material to British fans. Mick never dreamed of holidays. There was no reason not to play on Christmas Day – despite the Baker's objections.

'We'll play for all them who don't have a family blow-out and a kip during the James Bond film,' Mick said.

Everyone goes home for Christmas. We went home – to Portobello, for two gigs at the Acklam Hall, a local community hall which had the Westway for its roof. We had made Christmas-card tickets and a poster to be given away free: a photograph of the Clash in their best American finery, taken in Mick's nan's sitting room.

On Christmas Eve we picked up a PA from a bloke we knew with a limp, and worried about leaving it around the corner from the Baker's place in Barnes overnight. He got up in the middle of the night to check it hadn't been nicked. He took it to Acklam Hall on Christmas Day morning. I stepped out at 9.30 a.m. – no Tubes, no buses. I walked to Swiss Cottage and couldn't find a cab. There were no cars on the road, but eventually I flagged a bloke down. 'I'm with the Clash. We're playing today. I need to get there.' And he ran me to Ladbroke Grove. It must have been the season of goodwill. After all the American showmanship, we were back to me and the Baker and a Transit van. We had got a stack of booze in from the offie, and after the soundcheck we sat back with a few cans of beer and waited for the crowd to arrive. We were waiting for the guests to our Christmas party. We had a few big blokes on the door. People dribbled in in twos and threes – we couldn't understand it. A guy said, 'You realize people think this is a big wind-up. No one thought this gig was for real.' But we did the show anyway. It was the first time we had played to a half-full hall for years. The PA was ropey. Kosmo put on a silly hat and played a bugle. The Clash put on a good show. It was very pleasant. Mick's nan sat at the back, tapping her toes.

Lindy stayed at home and cooked a turkey. We were living in a flat in Hampstead. It was a GLC-licensed squat in an old servants' block, with tiny rooms and no bathroom. Rotten had shared a flat with Sid Vicious there. The old biddies round about still spoke fondly of Sid, the nice art student who carried their shopping up the stairs for them, turned the light on in their flats and made sure it was safe for them. Downstairs from us was a junkie gaff. Nancy had lived there. Keith Levene sometimes wandered up, out of it, to ask what the band he'd once played in were up to. I'd fob him off: 'They're fine, fine.' Paul and Debbie and Barry Myers, with paper hats on, joined us there for Christmas dinner. After the meal, Paul sucked on his cigar and said, 'Who needs the Savoy Grill?'

On Boxing Day I had to fight through the waiting crowd to get into the Acklam Hall. There was no back way in. We had left a roadie, tooled up, to sleep in the hall and deter thieves. Outside, it was like the 1923 Cup Final, and it was a good job the GLC safety officer never turned up. Doors were left open to get some air in, people passed out, people squashed on to the stage, waving their free posters, and still more turned up. Word had got round that the gig was for real. It was a struggle to get the band in there, and get them on-stage before more people passed out. It was an enormous reminder of how popular the Clash were.

The tour opened at the Friars in Aylesbury on the 5th of January, and it was all systems go. Aylesbury crowds were always enthusiastic, yet the tickets for the Clash gig were the

221

fastest ever to sell out. The audience loved the new songs. They'd had the record for a month or so. Ian Dury and the Blockheads played support, so Micky Gallagher had a long night. Blackhill, which also managed Dury, was firmly in control of all the tour arrangements. Kosmo said this was a favour in return for the Clash playing with Dury at a benefit for Kampuchea at the Hammersmith Odeon, and I remembered how awful that had been. It was a good cause but a shit place for the Clash to play. I had had a big ruck with the stage manager. I had set up Strummer's mike on the stage lip which hung over the orchestra pit.

'It's got to be back further. For security purposes,' the stage manager said.

'But the crowd are all going to be sitting down.'

Kosmo had tried to calm me down. 'This is the way it's done.'

'Why? People want to see him, don't they?'

But it was Dury's show – Blackhill's show – and that was the way things were done.

I had stood on the stage and smouldered with a fan's resentment. I knew the fan's frustration, having seen Abba just before the Kampuchea gig from Row G of Wembley Arena. As they'd launched into 'Dancing Queen' I was off up the aisle with a half-empty vodka bottle, and as I leapt for the stage Agnetha's eyes widened, although she didn't miss a note, and a giant security man caught me in mid-air like a flailing ballet dancer and packed me off back to my seat like a naughty boy.

As Dury delivered his wideboy repartee to the seated audience Kosmo persuaded Mick to go on-stage. There had been a row in the dressing room. Joe and Paul tried to talk Mick out of it: 'We are the Clash. We – not four Is. We're not here to prop up another act. Do you think you're a superstar?'

Guy Stevens wandered off to the bar in despair, as I strapped Jones into his guitar at the side of the stage. The

222

cue for 'Sweet Gene Vincent' came, and Mick said, 'Stick a fag in me mouth.' I said, 'This is fucking nonsense,' but I did as he asked and I hope he enjoyed it.

Backstage at Aylesbury I was running around, bad-mouthing lazy roadies and winding up the dressing-room atmosphere. I was taken to one side by Spider Rowe, Dury's bald minder.

'Calm down,' he said. 'Watch it. We can't be doing with this sort of agitation. It's not professional.'

'Mind your own business,' I said, but I watched him carefully. He wasn't having a friendly word, he was threatening. I thought he was going to deck me.

The tour was called the 16 Tons tour. Barry Myers, DJing, played the Tennessee Ernie Ford song as the Clash came on-stage. The halls all around Britain were now full of spiky-haired punk rockers, with rips, zips and safety pins, in contrast to the slicker, greased-back look the Clash now paraded. The set was smoother, but the homeward charge through 'Capital Radio', 'London's Burning' and 'Garageland' still sent the audiences wild. Paul had been working on his James Brown knee-drops, and hobbled around until he managed to get it right. Backstage, we all put on a limp to wind him up. Joe was able to take a breather, dutifully playing tight rhythm at a side mike nodding his head on auto-pilot when Mick gave it 'Train in Vain' from centre-stage.

He turned to me, off-stage, and made a face like he was being sick, and I grimaced back in sympathy. I usually wandered off for a drink during that number.

Blackhill's sound-crew produced a balanced, quieter sound through the monitors, but on-stage all four screamed and pointed frantically at their monitor speakers: 'I can't hear it, I can't hear myself.' Within days the levels were set as loud as ever.

Support on the tour was Michael Campbell – Mikey Dread – a DJ toaster from Jamaica. He was very tall and loose-limbed, quiet and humorous. When he spoke, it was with almost academic authority. He weren't no two-bit Rasta. I was impressed at the way he took to the stage alone with a tape recorder, which he set down and toasted along to. Supporting the Clash was no mean feat, as many bands discovered. A support band's presence was generally not required or appreciated by Clash fans.

Blackhill had arranged for a hippy catering company, Bubble and Squeak, to provide meals. After the soundcheck they'd put out tables and we'd all sit down to a big dinner, meat or vegetarian (no cheese: M. Jones). And it was kind of nice to sit down, all as one big happy family, to eat. The roadies appreciated it. They were out with the band every day, but this was the only chance they ever had to talk with the Clash. Roadies only ever eat to refuel: to pump nutrition into their bodies so they can go on humping gear. Mikey Dread didn't join the meals. He had the same meal every night: Kentucky Fried Chicken. He could have written a guide to fried chicken franchises around the country.

Two minibuses were provided to truck the band around. Huw Price was the tour manager. His cardigans kept out the winter cold. He was very genial, like a grammar-school Latin master, and treated the Clash like pupils on a school trip. He had a deluxe minibus with a great sound system and aircraft seats. The band piled into it, leaving me with the standard-model minibus, and Crocker. After the show in Sheffield Crocker and I shot off back to the hotel, and as we were getting our second round of drinks in the band arrived, dancing through the lobby.

They told us they had been getting in the van when a few kids asked for a lift. Price had said, 'They're not getting in here. I'm not insured to drive them.' He had refused to budge. Paul got out the van and started undressing. So did Joe. Paul was down to his underpants on the freezing cold night, with the gaggle of fans on the pavement watching open-eyed, until Price gave way.

In the Brighton Top Rank, the dinner-suited manager came to find me.

'There's someone at the door who's not on the guest list.'

Pete Townshend was in a bright red jacket, steadying himself on the arms of two women. He came and gave a nod backstage: 'Jam up with you boys later?'

'Yeah, all right.'

The band were towelling down before the encore. Townshend went back on-stage with them. He came on, fists punching the air, and I plugged his guitar in. No sound came out. I'd given him one of Mick's old guitars with a duff lead. I wandered off to replace it. I didn't hurry. He wasn't the Clash.

Driving out of Brighton, we saw the band's minibus just ahead of us. As we overtook, Crocker pulled out his famed expensive Dunhill lighter, which went in and out of the pawn shop nearly every week, and held it to the van curtain. He pulled open the sliding side door, dropped his trousers and waved hello to the band. Their faces cracked into laughter; Huw Price scowled at the vision of a naked, leering Crocker, framed in the van doorway by flaming curtains. Topper joined us in our van after that, throwing out a table to make more room, because it looked more fun to him. Then Paul joined us; then Joe, and Mick got the peace and quiet that he had never asked for.

Ray Jordan wore dreadlocks, and a hat which looked like it had been knitted by his nan. He was a terrific security man. I never saw him raise his arm. He kept his cool. He defused every situation before it could explode. He used humour to deflect trouble. I found out how cool he was after I had passed out on my bed during a drinking session after the bar had shut. I woke up freezing. I discovered I was on the balcony – still in bed. They had carried me out, bed and all. I got out of the bed, starkers, and the nearest thing to hand was an empty Rémy bottle. I threw it at Ray's head. He ducked and it shattered behind him.

'Warming up now, Johnny?' he said with a smile.

Topper playfully snatched his hat. Everyone stopped what they were doing. Ray's hat had dreadlocks poking out on all sides: but beneath the hat he was bald. Ray said, sternly, calmly, 'Can I have my hat back?' And it was sheepishly returned.

Barry Myers was a man who ordered a slice of toast in a café and then would ask, 'Don't you want that?' before eating everyone's leftovers. But he had splashed out to have a flight case specially made to hold his records. Barry was one of nature's worriers, which made him a natural fall guy for practical jokes. Paul and me were mucking about and swapped the records around in their sleeves. Topper went one further, and with a black marker pen scribbled swastikas and anti-Jewish slogans all over the new case. Barry was upset. He was devastated. He thought he knew what the Clash were about, and this wasn't it. He told Joe and Mick about the insult. Joe said, 'Yeah, but it's down to you, Barry. It's down to you to sort it out with Topper.'

Topper was getting out of control. He did the job on-stage, but some nights it was a close-run thing. He was letting himself slip out of his usual tip-top fitness, though while his arse was firmly stuck to the drum stool he could still deliver the goods. But it was becoming a worry. The Baker took it upon himself to deliver a series of lectures and sermons about Topper's responsibilities to himself and the band, but all he got back was, 'Don't be such an old woman. I can handle it.'

The Baker considered putting in a drum stool with a back on it. Topper had nearly fallen off a couple of times, leaning back between numbers.

We took two days out of the tour to hole up in Pluto Studios in Manchester to put 'Bank Robber' on tape. It had followed the 'Armagideon Time' route, from a soundcheck number to encore to vinyl. Mikey Dread was at home in the studio. His show was called *Dread at the Controls*. He had bought up the stock of farmyard-noise toys from a joke shop, which kept Paul going for hours on the minibus. Dread played with them on top of heavy dub rhythm tracks, spiralling out on top of tracks like 'Bank Robber'. Bill Price and Jeremy Green had come up on the train from London for this session, and there was a bunch of fans hanging around with us in the studio as we worked around the clock. We slept on the floor or in seats for a few hours, then carried on. When we came out, with a finished master, there was thick snow on the ground. We breezed into London for a couple of dates, with Joe Ely in support. The best-laid plans for smooth efficiency can go haywire through the simplest of things. We played the Electric Ballroom in Camden. The big hall, next to Camden Tube, was heaving. Its air-circulation system was linked to roof vents, which someone forgot to open. It became so hot on the stage that the band nearly passed out. Strummer ran back and forth from the centre mike to the side of the stage, where I stood with a big towel, billowing air. The next night, Blackhill got in two industrial fans at either side of the stage. But by then the air vents had been opened, and it was like being at the North Pole. It was a great show, though. Perhaps it had to be to keep warm.

The Clash had rejected playing London's bigger venues in favour of more intimate halls. We shot the video for 'Bank Robber' at Lewisham Odeon in the afternoon before the gig there. Me and the Baker, dressed in masks like cartoon robbers, were filmed by Don Letts running out of the bank, down Lewisham High Street and spending our swag at the Odeon box office on Clash tickets. We received some strange looks from shoppers down the High Street, but we were used to that. As Letts filmed the last shots – us running round a corner to the back door, the cameraman lying in the road with me and the Baker running up and jumping over him – two white Rovers came screaming round the corner with sirens blaring. Armed cops jumped out. We were up against a wall,

227

arms raised – Don too. He might have looked like a bank robber but we didn't. With bright knotted bandanas round our faces, we couldn't have drawn more attention to ourselves if we'd tried. We told the cops we were art students working on a project for our final grades.

'Well, get out of here quick, then,' they said, in almost comic-book Bobby style.

Ely joined the Clash for the encores at the London gigs. The Clash did his song, 'Fingernails', and Ely played 'White Riot' with the band. The Clash raced around the stage, and Ely stood with his cowboy hat on, trying to keep up with the frantic chords and keep out of the flying feet of Mick and Joe.

I was delighted to see Ely again. He played at the Hope and Anchor, Islington, between the Clash shows, and it didn't take much persuasion from me to stick a couple of guitars in cases and drive Mick and Joe up there. They were on-stage with him all evening, banging out his Texan Countrybilly music. At the bar afterwards, I said to Ely, 'Tell me stories of honky-tonks, sleazy mescal joints and greasy enchiladas.'

'I can do better than tell you. Why don't you come back to Texas with me and see it all?'

'I might just do that. But not right now,' I said.

Bandanas were big that winter. Chris Townsend, whose Fifth Column collective made our T-shirts, had just returned from San Francisco, and Mo Armstrong had sent us a present through him: a bunch of red and black FSLN bandanas with the Sandinista cowboy on them. He had brought them from the guerrilla supporters in Nicaragua. It was the first time we'd heard of them. I shared them out and we wore them and touted them round.

Donald came from Dundee. Donald was a drunk. After the Dundee show, Donald asked us for a lift to the next show, because he didn't fancy hitching. He didn't want dirty, petrol-rainbowed water from roadside puddles sprayed over his polished boots and Crombie.

He was an up-front guy, with close-cropped ginger hair. He'd been in the motor two minutes when he asked, 'Can we stop at the nick? I've got to renew my bail.'

We had a *Nationwide* film crew with us at the time. King and Jenner were trying to keep the film producers happy. The Clash were trying to keep Donald happy. One of his skills was attempting to drink the dressing rooms dry. But he was entertaining, and he once proved his fearlessness while, from the side of the stage, I watched Mikey Dread doing 'Rocker's Delight'. Donald came up and said, 'I feel like a bit of a skank,' and he was off on-stage, dancing with Dread. And he thoroughly enjoyed himself. Next night we played at Lancaster University – my old gaff. Donald got up on-stage and had another dance, and Strummer said, 'I bet you a jacks you ain't got the balls to do that.'

So I stuck a trilby on my head, a Sandinista bandana round my neck, borrowed a Crombie from Paul, and I was out there.

'Yeah, me and Donald, the dynamic duo,' I puffed, delighted, when we came off.

Next night I said to Strummer, 'I bet you ain't coming out there,' and as I went on to join Donald, from the other side of the stage came Strummer: Crombie, shades and bandana, skanking away. The audience never recognized him, or they would have gone mad.

And so Dread's backing dancers grew from being the dynamic duo to the funky four, the famous five, super six, then the magnificent seven, as the rest of the Clash gang gradually joined in.

I felt awkward, dancing on-stage. I wasn't used to performing, just running on and adjusting amps, or throwing people off the stage. I looked down at my feet to see my Doc Martens on fire. Then I saw Paul's grinning face at shin height. I had been right next to the monitors, and Paul had been lying behind them with a can of lighter fuel, pouring it on to my boots and flicking matches at them.

As the band came off after 'Garageland', Joe said, 'Right, three numbers and home. Go—'

'No. I'm not doing 'White Riot' tonight,' Mick said. 'I've had enough of it. No.'

Joe yelled, 'What do you mean?' He was fired up and he just slammed him with his fist, full in the face.

Jones slid down the wall and sat slumped for a few seconds. I dashed out, shouting to Ray Jordan to seal off the backstage area. I darted back, grabbed a towel and wiped the blood from Mick's nose and lip. He didn't say a word. Strummer was heading for the door, back towards the stage, and Paul and Topper followed him. I bent over Mick, picked him up, said something consoling like, 'You'll be all right.' I grabbed one of the Sandinista bandanas and tied it over his nose, put a pair of shades on him and half-supported him until he got back on-stage, where he bounced around, looking great. The band sped through the encore, into 'White Riot', and after the first verse Mick calmly took off his guitar, propped it against a speaker and walked off-stage. The others carried on as if nothing had happened. It wasn't mentioned again.

It was still my practice to wander about outside to see who was hanging around without tickets and try to get them in on the guest list, but it had become more and more difficult. The numbers were now tightly controlled. The days when I could add twenty-three names to the guest list were over. Out front had changed, too. Blackhill now had a merchandising stand selling T-shirts and badges with a star motif. It was run by Terry Razor, a hard-faced Scot, full of talk about 'punters' and 'units to be shifted'. I was appalled by it. It seemed thought-less and cynical. Every band had merchandising. But the Clash wasn't every band. It was a far cry from giving away Clash badges with Bernie. Terry Razor had some red Harringtons made for everyone backstage, with '16 Tons' on the front, reminding me of the Blue Oyster Cult road crew. I told him I didn't want one, but said as a wind-up: 'I dunno. A black one would be nice.' A few days later he came up with a black jacket he'd had specially made for me. He knew I didn't like what he did. I told the band I thought his stuff was shit. They quizzed him about what margin he was making on the gear, but he talked them round.

Donald was still around. We had to admire his front. He was a Crocker in the making. He was fearless. He stood at the side of the stage, then I looked up and he was down the front with the locals leading the slamming dancers, then he came backstage with half a dozen new mates. He walked around as if no door was ever shut to him. When he'd had a few drinks late at night in the hotel bar he started to show a strange interest in historical analysis. It very gradually came out ... he started talking about blacks being inferior, as if musing on other people's points of view. Then, one night at Coventry, he didn't dance on to the stage – he goosestepped on, went up to the microphone, delivered a diatribe that Goebbels would have been proud of and started *Sieg Heil*ing. He found a few takers in the audience, but also a seething mob of Clash fans longing to rip his head off. Donald had a lot of front – but we didn't know it was the National Front. I stood watching from the side of the stage as, with great restraint, Ray Jordan marched him off and straight out the back door. He had no train ticket and, I suppose, finally had to risk the puddles and condescend to hitch-hike home. Ray had declined to give him a kicking. He said it would have been pathetic.

Rude Boy limped home. After much to-ing and fro-ing on the phone I had to tell Mingay, 'The band ain't coming.' Mick also forbade me and the Baker from going to the premiere in Berlin. I took delight in telling Mingay on the phone, within Mick's hearing, 'See you at the airport.'

But at Heathrow the plane was delayed and we were looked after in the VIP lounge with free champagne. We reached

Berlin and the pre-film press conference was in progress. We walked in at the back, bags in hand. I threw my bag down, jumped over the table into a seat behind a mike. I wanted my fifteen minutes. The fame was due to the band, but the band wasn't there, and for once the Baker and I could step into centre-stage. At the showing we watched ourselves on the big screen from a balcony. I loved the film. I loved being able to sit back and watch the Clash perform without concentrating on what could go wrong. It overwhelmed me, and it did the audience too. I couldn't understand why the Clash objected to the film. Mingay said, 'I think Mick realizes his film image is at contrast with his self-image.' After the film I walked down the aisle of the two-thousand-seat cinema with Mingay and the Baker and the audience burst into applause. That was my pay-off. But I wasn't hooked. I didn't get addicted to fame. The Berlin Wall was famous. We never saw it. We went for a meal after the show, but the Baker was ill-at-ease and agitated. Eventually he said, 'I want to get a bird.'

'What kind of a bird?'

'Blonde, with white boots on.'

So we went driving around looking for a hooker in white boots until we found him one. We went back to the five-star Kempinski Hotel. In one of the salons was a display of art, with a painting on an easel in the foyer. As we passed I shouted: 'Karate kick to culture', and lunged my foot at it. I didn't mean to actually connect, but I put a hole through the canvas. Me, the Baker and his hooker cleared off quick to our rooms.

We had to be in Paris the next day. French TV were filming the Clash gig, and then we were to fly to America. As we walked out of the foyer the manager called me over.

'Sir, this is yours.'

And he handed me the painting with the boot-hole in it. Mingay had paid for it to get out of the fuss the previous night. We rushed to the airport to find the Paris plane cancelled. The Baker and I had blown it. There was a flight to Frankfurt taking off soon. I blagged us on to it because Frankfurt was at least closer to Paris than Berlin. When we arrived, we found a plane from Karachi to London had stopped over, and had been diverted to Paris because of bad weather. I blagged us on to it – it did a nice curry – and we were at Orly airport. I plied the taxi driver with fifty-franc notes urging, *'Vitement, vitement.'* We arrived at the hall during the soundcheck. Mick sat on the edge of the stage, dangling his legs. His shout echoed through the hall: 'Where have you two been?'

'Berlin. The film was fucking great. You ought to see it.' I was still clutching my new painting.

We set straight to work, tidying the stage area, as the French TV crews wired off an artificial orchestra pit at the front. They built a big rig that glided across the floor and raised or lowered a cameraman. When the Clash ran on-stage that night the crowd surged forward, trampling the wire. The cameraman was knocked from his seat and crawled up the stage like he'd been swept on to a beach by a tidal wave. The rest of the crew struggled to dismantle their equipment at speed, passing expensive cameras and stands over the heads of the heaving, sweating kids. Paul, usually so cool on-stage, was laughing all over his face. The gig was supposed to be filmed for French TV, but the Clash weren't going to stop playing now.

'Looks like Mingay got it right,' I said. 'He knew how to film you lot.'

17

Jenner and King had booked us into the Miyako Hotel in the Japanese centre of San Francisco, on a hill overlooking the bay. It had Japanese stone gardens and bonsai. It was modern. Guests got a free kimono, with a little tag that read: 'This is yours to keep.' The rooms had paper screens, and each had a big sunken bath with a wooden bucket to pour cold water over your head when you got out. It was very unusual, and just the novelty for jaded rock stars or jaded businessmen. I had a bath, poured water over my head from the wooden bucket, and wandered around the room in my kimono.

This tour was to be short and sweet, playing at the places that mattered. There were no trips to the deep Midwest. We were playing those cities where everything new that moved was high profile. The Clash loved playing to large, enthusiastic audiences. Blackhill loved it because it was easy to arrange, and CBS loved it because they had the Clash promoting *London Calling* to the people that were important to them, the national media.

We hired our stage gear at each city we played – everything but the guitars, our specialized leads and parts of the drum kit. The Baker and I went to collect this from the airport cargo depot in a hired van. The gear was late coming out of customs and so we went and sat in a bar with a woman from CBS who was handling the paperwork.

'This is really nice, Barry,' I said. 'This is getting big, really big, yet here's me and you in a Transit van picking up the gear – we could be back in Camden, two years ago.'

When we returned to the hotel lobby Paul greeted us excitedly: 'Lee Dorsey's here, he's arrived from New Orleans.'

His words took me back in a flash to my days as a mod in the Medway towns. The lift doors opened and there stood two huge minders holding up a shrunken, wizened man in a tasty two-tone maroon mohair suit. He was tiny. His eyes were bright. I stood forward: 'Lee Dorsey? Johnny Green. You taught me to dance.'

He reached forward to take my hand and fell over.

'I think a drink is called for,' he said.

We went into the Japanese bar and sat on the floor around a low table. Dorsey didn't look like he needed another drink but he had one. He was legless, slurring something about a motorbike. I was told later that he was recovering from breaking both legs in a bike accident.

The Clash were in rehearsal downtown. The band didn't need to rehearse after finishing the long 16 Tons slog round Britain but they put a few days' hard work in anyway. Kosmo had the rehearsal-room doors locked for privacy.

Down there that night it was dark, cold and raining. Mick and Joe asked me to get them something to drink, and I pulled my leather coat around me. The Baker and I stepped on to the rainy street in Castro, looking for the nearest offie. A bar on one corner was called the Stud. On the other corner was the Tool Box. The names only made sense when we reached the doorway and the Baker was stopped.

'Are you twenty-one?'

He had to show his passport to prove his age. The bar was heavy. The Clash looked heavy, but these blokes were heavy in a different way. The Clash wore leather and studs, but these blokes wore it in a different way. They wore coloured handker-chiefs protruding from different pockets, each combination conveying a different connotation of sexual preference. I leant over the bar to see what beers and cokes were on offer. Big moustachioed men with leather crotches pushed themselves at us in the bar. The Baker looked anxious.

We went back to the studio and a little group of people outside asked: 'How come we can't get in there?'

I didn't know the answer, and invited them to come in with us.

Gerry, the minder, said, 'What are these people doing in here?'

'They're with me.'

'We don't want them in here.'

I took a deep breath, and said, 'Fuck off. They're here with me.' I didn't want to mess with this bloke.

Joe looked up and said, 'What's the problem?'

'These people are cold and wet and want to hear you.'

'That's no problem. Give them a seat. Give them a beer.'

THE AuaiENCES all begAN to look the SAME...

In an old Edwardian theatre with burgundy velvet walls and curtained theatre boxes the Clash played one of their best gigs ever. The theatre had seats, but Americans don't break seats.

Bill Graham supposedly knew how to look after rock'n'rollers. Certainly the backstage spread was an impressive banquet-size, and exotic. A giant video screen showed highlights of the history of rock'n'roll: Elvis, the Beatles, the Supremes. Pity it ain't got Lee Dorsey, I thought as I watched it all. It seemed like Dorsey was playing a Royal Command performance that night, and I wondered how often he had a chance to do that these days. He was cool; it came from the heart. He didn't need gimmicks. Kosmo went out and bought him two cheap starting pistols for 'Ride Your Pony'. And the film didn't have the Clash on it.

There were some nights when the Clash knew they'd been bang on form but the audience hadn't appreciated it; some nights when the audience went mad but the Clash knew they hadn't quite gelled. And some nights, everything was spot on. This had been one of them. It took my breath away, and I had been seeing the Clash play every night, but at that moment I felt like a fan seeing them for the first time. This wasn't a film, it was now. How would this look in twenty years on a flickering screen? Not the same, because rock'n'roll happens in the present. Capture it on record, capture it on film, but it's not the same as being there when it happens.

And I was sharp then, on top of it all, running a tight ship, not strung out like on the previous US tour. I had made my contribution, getting the equipment on-stage in top working order and getting the Clash on-stage in top order – fired up. As the band came off-stage I saw the familiar, unpleasant, scowling face of Bill Graham.

'Great show,' he said. And to me, 'And nice to see you do it well – and sober.'

Strummer said, 'patronizing git.'

•

237

I went exploring next day, looking for America. Round the block I found an old dark and smoky wooden tavern with pictures of Jack London on the walls. London calling? I took Joe back there with me and we had a beer and I had pig's knuckle with cabbage. There were these old whiskered guys sitting there. Each one looked like their story would keep a man entertained for hours for the price of a couple of beers. A guy might think he's done it all, yet still feel humbled looking at ordinary blokes like these and the stories behind their eyes. Joe looked and listened.

Back for the second night's gig, I let in some fans waiting outside the stage door to come and talk with the band. I spotted a woman in leather trousers – one of the group I had let into the rehearsal rooms in the rain. I said, 'What did you reckon to that?' She was speechless. I went back to her place that night. She had a lovely house on one of those big steep San Francisco hills. We had a wildly erotic and passionate night. I had Mick Jones's stage gear in a bag on my shoulder, and I washed it out in her bath. She couldn't believe what I was doing. In his bag were some egg mayonnaise sandwiches I had had made up for a late-night snack. In the morning – I had timed it very tightly – I returned as the band were getting ready to leave the hotel. Jones said, 'Where's my bag?'

'Here it is, Mick, with some lovely sandwiches for your breakfast,' I said.

The girl came running up as we were waiting for the plane to LA, waving a ticket and throwing her arms round my neck. The band gathered round me cheering: 'Johnny's got a wife! Johnny's got a wife.'

It was true I was soon going to have a wife – Lindy, not her.

I shared the flights with Lee Dorsey. He couldn't tell me enough about his music and his life, growing up in that big chunk of America that was beneath us as we flew. I was fascinated, too fascinated to have a laugh with Paul or share a bottle with Topper.

I'M LEAVING

But I shared plenty of bottles with Lee Dorsey. In a cab with him in Philadelphia the driver was abusive about blacks, so I put him right. He made us get out of the cab and we both jumped on the roof, lying spreadeagled across it while I tried to stab the driver with a flick-knife through the taxi window.

We flew everywhere, up the East Coast from Philadelphia through New York to Boston. Ain't nobody feeling no pain ... it ran smoothly. 'Train in Vain' was out as a single and doing well, *London Calling* had been released, the Clash were doing press interviews everywhere, the product was moving.

I spoke to the Baker. He was my oppo. We'd argued constantly. We were chalk and cheese. We'd covered for each other. We loved each other. 'It's all getting safe, predictable. I'm getting bored. It's time to make a move,' I said.

As we took off from Boston I went and sat by Joe, Mick, Paul and Topper in turn and explained that I was leaving to join Joe Ely in Texas.

'I want to live America, not see it through the window of a tour bus,' I said. 'I've been in a bubble – the bubble of a tour bus, an aeroplane, a hotel room. I want to touch America.'

239

As they slept, the spirit of ELVIS Moved among them. Coked out on the good ship ARPEGGIO. .... Sept '79

The band's response was all positive: 'If it don't work out, come back – always. Good luck.'

As I sat down to tell Jenner and King of my decision, my back molar fell out: 'I just wanted to tell you that I'm ... aarrgh ...'

We played a benefit in Detroit that night. Jackie Wilson was in a hospital in a coma, and we gave the money from the gig to his wife for medical expenses. The Clash, the Baker, the entourage, left next morning. I heard a knock at the door. A Diana Ross lookalike, naked under a white fur coat, said: 'Johnny Green?'

'Yeah?'

'I'm a goodbye and good luck present from the Clash.'

'That's very nice of them. It's very nice of you. But ...' I said.

Afterword

Joe threw his guitar into the air, almost hitting the
ceiling. I saw it out of the corner of my eye, the Ignore
Alien Orders sticker visible as it spun. I caught it, of course.
His smile said it all. It was just like the old days. Except that
now we were in his kitchen, nearly twenty years on, talking
about Eddie Cochran. I'd sent Joe a rare photo of Cochran, the
last one taken of him before he died, and Joe had pinned it to
the door. 'Yeah, you can't have too much Eddie Cochran,' he
said. We lit a huge bonfire in his garden and sat beside it all
night talking about old times and looking forwards. Joe
pointed upwards. 'Hang me high from that tree if the Clash
ever get back together,' he said.

Well who knows what might have happened ...?

Finding myself in London with time to spare, I called round to
see Simonon at his west London home.

'Hello Johnny! Good to see you.'

'Here's a waif and stray turned up on our doorstep
demanding a brandy,' he called inside. 'Come in.'

'That's very nice of you, but I'll just have a coffee. I don't
drink no more.'

'Wow,' he said. 'Here's a funny thing. Joe's coming round
today as well. He'll be here in a minute.'

And there he was coming up the steps. Then Mick rang.

'Joe's here. And Johnny's turned up,' Paul said to him.

Twenty minutes later, Jones arrived in a minicab.

'So, do you three get together often?' I asked.

'Hardly ever,' said Paul.

241

So I was spot on with my timing.

'We've got some money matters to discuss,' explained his missus, Tricia, who seemed to be looking after that side of things. When a couple of suited lawyers turned up, I went to make a move, but Joe said, 'No, it's all right, Johnny. No need to go.' I was glad they felt they could talk in front of me, but I decided it would be more fun to go and help keep Paul's two boys entertained.

Later, we chatted about old times. 'Do you remember that time we nearly killed you?' Paul laughed.

It was a story I had forgotten till he mentioned it ...

I never told that story to Don Letts, either, when he finally got round to making his film about the Clash, *Westway to the World*. I'd gone round to his studio a few months before so he could film an interview with me. It felt odd having a camera pointed at me; it felt uncomfortable to be on the wrong side. As I nervously waited to start talking, a plastic cover on one of the lights burst into flames, which calmed me down.

Don was the original Rasta link going right back to the beginning of the Clash. While the light was being fixed, he said, 'Mick and Topper did their bit the other day.'

'How did it go?'

'Yeah, good. Topper took a great fancy to the rug I had in here. Said it matched his decor at home. He rolled it up and took it away with him. Drove off with it sticking out the taxi door.'

It turned into a long friendly chat with Don which he captured on film.

The première, in September 1999, was at the Coronet, a cinema in Notting Hill Gate. A good choice, as it was the only cinema left in London you could smoke in. Familiar faces from old Clash gigs – liggers, loyal fans, sound men – dotted the crowd, queueing down the road. As I strolled past them to go straight in, a couple came up and said hello. I knew their faces, but couldn't remember from when and where.

'Graham and Lydia,' the man said. I looked blank. 'We used to drink in the Caernarvon.' I recognized them from the Clash's old Camden local.

'Of course. How are you?'

'Great. We won the tickets for this in an *NME* competition.'

'What are the chances of that? There is some justice!'

'I work at London Zoo now.'

'Any chance of some free tickets?'

'Of course. You got us into enough gigs. Time to return the favour.'

'Can you show me round backstage? At the insect house?'

And he did, me and my kids, a few months later.

Don's film brought it all back. It seemed to for the whole crowd, who shouted and cheered at the screen. My old mate Jock Scot was on his feet yelling 'Punk rock!' and was asked to leave. Then, as we walked out into the drizzle, Crocker, now going by the name of Robin Banks, said, 'So none of the band was there.' As we drifted across the road, I said, 'There's one.' Sure enough, spying from behind a pillar, was Mick with a hat pulled down and a grin.

'Out for a stroll? You missed a good film.'

'I lived it,' he smiled. 'Coming to the party?'

'Oh, all right then.'

It was in a fancy joint at the top of Ladbroke Grove. I noticed Paul and Joe there straight away. Joe pushed his way through the crowd and came straight over to me.

'Give us a hand, Johnny. Terry's stuck outside with no invite.'

We shot down the stairs where, after extended haggling with security men, all shaven heads and earpieces and identical Burton suits, trained to keep people out, not let them in, we succeeded. Terry McQuade, the little skinhead in *Rude Boy*, said, 'Cheers lads' as he raced ahead of us to the free bar.

'All the new stars are here,' said Robin. 'There's Sharleen Spiteri from Texas.'

'Yeah, good-looking bird, but look there.'

We stood transfixed by the ageing beauty of Anita Pallenberg in leather trousers, thinking, 'There's hope for us yet.'

A drum kit and back line was set up on the stage of the club. I lost count of the times people came up and asked, 'Are They going to play?' I was thinking, 'You never know with this lot,' but the only answer I gave was a wink and a shrug.

Shane MacGowan was passed out in a corner. He roused himself, took ten minutes to get on-stage and did six songs with a band, never finishing one of them. It was terrific.

A few days later, Topper asked, 'How was the film?'

'Only a mate like Don could have made a film like that.'

'Yeah, it was easy to open up with him.'

'You look a lot better now than you did on the screen, though.'

'Swimming and walking the dog.'

We both looked down at Yowsah, his brindle Staffordshire bull terrier. Women had come and gone, but Topper had always had a dog by his side.

'Have you got a moment to help me clean the house?'

I looked around at the neat room, clocking the rug that must have come from Letts' studio.

Topper explained. 'The dog's got fleas.'

I used to drive around in the middle of the night fetching drugs for him, buying food, bringing alcohol. Now I was driving around trying to buy flea powder for his dog. I vacuumed his house, but I'd rather have been putting up a drum kit.

Joe was moving on. It was about time I saw him play with his new band, the Mescaleros. I checked his itinerary, and Norwich seemed the one. The London shows were out: I get lost in twenty years' worth of liggers, and you can't park the motor by the stage door. I told Banksy, and he was keen as mustard to come along.

'Why don't you bring Topper?' he suggested. 'He's down your way now.'

Topper sounded up for it.

''Ere, I'd love to do "Rock the Casbah" with Joe. D'you reckon he'd do it?'

'I'll find out.'

I knew Topper had never played the song live, even though he had written it. I rang Joe and spoke to his wife, Lucinda. 'Terrific. See you there.'

Cometh the day, cometh the man. But not Topper.

'Where is he?' asked Joe when Banksy, me and my teenage son Earl strode into the cold dressing room after the soundcheck.

'He didn't want to blow it by playing without a rehearsal.'

'That's a pity,' Joe said, rifling through his plastic bags, dumping his coat on top. The young Mescaleros were putting their coats on hangers. A bloke with a laptop was sitting designing stickers for the Mescaleros' dressing room. He never touched the free brandy. It looked like he was there to stop hysteria, panic and mania: a bit of a shame, I thought ... The only man in the crew with a bit of sparkle was Andy, a Rasta roadie.

'I like your man's style there,' I said to Joe.

'Yeah, me too, but no one else does,' he replied.

'What's your lapel badge, Johnny?' Joe asked as we made to leave.

'Gillingham FC. The finest football team,' I said.

He smiled wryly and shook his head as if he despaired of me.

'Have a good one,' I said as we drifted out to catch the show from the mixing desk, leaving Joe to psych himself up. It wasn't my job any more. It wasn't the Clash.

Driving south, my son was still buzzing because Joe had yelled, 'This one's for you, Earl', before launching into 'White Man in Hammersmith Palais'. Banksy chewed over Joe's new songs. 'Next time we'll make sure Topper comes.' But he didn't.

Jones had been producing records for other bands, but was typically vague when I asked him what he was up to. 'Mucking about sticking music on film,' he replied.

'Do you fancy meeting up at the football?'

'Yeah,' he said, with enthusiasm.

Jones was a long-time QPR fan and had always mocked my lifelong love for Gillingham FC. He went to home games with Glen Matlock – Loftus Road is bang opposite the council estate that spawned most of the Sex Pistols. Now the Gills were in the same division as QPR, and they were playing at Loftus Road. I arranged to meet Mick at the players' entrance after the match. A 2–2 draw prevented either of us being smug. We drank Turkish coffee in a place on Shepherd's Bush Green and talked about the match. It wasn't very rock'n'roll; just two middle-aged men doing what middle-aged men do.

'I couldn't believe it when they played "London Calling" over the tannoy before the game and the crowd sang along,' I said. 'Did they know you were there watching?'

Mick just smiled, but I knew it must have been fantastic for him to hear a song he'd written played at his home ground.

Mick said he'd just moved to a new place over the other side of the roundabout.

'It's handy for walking here,' he observed.

'You? Walk?' I mocked.

He asked about my life and my family. Jones had grown into a wiser, kinder man, and I traced a change between us to a conversation at his old one-bedroom flat in Willesden about a year earlier. He'd told me about how he had been seriously ill in intensive care; it had been touch and go, and I'd had a similar scare. We'd compared notes on our near-death experiences, relieved at our close shaves and he'd even offered to make me a cup of tea.

'First time for everything, eh Mick?' I laughed.

'I'm sorry,' he said.

'Why, ain't you got no sugar?'

'I'm sorry if I treated you badly in the old days, Johnny.'

'Thanks,' I said. 'But you know, it was all worth it.'

The Mescaleros were playing support to the Who at Wembley Arena. I wondered how it was to play second fiddle to a band you had been at least the equal of.

I left it to the day of the gig to ring Joe's wife, Lucinda.

'I'm not sure you'd care for all this, Johnny,' she said.

'I'm not keen on stadium rock,' I replied, 'but I wanted to hear Joe's new stuff.'

'It's not that. It's just tricky with the passes. We had a load of people backstage last night. They drank up the Who's rider. The accountants took back our pass allocation. But if you are going to come, I'll look for you out of the stage door and try to wangle you a pass.'

I didn't fancy hanging around in a cold car park like a punter.

'I think I'll give it a miss,' I said.

Nobody missed the Novellos. Tricia Ronane, Paul's missus, had rung me.

'The band are going to get a lifetime achievement award at the Ivor Novello awards ceremony.'

'Are the others all going?'

'Yes.'

I was surprised. I knew they didn't do showbiz, but this was different. It was a recognition of their songwriting talent.

'About time too.'

'Are you coming to town by train, or shall I send a limo?'

It was a tough choice.

•

I was checking my watch nervously. The limo was late. Pro drivers aren't late, but the limo wasn't there, although I'd seen it up the end of the road half an hour before. I rang Topper to warn him of the delay. The doorbell rang, and a man covered in sweat panted, 'Mr Green?'

'On my way now,' I said down the phone to Topper.

'Where were you?' I asked the driver, as I settled into the luxury of the Mercedes.

He had a cut lip, blood dripping down on to his crisp white shirt.

'This has never happened to me in all my time,' he said. 'I've driven all the stars, the Spice Girls, Shirley Bassey ... Look at this.' He held out a smashed mobile for me to inspect. It turned out that some old woman had objected to him blocking a church entrance. He'd said, 'Excuse me, I'm on the phone,' and she'd snatched it from him, cutting his lip, and hurled it on the ground. He'd punched her in the face, just as a builder's Transit was coming by. The builders had piled out ready to teach him a lesson, so he'd scooped up his broken phone and shot off. He'd spent the last half-hour hiding up a cul-de-sac. We left town by the backroads.

We picked up Topper. He came hobbling out on crutches. He'd been in a fight the week before and broken his leg.

'Tell him what's just happened,' I told the driver. And me and Topper roared.

'Every day was like that with the Clash,' said Topper.

We were running late when we got to Park Lane, having stopped for a livener on the Old Kent Road. The do was in the Dorchester ballroom, down a magnificent staircase, perfect for making a grand entrance. Topper, in plaster, couldn't get down the stairs. We went in the service lift, down into the kitchens. We followed a line of waiters into the ballroom, and spotted the rest of the band at their table.

Paul, in a light tan suit, looked like a cool French gangster.

'No suit?' said Paul, pointing at Topper's jeans.

'I ain't cutting up my good suit to fit over the plaster,' he replied.

Mick laughed, but Strummer nodded knowingly. 'I only had my plaster off last Saturday. Football,' he added.

'Old crocks,' I said, realizing this was the first time the four of them had been together in public for eighteen years.

On each seat was a goody-bag of sweets, an Armani catalogue, and an Armani presentation set of pen and propelling pencil. I checked round later to see if anyone had forgotten theirs, but although these people were rich, they weren't stupid.

There were faces all around us: Stevie Wonder, Pete Townshend, Leo Sayer, Des O'Connor. But all eyes were on the Clash, yet they were only looking at each other, delighted to be together again. As the champagne flowed, Mick became talkative and charming. Joe, in a striped suit, was sharp-eyed and inquisitive.

He pointed to my lapel. 'What's the badge?'

'Captain Haddock.'

'I didn't know you were a TinTin fan. Why?'

'Because Captain Haddock drinks like a fish, smokes like a chimney, swears like a trooper and is always losing his rag. He's a mess, but he gets there in the end. What a great message to all children everywhere.'

Joe smiled: 'Yeah, never trust a grown-up.'

I looked round the ballroom at the record-company executives and agreed. Mick's guest was his daughter, Lauren, and Paul had blagged a couple of extra tickets for his boys, hidden away at the back.

Stevie Wonder sang 'I Just Called to Say I Love You' in a cappella style, Paul Gambaccini droned on, Iron Maiden looked like ageing garden gnomes, although I was astonished at how many records they had sold, and at how sharply and intelligently Bruce Dickinson spoke. And then Townshend introduced the Clash; full of praise, low on gushing flannel. Behind him, giant Pennie Smith pictures of the band flashed on three big screens. Their music pumped out, and up the four of them went. I found myself on my feet, taken over, roaring as if Gillingham had scored.

Later, upstairs in the award-winners' bar, celebrities mingled. The Clash sat around a table and talked to one another, absorbed. They attracted attention because they were so self-contained. I went to the bar to buy a round, and was embarrassed to find I was losing my touch. I was reaching into my pocket for the cash when the bloke next to me, who I later discovered was Craig David, said: 'No, it's all on the house.'

I put the drinks on the table and nudged Mick. 'Oi, there's Roy Wood over there.'

He looked up and saw Wood talking to Chris Tarrant. 'Two Brummie boys together.'

'He's just asked Tarrant how long till Christmas, 'cos he's a bit short.'

I've got a loud voice. Wood heard me, smiled and gave me a double thumbs-up.

Topper was less at ease, and wanted away. I popped around the corner to check the driver was there waiting, and bumped into Strummer, also on his way out. Mike Reid came out, with his schoolboy fringe and polished smile, put his arm round Joe's shoulders and said: 'Well done, well deserved.'

Joe greeted him politely, but as the ex-Radio 1 DJ walked away, Strummer muttered to me: 'See what I have to put up with.' He looked thoughtful. 'He never played our records back then.'

'That's showbiz, Joe.'

On the way home, Topper dozed. Suddenly, he was awake, alert and talking with great authority and knowledge about the shortcomings of the Blair government and his discontentment with it. The driver was surprised, but I was delighted. It showed he hadn't lost his marbles.

Robin Banks met me off the train at Victoria.

'Where are we off to?'

He never knows, since he never gets invited because of his reputation for mayhem.

'To the launch party for Bob Gruen's book of photos of the Clash.'

When we got out of the tube at Camden Town, the high street was smarter than we remembered it.

'They've even got a fucking art gallery here now.'

A battered old red car pulled alongside. Someone shouted from inside, 'Oi, Johnny, where's this show?'

'In the art gallery.'

Our one-time security man, Ray Jordan, leant out the window. Jones got out the other side, elegantly, as if he was getting out of a Mercedes.

'Still looking after him?' I asked Ray, nodding at Mick.

'No, he don't need it now.'

As we entered, Mick was swallowed up by the heaving crowd of young media types whacking back the free Miller Lite. I doubt any of them were old enough to have seen the Clash, except in photos. Robin was wearing a Mao Tse Tung-style jacket. A photographer came up and said: 'I'm shooting the most fashionable people here. Can I take your picture?'

I roared.

I was surprised to see Barry Myers, the old Clash DJ, playing the records.

'I thought you'd given this up to be a photographer?'

'Yeah, but Gruen asked me for old times' sake.'

Gruen, the American photographer, had come on the road with us, and his claim to fame was blowing the bugle a couple of times to announce the Clash's arrival on-stage.

The gallery extended into the backyard, covered by a huge marquee. I pushed my way through. There were Mick and Joe, as expected, chatting with fans.

I was surprised to see Pennie Smith at another photographer's show. She asked about Ray Lowry.

'He's holed up in his northern cottage, high in the Pennines, wearing a baseball cap to keep out the rain, with a walking stick and every Elvis Presley record ever made.'

A BBC film crew was in action. The producer said to me: 'Bernard Rhodes is here.'

'Someone's having you on, mate.'

He showed me a poster for the event. He was getting it signed by the band, and right there at the top was written: 'I started all this. Bernard Rhodes.'

'I believe you,' I said. 'Only he could have written that.'

And sure enough, I soon found myself bending down to listen to Bernie.

The large beret he was wearing marked him out as a creative man.

'Listen Johnny. You got what you wanted out of all this, the sex and the drugs.'

'Yeah, that was very nice Bernie, but that wasn't why I did it.'

'The world don't need rock stars.' He gestured towards Strummer and Jones. 'You have no idea of the radical impact of US basketball stars in the Ukraine. Have you got a radio mike on you? I need to speak to everyone.' And he pulled a speech out of his pocket.

I turned to Pennie Smith and whispered, 'Have you got your camera?' Silly question.

She fumbled in her pocket. I was worried Bernie was going to leg it, as he always did in front of a lens. I'm not big on mementoes, but I wanted this moment captured. So did Joe. Seeing what was happening from across the crowd, he waded his way through, shouting, 'Hang on, I want in on this,' and appeared the other side of Bernie, so the three of us were cheek to cheek, just as Pennie pressed the button.

Bernie had spoken to Pennie as well.

'It was just like he was picking up halfway through a conversation we'd had twenty years ago,' she told me.

'Yeah, it was the same with me. He must do that with everybody.'

On my way out I was looking for a copy of Gruen's book to have away but there were none lying around. I asked to see the gallery owner. His name was Proud, but not as much as I was.

'Can I have a copy of the book?'

'Yes. They're forty-five pounds.'

'I've got a problem putting my hand in my pocket when giant photos of myself are winking at me.'

He looked up at the picture, then back at me. 'Camilla, get this gentleman a free copy.'

It was a good flick on the train home.

Concorde 2 was just my kind of place for a gig, old wood and new chrome. It's a converted bikers' joint, right on the seafront at Brighton. Joe was working it with his new line-up of Mescaleros. I arrived in time for the soundcheck, as always. It was a bonus to find my old drinking mate Wreckless Eric knocking around. I'd last seen him when I wrote off his red Morris Marina. He was playing support.

It was easy to find my way to Joe's dressing room by the computer-generated arrows pasted on the walls. They were a bit unnecessary. It was hardly Shea Stadium.

'How're the new boys in the band?'

'It's coming along good.'

'Writing much?'

He grunted and nodded, sipped a lemon-and-honey. I knew better than to ask him to speak much before a show.

'Some writer posted this to me to pass on to you.' I handed

him a novel. 'It's not bad. Quite a good read, actually. Try this as well.'

I passed him a new biography of Jack Kerouac with loads of photos.

'Yeah, you can't have too much Jack Kerouac.'

As I was going out front, I did a double take as I saw Strummer crouched in a small space behind the amps. He was fully engaged in getting his breathing right, pumping his breath up before going on-stage. He seemed a lonely figure to me, but he wasn't. It was just that I was used to him in the Clash, everyone geeing each other up before a gig. Here, Joe was the only front-man. But what a front-man he was, as ever.

The researcher from the BBC had been very polite when she'd invited me to record a radio interview with Tom Robinson, so I guessed that she had been unable to persuade any of the Clash to do the slot.

After the interview, we went for a bite to eat. He paid. I had to shoot off because I'd arranged to meet Paul outside Oxford Street tube. He arrived carrying a box of Bob Gruen books.

'Will you get Topper to sign these? They're going to be competition prizes for a music mag. Here's a couple of legal letters for him to sign as well.'

'Yeah, sure.'

'Fancy a sandwich, Johnny?'

Bloated as I was with Tom Robinson's free pizza, I said, 'Yeah, lovely.'

I told him about the radio interview.

'When's that going out? I'll listen in.'

'Dunno, it's on Radio Six. You got digital radio?'

'No.'

'Robinson's a changed man now.'

'Yeah?'

'We were sitting in this restaurant, right, and he got out a

254

laptop, pressed a few buttons, and up came two portrait photos of his smiling children. People used to whip photos of their kids out of their wallets to show you, and I never used to know what to say to them then.'

'Yeah, right.'

'How's the painting going? Finished the kitchen yet?'

He was taking his art seriously these days.

'I'll show you when you bring the books back.'

So I set out for home, lugging a load of books with me. They weighed a ton. He could have sent them by courier, but I was pleased he hadn't. He was still doing things the old Clash way, with a personal touch.

When I brought the books back, I met Paul at Cleopatra's Needle on the Embankment. I was surprised – he was wearing a dark blue suit. As a musician he had splattered paint on his clothes. As an artist he didn't.

'I've been painting up there on the roof,' he said, pointing at Somerset House.

'What? You do it from up there, not from photos?'

'Yes. I do it the old-fashioned way.'

He pointed out various landmark buildings, like the National Theatre opposite, where he'd been working from the rooftops, getting perspectives on the River Thames.

'How do you get up there then? Someone fix it for you?'

'No, I just ask them.'

'Do people know you're Paul Simonon from the Clash?'

'No. The only hassle I got was when I set up my easel on Waterloo Bridge.'

'What, people stopping to gawp at what you're doing?'

'No. It was just difficult when I wanted to go for a piss.'

'I'll show you how I work,' he said, as we went to a little café across the road and sat on the verandah of the little wooden chalet.

From a big leather portfolio he fished sheets of paper with diagonal grids drawn on.

'I start like this,' he said. 'I sketch it all first.'

'What, and then work from home?'

'No, I like to finish it off on the spot.'

He'd just been out to the Caribbean.

'Was that lovely?'

'Yeah, but the best thing was coming back into Heathrow. The river looked fantastic.'

I realized his fascination with the river, and why he kept painting it again and again. It was good to see a Londoner who's proud of his city. And nice to see Paul still so enthusiastic about his work. He spoke in great detail about how he worked on his art.

As we walked up Charing Cross Road I asked him, 'See much music these days?'

'Not a lot. You?'

'Very little. The Clash is a hard act to follow.'

Paul just grinned, but he wanted to talk about his art, not the Clash.

'I've got an exhibition coming up. Do you want to come?'

'I wouldn't miss it for the world.'

I was a bit surprised when my wife Janette and son Earl started hustling me to take them to the Fleadh, the annual Irish festival in Finsbury Park. I put up a strong rearguard action. Big gigs, out of doors, muddy fields ... but they had me over a barrel. Shane was back with the Pogues, and Joe and the Mescaleros were supporting. Despite my reservations, I sorted out a family's worth of backstage passes. We strolled into the liggers' area, all canvas, decking and drinks which had to be paid for. I knew very few people there. I wasn't really in this world any more. For me, it was a family day out, so we kept on moving. I didn't want to be there. There was music blaring in the background from the main stage and another stage in a tent, but I had most fun with my daughters, Polly and Ruby, at the super kids' play area.

The crowds, all Celtic shirts and sham rocks, were drifting and drinking. It all seemed a bit aimless. Old habits die hard, and I wandered in and out of the backstage bar, but it was all a bit boring to me. The words gig and chill-out don't go together for me. Things sharpened up as dusk fell and the stage lights came on. I only got really interested when Strummer hit the stage. The Mescaleros stuff went down well. The Clash numbers went down really well. Persuading other people to move on is a long hard job. My son Earl went right down the front. I watched from the mixing desk. Earl said Joe was really driven, pushing the music on, to the point of throwing a mike stand at the drummer. The set really had me moving, banging my heels, Strummer-style.

'Come on, I'll introduce you to the man,' I said to Janette.

Easier said than done. The blokes guarding the inner sanctum of dressing-room caravans were identical to the others I always seemed to come across.

Although I had a backstage pass, I didn't have a dressing-room pass. While we were hustling, we watched Shane MacGowan staggering his way down the ramp off stage.

Eventually I walked through with Luce, with Earl sticking real close. The dressing-room caravans were drawn up in a circle like a wagon train preparing to fight off marauders. Strummer was talking to an American guy as I walked up.

He introduced me. 'Tell him,' he said to the American. He rattled on about a benefit he wanted Joe to play. Sounded very worthy to me, but he was giving it a big pitch. Strummer was polite to him, but still in a post-gig distraction.

'What do you reckon to the show?' Strummer asked me.

'It's getting better every time. But I couldn't really hear. The PA cut out three times in the first ten minutes. The mix was a shambles. The top end floated away. The bass was like the mud on the field.'

'Vocals?'

'So-so. The Pogues sounded right on the button though.'

He turned to Tymon Dogg, one of his oldest musical pals and now a Mescalero. 'Yeah, I thought as much.'

The oldest rock'n'roll dodge is making sure the support don't upstage the headliners. Except with the Clash. We were always under instruction to look after support bands.

I had to break off the conversation.

'Hang on a minute, Joe. Family business.'

I'd been watching Earl standing near Shane MacGowan who was talking to a woman. Earl was poised stiffly next to her. MacGowan took his loitering presence as a threat, and was giving him the eye. He pulled his fist back. I lunged forward, with visions of bloody mayhem with security men and Irish road crews. Earl beat me to it with an open palm.

'I'd like to shake your hand,' he said to MacGowan. 'I love your stuff.'

I turned back to Joe with relief.

'I really like doing these outdoor shows,' he said. 'I'm doing the Cambridge Folk Festival.'

'I think I'll give that a miss,' I told him, and realized my missus wasn't with me.

I found her outside. She'd been asked to leave the backstage area forty minutes before.

I'd been warned that Paul's exhibition preview was a smart job so I wore my best dark suit. I thought I looked like a security bloke, but the staff on duty at the gallery in St James' wore tailcoats. I arrived early to have a wander around those few little streets that house the expensive galleries. I found the place where Paul's exhibition was by the shop number. There was no name in lights above the door. I passed on the champagne, but had a rare bite of caviar. There weren't many people there yet, and I went up to Trish.

'This is a big step up for Paul in the art world,' she said.

'He's really keen to be recognized as an artist in his own right, not because he was once in the Clash.'

He had a little cream peaked cap on. It looked like he'd just thrown it on the back of his head, but of course on him it looked stylish and perfect.

'Good of you to come,' he said, his face radiant and excited. He was already chatting to elegant, conservatively dressed people, who wanted the artist's take on the exhibition, From Hammersmith to Greenwich, before considering buying the pictures. They wanted the personal touch. It continued for an hour or more, low voices and discretion. Paul was kept busy as a charming host.

I chatted to people, then realized the room had got more animated. The city people were drifting away and more glamorous people were arriving. Harry Enfield. Ben Elton. Mick Jones. This little bloke went up to Paul and put his arm round him. Paul seemed pleased to see him.

I said to Mick, 'Look at that cunt. He's got the same hat on as Paul.'

But he was wearing it properly, brim pulled down.

Mick looked over and the little bloke looked up and gave a huge grin. It was Ewan McGregor. He might have been wearing the same hat as Paul, but he didn't look half as good.

A few of the old gang had gravitated towards the gallery. Don Letts was there, and a camera was going round. 'I'm bringing on the next generation,' he said, pointing at his youngster who was behind the camera.

Plaxy had been a founder of the Camden Town Ferrets, who had hung around Rehearsals. She looked glamorous, with an elegant Italian man, but I recognized her immediately.

'What you up to these days?'

She gave me a card. 'I run a restaurant with my husband. You must come and eat there. I want to return all the favours, the backstage passes.'

I caught Paul's eye as he paused in between talking to prospective buyers.

259

'What about Plaxy? You been to her restaurant up Bond Street?'

'Coo yeah, it's very smart.'

I joined Pennie Smith for a fag on the front steps. We both spoke of how pleased we were to see Paul doing well and so proud of his work. Some suit with a big cigar turned to me and said, 'I know you, don't I? You use my merchant bank.'

'I'm lucky if I don't get shown the door down my local NatWest,' I said.

I moved the conversation on to the art work. He said: 'I'm friends with one of the partners in this gallery. They're very excited about Mr Simonon's work. It's a radical move for them. They usually specialize in established artists.'

'I used to have a Simonon on my wall. But I moved.'

He looked blank. I didn't bother to mention it was the car mural on the wall of Rehearsals.

Mick joined us, and also raved on about Paul's work. Everyone else was raving about Mick's work. He was on the up, winning fresh recognition as a hip producer with The Libertines.

There were two blokes on the other side of the road, just staring across. I realized they had been there all evening. I hadn't noticed before, but Mick had. He went and spoke to them, and I joined him. They were fans. Said they ran a Clash website. Mick happily autographed their pile of albums and said he would get Paul to come out, which he did.

As I left, I went up to Paul and said, 'Brilliant.' His eyes twinkled. He was really geared up and full of it.

'Thanks for coming.'

'I wouldn't have missed it for the world.'

And I was impressed by the way he handled that world. He was cool, as always, perfectly at ease discussing his work with businessmen, who might buy them, and with mates, who couldn't afford them.

Trish put her hand on my arm. 'Things are moving. I'll give you a call.'

When I spoke to her on the phone a few weeks later, I saw what she meant.

'The band are going to be inducted into the Rock'n'Roll Hall of Fame.'

I wondered what weird ceremony the induction would involve.

'When's this happening?'

'Next spring. Do you want to come?'

It was a tough choice. But I knew I wasn't just being asked along for the ride. It was understood that my role was to make sure Topper came along, and to look after him on the trip.

Things were happening. There was already a reheightened interest in the Clash that had been building up over recent years, since Don's film, the release of a live album, *From Here to Eternity*, Gruen's book, articles and speculation in the music press about them reforming. I knew they'd already turned down big millions to do that a few years before. My phone started getting hot, old Clash people I hadn't heard from for a while.

Mick phoned. 'What do you reckon? Isn't it great?'

'It's brilliant to be recognized as being an all-time great,' I said, with one eye on a free trip to New York.

Trish called, and said Paul was having doubts about going. 'He'll go if the others go.'

Mick asked how Topper was. 'He said he'll do New York if he can go by boat.'

I told Mick how he'd put on weight and was working out, particularly from his drum stool. We'd got him a new Pearl red sparkle stage kit and a small silver jazz kit to practise on. He'd done a good DIY job at soundproofing his spare bedroom. He needed to, because he didn't practise at half volume. He still hit them as if he was playing at the Lyceum. Trouble was, there wasn't any ventilation in his spare room, so he'd emerge from it looking like he'd come out of a sauna, while I made

261

him a cup of tea downstairs. His sound system, which usually blared out Herbie Hancock or Buddy Rich, was now occasionally blasting out his tracks off the live album. I was curious.

'Fancy a day at the seaside?' I asked him.

'I live at the seaside.'

'No, down at Hastings. Strummer's playing there.'

I knew about this gig because Barry Myers had rung me, delighted to be working with Joe again. He'd seen the Mescaleros, and was knocked out by them and had asked Joe for a job as DJ. He'd been with the band in Irving Plaza, New York, for a week of shows and was now on the road full-time with them. Joe had got a young band, but a DJ from the old team.

'Did they love him in New York?' I asked Barry.

'They went fucking mental.'

'What are you doing here?'

'There's nowhere else I'd rather be, Joe, on a cold wet winter's night, than stuck here on Hastings pier. Brings it all back. When's the soundcheck?'

'No soundcheck,' he said, in a tone of voice which would brook no questions. I was surprised, but as always, just when you thought you'd got an angle on Joe, he'd do the opposite.

'Topper?' he asked.

'It's a long drive, Joe.'

'I guess there's no rush. Is he drinking?'

'Well, I'm not with him at closing time every night. But he's fit and well. He's doing a small-town gig with some old mates in a few weeks.'

'That's a first. Are you going?'

'Of course.'

'Let me know how it goes.'

He trudged off down the pier deep in thought, back to his big tour bus.

I continued on into the familiar ballroom, with roadies buzzing everywhere. The gig was running late.

'Where's Barry?' I asked.

'No Barry here, mate.'

'Yeah, the DJ?'

'Ah, you mean Scratchy,' and the roadie hoicked a thumb over his shoulder towards the mixing desk.

'Hallo Scratchy,' I said as I met Barry.

'Oh yeah. Well, you've got to keep up with the times,' he said.

We walked down the pier, through the amusement arcades.

'Do you still have to push all the gear up here by hand?' I asked.

'Yes,' he said.

'Sorry I wasn't here to give you a hand,' I lied.

'Some things change though. No hotels now. We live and sleep on this beauty.'

It was a beauty. A double-decker tour bus, with sumptuous lounge, video screen, sound system, kitchen, wall-to-wall bunks upstairs.

'Actually, I've only just got up. It was a long night in Portsmouth last night.'

'What, Joe too?'

'He comes and goes. But mostly he keeps himself to himself, up in the front part of the bus,' said Barry.

'The tour manager, Fozzy, rents a couple of rooms in the hotel opposite so we can use the showers.'

'How great is it to have the music every night?'

'As you always say, you can't have enough Joe Strummer.'

Bang on cue, while Myers shuffled his CDs, Joe hopped off the bus in a thick coat. He still needed a bit of space to himself before a show. Before it was my job to keep an eye on him. Now I was a guest.

'Mind if I tag along'?'

Mostly it was silence in the dark as we stepped out along the promenade. He stopped, looked me straight in the face, and said, 'You would tell me, Johnny, wouldn't you'?'

'The truth, always, Joe.' That's what he gave, and demanded from those around him. I was very flattered he was sharing his doubts and vulnerability with me. The world didn't often see the tough guy's soft side.

The joint was full and buzzing when we got back. Barry spun me some of my favourite acts like Big Joe Turner and Dr Alimontado. It was my own loud Desert Island Discs, and I could see why Strummer still used him.

The supports were local acts. The sound was immaculate, and they were going down well. I was pleased to find the dressing rooms warmer than I remembered. They had filled in the gaps between the planks, although I missed seeing the sea through the floor. Joe was putting on his stage shirt and I was about to leave him to it. He had played a benefit for the striking firemen at Acton town hall five days before. Mick had joined him for the encore. He had joked on the phone to me about how he had felt like Nigel Tufnell from Spinal Tap standing in the wings as he waited to be invited on stage.

'Yeah, but how good was it to have a guitar strapped on you again?'

'Wonderful, Johnny.'

'How good was it to play with Mick the other night?' I asked Strummer.

'You ought to fucking know,' he replied. I certainly did.

I listened to the set. New songs and old were received with equal acclaim. The crowd was pumped up and dancing. Strummer weren't coasting either. His veins stood out as he pushed it to the maximum. I was intrigued that his nod to his past catalogue took the form of old Clash cover songs like the Maytals' 'Pressure Drop' and Sonny Curtis' 'I Fought the Law'. Halfway through the set, Barry Myers said, 'This new one's a cracker,' and I left the mixing desk to sit down at the side, put my feet up and listen to the song. I sneaked a look at the set list stuck on a monitor, so I wouldn't look green later. The song was 'Coma Baby'. Backstage, Joe said, 'Brandy Johnny? Sorry, you don't. I forgot. What do you reckon?' he asked, as he whacked back a big one.

'If Eddie Cochran had kept on going, he'd be doing it like you're doing it now. I really liked the new one, "Coma Baby".'

He was pleased I'd named the song, and I knew he'd be pleased, which was why I'd taken the trouble to check the name.

'Yeah, we're still working that one up and adding bits every night when we play it.'

'I did wince, though, when you went into "White Riot",' I said. Everyone used to go mental during that song, and it was really hard work dealing with the stage invasions.

'Now you've got the drummer leading with a cool groove.'

'Tell him,' said Joe, calling the drummer over.

'I was well impressed,' I told him, 'and I've been used to working with a five-star drummer.'

He knew I was talking about Topper. 'Thank you,' he said.

Joe had surrounded himself with a band that was not only young and high-grade, but also ready and willing to move into new areas, not wanting to sit back on Joe's reputation. It was a familiar scene as Fozzy opened the doors and the room flooded with eager fans, some bald and wrinkled, many young. Joe had time for every one of them, treated them all as special, even though so many were still treading over old Clash territory.

'I'd never heard any of your stuff before,' said a young man with wild eyes, 'but that just blew me away.' Joe absolutely beamed. The dressing room gradually emptied, and I sat in a corner with Joe.

'Looking forward to Cleveland?' I asked.

'No, we're doing Sheffield, then Liverpool,' he said.

'I don't mean petrochemical works on Teeside. Cleveland, Ohio. Rock'n'Roll Hall of Fame?'

'The museum's in Cleveland, but the awards are in New York, as a matter of fact.' He knew all the details.

He was smiling as he bent close and whispered, 'You know the problem?'

I nodded. 'Simmo? I know,' I replied.

'Is he for turning?'

'Well, he's got a point, eh?' I said. 'I can just see it now, Joe. The lights shining off polished bald heads and expensive gold jewellery as the record company executives applaud your induction.'

He covered his face with his hands. 'Don't! Don't!'

As I stood up to leave, I added: 'But there are more ways than one to skin a cat, Joe.'

He looked up with a big smile. 'Yeah.'

I wondered just what he would say to the assembled music business when the day came.

'Don't forget to tell me about Topper,' he said, as I left to drive home.

'Stick your moniker on here four times,' I said to Topper, putting a blank sheet of paper in front of him.

'It's for the Rock'n'Roll Hall of Fame.'

It was to be etched onto a piece of glass for the museum, to go with an exhibit of Clash artefacts like their stencilled clothes and Paul's smashed-up Fender Precision bass.

'And you've also got to sign this.' It was his passport application. He'd asked me to sort it all out for him in time to go to America for the awards.

'What's the date?'

'December the twenty-second.'

'I haven't needed a passport for fifteen years,' he said. 'You know I don't like travelling.'

I'd gone to his place with Pat Gilbert, editor of *Mojo*. He'd wanted to do this interview personally. He was a Clash fan. He was talking to all four of the Clash members for the issue in the run-up to the Hall of Fame job. I left them to it and took Topper's dog Yowsah for a walk, trying to stop him from attacking the swans in the park.

On the way back, Pat said he hadn't realized till then how hard the break-up of the Clash had hit everyone.

'It's taken a long time for them to build up separate lives. But there's a buzz in the air now, eh? Do you think they'll play again?'

'The Hall of Fame want them to,' I said.

'Doesn't everyone?'

'I don't.'

But I nearly changed my mind that night when I went back alone to watch Topper play a set in his local. I was wedged in next to the bass player, Nigel, a mate of Topper's. The whole pub was a mate of Topper's, except they all called him Nick. The three-piece belted out old R'n'B favourites. I was staggered to see and hear that Topper was as great as ever – slick, flash and driving. After a second encore, he came over to me covered in sweat.

'How was that?'

'Where've you been all these years?'

'The only thing missing is a bit more stamina, but I'm working on it.'

He started to unscrew his cymbals, but I said: 'Leave that. Top drummers don't strip their kit down. I'll do it. Have a drink with your mates. Give us your key, and I'll drop the kit round at your house.'

I'd just finished stacking it in his spare room when Topper walked in the front door.

'Fucking brilliant,' I told him. His face showed the same euphoria I was feeling. He glowed with pride. He was bouncing around the room.

The phone rang. He picked it straight up.

'Hello? Oh, hello Mick.'

I watched Topper stand stock still. Then his legs seem to

melt into the carpet. There was a long silence, Topper still with the phone to his ear.

He shouted, 'Fucking hell,' and threw the phone across the room.

I went and picked it up.

'Hello, Mick,' I said cautiously into the receiver.

'Johnny? Joe's dead.'

Afterlife

Eight days later, I drove Topper up to the funeral in pouring rain. We were both still in shock. Joe had died the most peaceful death possible. Who'd have thought that of him? He'd been out walking his dogs at his spread in the West Country. He'd got back home, stretched out on the settee with a paper. Luce had come home and thought he was asleep. He'd blacked out, then had a heart attack. He hadn't felt a thing, said the doctors.

We were bang on early for the funeral in London West 11, Strummer's old stamping ground. And Topper's.

'Time for a quick one,' he said.

We went into a pub in Ladbroke Grove. We both had cola. Topper left most of his. We saw an old face from the past, Slim, a huge fat squeezebox player, dressed up for the funeral in rockabilly chic. A group of seven or eight people at the back of the pub spoke to me. Fans seem to think I live in a Clash museum, surrounded by tour T-shirts, backstage passes, every free badge made and rare Capital Radio EPs. I'd given all that away at the time. All I have left is one moody monochrome photo of Joe and me, outside the stage door, New York Palladium, stage gear in a paper deli bag.

'We've come down from Leicester for the funeral, but don't know if we should go,' they said.

I knew the answer after talking to Mick and Paul. Their

answer to such enquiries was, 'If you think it's appropriate, come along.'

It was a reminder of how many people felt personally connected to Joe.

I gave Slim a lift to Kensal Green cemetery, worried about my suspension. As I turned off the Harrow Road, Topper wound down the window and yelled, 'Keep the boots on darling.' I was shocked. All we could see was mini-skirt, legs and boots beneath an umbrella. She looked up.

'Sorry, Pearl,' said Topper. It was an old girlfriend of Paul's. Trying to keep our suits dry, we dodged the massive puddles and saw two fire engines parked up with their crews milling about.

'What, is the crematorium on fire?'

They were there as a guard of honour, returning the favour of Joe supporting their strike.

Despite the weather, there was a large crowd gathered: fans, faces, film crews. It was like walking into the set of *This is Your Life*. Pennie Smith was standing at the entrance smoking a Gitane. Topper joined her, pleased to see her after so many years. They both stubbed out their fags and walked into the lobby. I broke away to speak to a woman.

'How are you Sheila? Is Bernie coming?'

Sheila was his ex-missus. 'As he would say, who knows, who cares?' she said.

As we went in, someone shouted, 'Fire'. Flames were leaping from the rubbish bin, sparked by one of the discarded fags. One of the firemen came and carried it off.

'Only you could have done that, Topper,' I said. He ducked through a door to hide his laughter, to find himself among the long sad faces at another funeral.

Those of us with invites went into the chapel, nodding to friends past and present. Me and Topper took our seats with Mick and Paul. A lot of Joe's family was there, mainly from

Scotland. I was taken aback to see so many of them. I just didn't think of the man's life outside of the Clash. You think you know a man, but you don't.

The chapel was decorated with brightly coloured flags, some of Joe's favourites. The coffin had radical stickers all over it. His straw cowboy hat was sitting on top. They played his music, old and new, and people spoke about what he meant to them. Speakers relayed the ceremony to the people outside – considerate to the fans to the last. I knew Simonon was going to speak and I was surprised at that. I didn't think that was his scene, but how wrong can you be. He was articulate and eloquent, telling of his friendship with Joe. He told a simple story from the early days. Walking down the Portobello Road, Joe had dived into a shop and emerged with a pair of mirror shades, which Paul had admired and envied. When they got to Rehearsals, Joe reached into his pocket and gave Paul another pair. 'I got these for you,' Joe had said. Paul said that summed up the man.

People filed out, saying their farewells to Joe.

The wake, which was more like a post-show lig, was at the Paradise round the corner, a favourite den of Joe's. There was no Burton-suited, shaven-headed St Peter on the door. Everyone was there. Lucinda greeted us all with warmth and dignity. It was getting so packed it was hard to move. Upstairs, a sound system was whacking it out courtesy of different DJs who'd worked with Joe through the years; Don Letts, Barry Myers and a crew from Manchester. Joe had been no slouch at DJing himself. There was a drummers' convention at the corner of the bar: Topper, Terry Chimes and Rat Scabies.

'Doing much?' I asked Rat.

'Yeah, some sessions. Thank God he's not working,' he said, pointing to Topper, ''cos I'd get a lot less work if he was.'

It was delightful but exhausting, having similar conversations over and over with so many people: Chris Townsend, who'd done the old Clash T-shirts; Kosmo Vinyl, who'd arrived

270

in two-tone correspondent shoes at the last minute; Dave Mingay, director of *Rude Boy*. Everyone had gone in new directions, in particular Mickey Foote, Joe's old mate from Newport, who had been with him right through the 101-ers and who produced the inspirational first Clash album, always my favourite. He's a plumber now. Pointing at Paul Cook, the Sex Pistols drummer, across the room, he said: 'I took a call from him on the phone, but I sent my mate along in case, when he saw me, he asked for a discount.'

Simonon was holding court over a brimming plate from the vegetarian spread.

He called me over. ''Ere, Johnny, tell them about the time we nearly killed you.'

'What, that motor in Aberdeen? Joe behind the wheel when he couldn't drive? Me screaming, him crying? ... Nah, not now,' I said. 'I've just been talking to a personal friend of yours.'

He beamed. 'How is Howard Fraser?' He stroked an imaginary drooping moustache.

'Clean shaven now,' I said.

The attention was getting to Topper. 'Can we go?'

We found Mick and said our goodbyes. As we neared the door, I said, 'Give us two minutes, Topper.'

In a sharp western suit was Joe Ely. 'Nice tie, Johnny,' he said, pointing at my bootlace.

'I bought it with you in Texas. How are you?'

'Fine. So you haven't needed me to save you from getting shot dead recently?'

I laughed, remembering the wild days with Ely.

'I blagged the last airline seat out of Texas to get here,' he said.

'I'm glad you did. It's lovely to see you.'

I nearly crashed the car going back down Ladbroke Grove. Topper screamed. A big Jag pulled out on me and I did a controlled skid past it at the last second. I don't get to do many of those these days. Banksy, in the back seat, was pleading with me to stop so he could get out and do the bloke. I declined and dropped him off at Victoria.

We drove across the open spaces of Blackheath, bleak in the rain. Topper looked across.

'It should have been me who died, not him, the way I've lived my life.'

He paused, then added, 'Would you think I was a bad man if I said bad things about Joe?'

'No, I could probably match you on those stories any time. He was a wonderful bloke, but he was just a bloke. He could be a right bastard when the mood was on him, and he could fuck up, like we all can.'

We took off the rose-coloured glasses. Topper said how it had hurt him to be sacked from the Clash, and blamed himself for the band breaking up, although he agreed that he'd been so out of his head most of the time that he'd given Joe no choice but to sack him.

'The funny thing about that, Topper, is that Joe always blamed himself for breaking up the band by sacking you and Mick. And not only that, but Mick takes the blame for being so difficult.'

We spent the rest of the journey home slagging Joe off, recalling incidents and arguments. For all his faults, perhaps because of his faults, we both loved the man.

All the people who'd been pestering me, asking me if the Clash were going to play in New York, suddenly stopped. That dream was over.

Mick was still red-hot to go. Paul had reservations. He didn't want it to be a big Joe slush-fest. Topper wavered between the two points of view. He wanted to know if the Baker was going to be there.

'I've tried my best to track him down,' I said, 'but he is lost in America and has buried his traces.'

Although Topper was pleased to have a new passport, he was less sure about using it. Seven hours in a 747 terrified him. And he said he wanted to draw a line under the Clash.

I understood all the arguments, but mostly I resented the fact that the award was coming so long after the band's great years. I wanted them to receive their just plaudits, but I didn't need some record-company clown in an Armani suit telling me how great the Clash were, twenty-five years on. I always knew they were magnificent. But if the record company was going to pay for a luxury trip to New York, I wasn't too proud to spend their money.

Tricia gave me the itinerary. Topper's bags were packed ready when I called to pick him up. The limo driver was waiting outside.

'I ain't coming, Johnny.'

I wasn't surprised. 'The flight?'

'Yeah. And Joe ain't going to be there, so what's the fucking point? Let's just draw a line under the whole business.'

I argued with him, pleaded with him until as late as I could leave it, but I knew it was no use. I cut and run to the airport. Lucinda was in the first-class lounge with Joe's daughters, Lola and Jazz, when I walked in. 'Where's Topper?'

'No show. I did my best.'

'I'll have a go,' Lucinda said. She tapped the numbers into her mobile, and I heard the familiar unsuccessful arguments.

'Well, we gave it our best shot,' she said.

'How are you?' I asked.

'It's been a difficult couple of months, you know?' I did know. I told her how my wife Lindy had died from meningitis twenty years before.

'I never knew that,' she said. 'You understand, then.'

'Joe understood too. He helped me out with the funeral costs, and he paid for me to clear off to a Greek island to get over my grief. Banksy came with me. It turned into a riot, of

273

course, but it helped. But that's another story.

'That was the only other time I've flown first class. It's good here, eh?' I said, looking around the sumptuous lounge. You could get your suit steam-cleaned while you waited; there was a bar, massages, manicures and sushi. I had a chicken-salad sandwich. On the plane, I spoke to Terry Chimes, the first and last Clash drummer. He said his invite had been addressed to Tory Crimes, his nom-de-plume on the first Clash album. He was pissed off about that.

'Still drumming?'

'No, I've moved on. I'm a chiropractor now. I've got a practice in Rio de Janeiro. And one in Milton Keynes.'

I had a steak on the plane, cooked to order, waitress service.

I was used to being pulled at airports. At Kennedy, I was stopped at immigration.

'Flying the flag for your country?' the man said, pointing at my blue lapel badge.

'No, Gillingham FC,' I said. Here we go, I thought.

He asked the purpose of my visit.

'I'm here with a band to receive their rightful place in the Rock'n'Roll Hall of Fame.'

'What band is that?'

'The Clash.'

'Wow,' he said, and waved me straight through. It was all so easy now. In the Clash days, everything was a struggle.

Outside, there were a couple of dozen people in Clash T-shirts, shouting 'Topper!' Terry signed autographs. I looked for our limos. They dropped us all off at the Waldorf-Astoria. As I waited for my room key, Simonon came flying past me across the lobby. All I glimpsed was hat and overcoat. 'I'll catch you later,' he called as he disappeared into the lift. He and Mick had flown over a few days earlier to do press interviews. I blagged Topper's hotel room for myself. He wasn't going to use it. The liveried bellboy took me up to the 34th floor and opened the door. It wasn't a room, it was a six-room suite. We walked through the vestibule and he showed me the lounge, with the biggest television I'd ever seen, disguised in an antique wardrobe, with CNN Iraq war-coverage blasting out. He showed me the office, with fax and internet; the well-stocked bar; bedroom, dressing room, and marble-tiled art-deco bathroom with gold fittings. Outside the window, the sunset was glinting off the nearby Chrysler Building. I went to tip the bellboy. That's what they do on films.

'No, no sir, that's all taken care of.'

A phone rang, and I didn't know which one to pick up. A waiter arrived with a box of chocolates, vintage champagne and a basket of fruit, 'Courtesy of Sony Records'.

I picked up the phone to make a difficult call. I rang Mick's room.

'I fucked up. Topper bottled out,' I said.

'That's really a shame,' he said. 'I'll be right down.'

Mick arrived with his missus, Miranda, and his baby Stella in his arms.

'How was the flight? Wow, nice spread,' he said, looking round the suite.

'What, ain't yours like this?'

'No.'

'I suppose you'll be wanting to swap.'

'No, no,' he said with a smile. 'You enjoy it.'

He really was a changed man.

After a night's rest and a blast of room service, I was ready to take to the streets. I rang Mick.

'Fancy a stroll?'

Mick was never one for strolls when we were gigging, but Joe always was.

It was clear blue skies and freezing as Mick walked me down Fifth Avenue. I'd been to New York many times, but never seen it sober or in daylight.

We went into a big bookshop. Mick was thumbing through history books. I was in the music section, but always looking over to make sure he was all right. It was a reflex action. I was checking on him because that had always been part of my job. He bought a couple of books, and I reminded him the time was getting on, because that's what I'd always done.

We all met up in Mick's room, in time-honoured fashion, drinking, smoking, laughing. We were aware we were only half a team, but were in good spirits – eye contact, in-jokes. We were joined by Kosmo Vinyl, Rudi Fernandez in a bright-red jacket; and Bob Gruen, corpulent in tuxedo, bow tie and cummerbund.

'Where's Bernie?'

'He can't be with us,' said Tricia.

Bernard Rhodes had been Joe's controversial choice of guest for the event, and after Joe's death, the others had stuck to his wishes. He had decided not to come. He said he wasn't going to be treated like a piece of furniture. Whatever that means.

We were in dark suits, Paul with an immaculate white brushed hat, which he didn't wear, but held lovingly on his lap, stroking the material. As we walked to the lift for cocktails, his boys, Claude and Louis, snatched the hat and danced off delighted down the corridor. Paul couldn't help laughing.

'Like father, like sons,' he said, with some pride.

Waiting for the lift, I noticed Lola was wearing black Hudson's buckled biker boots. Joe's boots.

'No one else might notice them, but I have,' I said to her. 'I've just got to say it's a nice touch.'

We stepped out of the lift into the fin-de-siècle lobby. Paul was surrounded by a scrum of guttersnipe fans, pleased with themselves for having beaten the security. In the unexpected sudden burst of chaos, I pulled his sons close to me for protection. I was working again. Hotel staff looked to me to get them through into the cordoned safety zone, but Paul refused to be hurried. He signed autographs on photos, albums, guitar scratchplates. Later I read about a scam involving White Stripes, where these signed plates were screwed onto guitars which were then sold as the genuine White Stripes item. Were we so off the game to have missed this trick?

We took our seats. It was tightly packed. I had to ask Elvis Costello to hold his gut in so I could squeeze past. It was chock-a-block with record-company executives on their big night out, all polished bald heads and expensive gold jewellery, their women on their arms and their star acts. The grinning Mexican death's head, Rudi Fernandez, materialized in the seat next to me. We tucked into the menu: Rack of Lamb, Cannallini Beans, Cherry Tomatoes, Spanish and Calamata Olives, Roasted Garlic and Rosemary Jus d'lie. I asked Rudi, 'What's this, Spanish hot-pot?'

'Nobody touch the bread rolls,' I said. 'They're going on Sting's head.'

I turned to look at the stage, and just caught Sting's eye. He was nervously grinning at me from the next table. The grub was cleared, and the awards began. But there was a problem. Here we were at the very pinnacle of rock'n'roll fame, and you weren't allowed to smoke a fag, let alone anything else. We all sloped off to the bogs for a cigarette like schoolkids. The girls went into the ladies, offering support to Luce, who was going to deputize for her old man on stage for the first time.

There was an audio-visual presentation on each act that was to receive an award. The stage set was real punk rock – on Broadway. The Edge, from U2, with a tea-cosy on his head, introduced the Clash. He told of an autumn night in 1977 when he and Bono had seen them live in Dublin. They'd come out of the gig and their lives had been changed. Hadn't we all?

Mick was first to reply. He thanked the Sex Pistols, without whom none of this ...; Bernie, me and the Baker for seeing it through; and lastly his old friend Robin, now out in Baghdad as part of the human shield peace protest. Baghdad Banksy. This bit was chopped when it was broadcast on TV.

Paul and Terry Chimes were equally brief and cool. Luce stepped up nervously. The whole place stood and applauded as she received Joe's award. It was not until this moment that the penny really dropped. The finality hit home. It wasn't just the man that was missing. Ever since it was announced about the Hall of Fame the band had been under big pressure from the organizers to give it one last shot live on stage here. They'd chewed it over and over, even fantasizing about doing a runner from the glitterati and doing a one-off gig at some secret club down the road – still putting up two fingers to the system. And even though you knew it was stupid, even though you would shrink from seeing our four heroes as middle-aged men running through 'I'm so Bored with the USA', even though you didn't want that to happen ... if it was going to happen, you wanted to be there, to peep in curious horror, but also in excitement, to see if the thrill could be captured one last time – didn't you?

And at that moment, when the crowd rose to its feet for Joe's widow, came the realization that we would never hear the music again. I thought of Joe pointing to the tree in his garden. 'Hang me high if the Clash ever play together again.' That won't be necessary now, Joe. The game's up. There's no Clash without Strummer. They weren't a band any more. Joe was dead.

It took twenty years for me to realize the Country and Western saying that you can't drink it off your mind. No amount of booze or heroin can capture the hit, although occasionally, very occasionally, when I hear 'White Man' or

'Complete Control', a whiff of it hits me: the thrill of setting up the equipment, hearing the soundcheck, seeing the Clash rock the stage and being part of it. And when I catch that whiff, I'm overpowered. It's only cheap-shit rock'n'roll, but it's powerful stuff. And now Joe's dead, and the finality hits me. But it was never meant to last for ever.

While the others went off to do the obligatory press photos, I waited outside with Kosmo. It was an emotional time. 'I had you figured wrong,' I told him. 'I'd always figured you for a joker, but Topper has told me how you helped him through his bankrupt junkie days.'

'That's all right Johnny,' he said generously.

'I liked your speech, The Edge,' I said to the Irishman. 'As a matter of fact, the gig you mentioned was my first one too.'

Costello played a neat set. AC/DC played tightly, as you'd expect from a band that lives on the road. The Police set roused my vitriol. What Sting had failed to realize is that being note-perfect without the passion is a waste of time. Going through the motions is obvious to me and you.

There was no faking the pride of the families of Motown drummer Benny Benjamin, Nashville piano man Floyd Cramer and sax player Steve Douglas as they received the 'Sidemen' awards on their behalf. And the Righteous Brothers were enjoying every moment of it, exuberant, glasses of wine in hand, mullets flapping. It had been a long hard wait for them.

I was carrying round Topper's award like it was the FA Cup. It was a black 18-inch statue of a figure holding a gold disc on a marble plinth. The plate read Nicky 'Topper' Headon.

'Nicky? No one calls me Nicky,' Topper said when I gave it to him later.

People were milling around shaking hands. Seeing me with an award, they came up and shook my hand. 'Well done fellah, very well deserved.'

I beamed back at them. 'Why, thank you very much.'

Luce came up to me and said quietly, angrily, 'Some bigwig just came up to me and said "I feel Joe is here with us tonight." I just smiled and hoped he'd go away, but I felt like screaming "Fuck off, because he's not".'

The parties flowed into the night but I didn't have the heart for them. I sat down for breakfast at noon in the swanky restaurant. There was only one thing I could possibly have ordered. 'I want a Waldorf salad.' And don't mention the war.

As we stepped into the first-class cabin, the flight attendant offered us newspapers. 'Sorry, Johnny, they ain't got the *Beano*,' shouted Paul. It was a smooth ride home, except that somehow Terry Chimes' Hall of Fame award got smashed to fuck in the luggage hold.

'Don't worry,' I said. 'They've probably got a warehouse full of them on some industrial estate in Ohio.'

It was the crack of dawn at Heathrow as I waited with Paul and his boys at the luggage carousel, jet-lagged.

'What do you make of all that then?' I said.

He looked at me with the biggest grin I've ever seen.

'Not a lot.'

Epilogue

In homage to Charles Dickens, a fellow son of the Medway Towns, with his prophetic introduction to *A Tale of Two Cities*:

It was the best of times, it was the worst of times ...
People are always asking me: 'Well how was that, working with the Clash, travelling the world with them?' – and my answer is always the same: 'What do you think? It was fucking brilliant.'

It was the age of wisdom, it was the age of foolishness ...
As the years roll on, these questions never seem to dry up. If anything, the queries become more urgent – affectionate, of course, but somehow with the passing of time, I notice a certain desperation to get a grasp on that era again. I don't feel that. The memories that I've put out are as vivid and meaningful as they ever were.

Again, people say to me, 'Well, that must have been the best time of your life.' I can understand why people would say that to me, but it ain't true. I've had a fabulous time elsewhere in my life – with other people, in other places. Nevertheless, my response is, yeah, it was pretty damn good. I don't spend my days forever thinking back to the good old days, but, on request, I find it easy to access my Mind Palace. It's all still there. It is joyful to summon up my time with El Clash combo.

That doesn't necessarily hold with all our companeros from that remarkable burst of energy. Take my mate The Baker. We were oppos in the military sense – comrades in arms, opposite numbers, doing the same job. And 'opposite' is apposite: we were like chalk and cheese.

It was the epoch of belief, it was the epoch of incredulity ...

In these days of large entourages surrounding The Act, it is worth bearing in mind that The Baker and I were the entire entourage for the Clash. We did the lot, from lengthy every-day rehearsals to all-night recordings in the studio to manic full-on gigs, night after night after night – always, him and me, a shared experience. We two, we happy two, we band of brothers ... There were times when you could look at the whole Clash operation as like being in the army. Photographer Pennie Smith said being on the road with the Clash was like being on a commando raid with the Bash Street Kids – it was frantic, but not without its laughs.

We each had our individual expertise but could easily overlap tasks, jobs and duties. He could wield a soldering iron, but I was a dab hand with the gaffer tape. I could rabbit on with anyone, but he saw things through. We were a team. A tiny team, but we had our fingers on all the buttons. Every night at the soundcheck, we'd catch up on needs, requirements and of course, gossip – the state of play with the outfit was a constant source of delight to us.

We came to be the Clash's road crew from very different directions. He was just seventeen, from south London, transpontine; I had ten years on him, and had moved around a lot.

He lived at home with his mum, I was already divorced with two young kids. He was a real soul boy, the music of Stax and Tamla. I was a rock 'n' roller, Keith Richards was my man. Punk rock fitted me perfectly, like the suit I never owned. Nevertheless, The Baker got it. He understood well the anti-social message blaring out of Rehearsal Rehearsals in Camden Town – but he didn't live there 24/7 like I did.

It was the season of Light, it was the season of Darkness ...

Away from there, out on the road, we initially shared hotel rooms. It was a cheapskate production. It was not to last. The phone would ring constantly with requests and demands from band members, promoters and irate hotel managers. The Baker was looking for a spot of peace and quiet away from the decibels on stage. I was quite happy to ramp up the chaos. He needed his sleep, I was up all night, speeding away underneath the yellow light. And then there were the chicks ... shouting was involved. So we separated to individual hotel rooms, but stayed as close as ever, and it has always been that way. We have remained the best of chums down the years. Although he's been a long time living in the States, and I reside in Blighty, we talk. We talk a lot, on the phone, pen and paper, email. And here's the thing: for the best of friends, we don't see eye to eye. I don't mean Donald Trump, gun law, Brexit, and the state of the world; what does concern The Baker and me is what we got out of it all, the Clash years. On what shore have we individually washed up? Like shipwrecked mariners, it has taken all of us a long hard swim to plant our feet on the beach.

It was the spring of hope, it was the winter of despair ...
Whatever it was that we went through, and whatever it is that we got from it, they are not the same. As I keep rattling on, for me it is a delight to keep on bumping into and chewing the fat with ageing punk rockers throughout the length and breadth of the British Isles, not to mention around the world. I was in Vietnam recently and was astonished at the number of Clash T-shirts I saw on the chests of the locals parading round the streets. I've seen a life-size mural of Paul Simonon on the wall of a taverna on a Greek island. Australians love me to recall the good old days. Yeah, OK, but I'm also right there with Viv Albertine, ex of the Slits, who says: 'Punk? Yes it was fabulous, but it's gone – gone in a flash, and if you weren't there, hard luck, I'm sorry, but don't try to recreate it.'

She said that in a Q&A onstage at the 100 Club to mark the 40th anniversary of 'punk rock' in that dark, airless, sticky cellar. Bernie Rhodes was also there, the great svengali of the Clash, who had been sacked then reinstated, according to Strummer's wishes. He burst into the conversation, indignantly shouting at the poor wretch in the audience 'What are you doing sitting there asking retro questions at the "stars"? Why aren't you out there doing something with your lives?' Fair point, Bernie – that was always the statement the Clash would give to young fans asking for autographs back in the day. That's how punk rock thrived.

This would not happen to The Baker. He keeps his distance, a considerable distance. He would tell me that I'm milking it, flagging up old memories, riding on the back of their immense reputation as if it was some wondrous fairy tale. I got what I wanted from being with the Clash – he didn't. I treated it as a blast, never sure how long it would last. But for The Baker, it was a long-term affair – or should have been. In the Clash, he had found something that he could relate to, that he felt part of, a sense of belonging. What's that going to do to a guy when you say: 'No, it's all over. Sheboom. Off you go.'

We had everything before us, we had nothing before us ...
In the analogues of rock 'n' roll history, the Beatles always said that they didn't know if it would last until the next year. Back in the mid-Sixties, Mick Jagger reckoned he couldn't see the Stones continuing beyond another five years. Really. At the Rock and Roll Hall of Fame in 2003, I was talking backstage with The Edge. Over a cuppa, The Edge lamented the sudden brief demise that was the Clash. 'So sad,' he said to me, 'that it didn't last longer.'

'Not at all,' I replied. 'It was destined to explode like the finest sky rocket you've ever seen. And then it was gone.'

Had he been there, The Baker would have seen eye to eye with The Edge. not just because they both had the same first name – The! – but because The Baker was in for the long haul. He figured it as the family that always stays together. To be turned out on his ear with everyone else, with only memories in his wallet, was a blow.

We were all going direct to Heaven, we were all going direct the other way ...
He was looking for stability, purposefulness and a continuation

of the intimacy that we had enjoyed as 'the last gang in town'. He wasn't alone in that. Self-recriminations abounded after the grand schism. It was always my wish to stick a pair of boxing gloves on both Joe and Topper, shove 'em in a ring, and let them slug it out as to who blamed himself more for the break-up of the Clash. That's as may be. I'd already ventured to pastures new in West Texas, looking for kicks in the honky tonks there. You know what they say: old rockers never die, they just turn to country music. That was me. But The Baker drifted. To and fro he went, across the fifty-two states, up to Oregon and back to the New Jersey, none of the time looking for another band to work with. How could there be another band to fill the void that had been filled by the Clash? He was a bookseller, a chauffeur, a house builder. Nothing seemed to replace that sense of being 'us against the world' – contra mundum. And he blamed them. Blamed them for leaving him marooned on that desert island shore like Ben Gunn, with his catchphrase 'Would you have a piece of Christian cheese about you?'

The Baker says: 'I had thought I'd be able to walk away from it all without a care and adjust to civilian life seamlessly. I was dead wrong. Unable to escape the shackles of the Clash, I have sleep-walked my way through life ever since because I spent too long in a world in which I didn't belong.'

The trouble with that way of thinking is that his present state of mind wipes out the past. The man he is casts a long shadow over the lad he was. He used to whistle. A lot. Go and listen to the introduction to Jimmy Jazz on London Calling. That's The Baker. A happy-go-lucky soul, fresh in the world, with a stupid baseball cap on sideways, to show the world that he didn't give a fuck. His one-piece khaki flight suit and highly polished Doc Marten shoes said different.

Frequently he could take or leave the music that they were inventing, creating, but he always bust a gut to make sure that everything was perfect for them. His commitment was full tilt. We all knew that.

I meet The Baker in strange places these days to discuss ifs, ands and might-have-beens. I do this with the others as well – I'm a chatty sort of fellow. Paul, painting views of the Thames on his easel up on Waterloo Bridge; with Topper, walking his dog along the White Cliffs of Dover; with Mick, around the back-streets of Soho, he, ever the flaneur. The Baker chooses more idiosyncratic locations: we have walked the Pilgrims Way to Canterbury with a pack of roast beef sandwiches in the footsteps of the Summoner and the Pardoner. We have incurred parking fines in motorway service areas because we've chatted there for five hours; we have crunched the pebbles on the beaches of the mighty Thames estuary; we have stared over the abyss that is Beachy Head. All the time, we have discussed the meaning of life, and death, the possibility of alien existence out in the cosmos, and what it was exactly, specifically, that was so special about the Clash. We are not alone!

From time to time he is asked to revisit his recollections: 'People from the past who knew me have said, in their well-meaning naivety, "just think of it as something great that happened, you were lucky to be part of it. At least you have your memories." I know they don't mean to degrade it, or make light of it, but it seems so glib, so shallow and trivial. As if it was all just a meaningless day at some demonic funfair. A harmless ride on a chaotic, rampageous helter-skelter. It wasn't. It was my life. It was like the Wild West – the new frontier. Such important life-changing crossroads were navigated on a whim, or the spin of a coin. I never envisaged a time when life would be any different.

'Now I find that most everyone that worked with them or for them for a lengthy spell has paid a price. Whether it was drugs or alcohol addiction, or like me, just wandering the planet like a lost soul, desperately keeping the past at bay, living a life of regret, there are virtually none who aren't damaged and few who have lived up to their potential.

'But the music stopped long ago and after the intervening decades, just haphazard scenes and random images remain in my memory – the individual minutiae of each gig now lost. What was there to do? I reasoned that I must either be merely socially delusional or a kind of inverted snob, disassociated and sundered by my own innate detachment. I wondered if I had been suffering an existential crisis caused by dissatisfaction with my life ever since I stopped working with the band.

'I thought having worked for the Clash I would be qualified to do anything, exporting £500,000 worth of equipment around the world, dealing with foreign customs officials, finding and booking rehearsal rooms, recording studios, rental cars – who wouldn't want to employ me? I was dead wrong again. My skills were unrecognised and unwanted. As Sylvester Stallone in *Rambo* put it: "In the field, I was in charge of a million-dollar tank, now I can't even get a job pumping gas."

'Army veterans coming back from the war said that the hardest part was that people just did not understand what the fuss was about. Weren't they happy to get home, and just to get on with life? Mostly they had no answers and would turn away, saying nothing. This resonates.

'Substitute the word war for tour, and it was describing my feelings and internal misplacement completely. Now I'd never be so presumptuous as to suggest that my seven years' service to the Clash was in any way akin to going to war. That would be a ridiculous insult to all servicemen. But the similarities in the after-effects were strikingly similar.

'During those seven years my former friends and family too had moved on – got married, had children, moved away. Some had even died. I had had no Christmases, no Easters, no FA Cup finals, no World Cups. Politicians, TV shows, celebrities had come and gone. The fabric of life as I had known it was completely changed. It was as if I had been whisked away to another planet and had little contact with reality. I had been travelling along my own timeline, being myself, accepted and acknowledged by my family and friends, when suddenly it was stopped in its tracks, only to be restarted seven years later as if nothing had happened. Dropped back to earth from outer space.'

Ah, Baker Boy, if only you'd milked it a bit more! I don't hold on to his position. People often assume that I live in some kind of Clash museum – memorable pieces of clothing by Alex Michon in my wardrobe, myriad backstage passes pinned up on a cork board, badges – always, old badges, and of course photographs festooned across the walls. How wrong they would be. The only artefact on display in my gaff is up in the loft – a black and white photo in a cheap frame, sent to me by some chick from New York City – I don't even know her name. It shows Joe Strummer and me at the stage door of the New York Palladium. We're both wearing black leather jackets, glistening in the rain. I'm holding a brown-paper deli bag. It contains Joe's stage shirt. We'd shot off for an hour's solitary silence before the show – yeah, that show – the one where Paul smashed his bass up, on the cover of *London Calling*. The bloke on the stage door wouldn't let us in because we didn't have AAA passes (who the fuck wears backstage passes? Well, fuck him). This one photograph says it all.

Sure, I could lose myself on YouTube with old clips of the chaps. I play the records, now and again – did I ever tell you that 'Protex Blue' is my all-time favourite? But I don't wallow in it. Nor does The Baker. And yet ... and yet ...

In short, the period was so far like the present period, that some of its noisiest authorities insisted on its being received, for good or for evil, in the superlative degree of comparison only.

Over a cup of tea and a slice of Victoria sponge, and sniffing the wind in the right direction, we can be transported back to those few halcyon years. It only takes the nudge of a mention of Cardiff Top Rank ... Slob Ray ... filming homespun videos in the rain with Don Letts ... Bernie ('It's not Bernie, it's Bernard') ... a riot in Paris ... and it starts to flow. The details stack up, the picture colours, we start to smile, we talk faster, we laugh – always, we laugh.

The bond is there – always still there, as strong as ever, for all of us. And then there's the music.

Will you, won't you, will you, won't you, won't you join the dance (the Lobster Quadrille, *Alice's Adventures in Wonderland*).